Browning's Experiments with Genre

Browning's Experiments with Genre

Donald S. Hair

University of Toronto Press

UNIVERSITY OF TORONTO

DEPARTMENT OF ENGLISH STUDIES AND TEXTS

19

©University of Toronto Press 1972

Toronto and Buffalo

Printed in Canada

ISBN 0-8020-5264-9

ISBN microfiche 0-8020-0147-5

LC 75-185715

175727

FOR ARLENE

Contents

Preface

Throughout his life Browning worked at the lyric, the dramatic, and the narrative – and at combinations of these kinds – and tested the structure, conventions, and techniques of each in a restless search for ever more effective ways of realizing his chief interests as a poet, and of stimulating an imaginative response in the reader. In thus experimenting Browning was very much a man of his times. No student of nineteenth-century poetry can fail to be aware of the constant shifts, modifications, and combinations of poetic forms, and none was more ready to exploit these possibilities than Browning. His work gives evidence of both continuity and change; for Browning borrowed freely from the generic conventions he inherited, but reshaped genres just as freely when he felt them inadequate for his purposes. In my investigation of the literary kinds and modes with which Browning worked I have emphasized the literary relations of his poems – the kind of relations that become evident when the literature of the nineteenth century as a whole is surveyed from the perspective of the following century – and I have tried to show that a knowledge of such relations helps us define Browning's modification of conventions and his treatment of particular genres or combinations of genres. To study literary relations is not to trace sources and influences (though a knowledge of these often provides valuable clues for the critic); nor is it to trace the development of the poet and his changing attitudes and beliefs (though to study the poems in chronological order, as I do, inevitably raises questions and suggests problems for the biographer). My primary interest is the structure and character of Browning's poems, and in dealing with these it is literature rather than biography which has proved most helpful.

Browning's interests as a poet remained remarkably constant throughout his life, and are perhaps best defined by the well-known statement in his 1863 preface to *Sordello*: 'my stress lay on incidents in the development of a soul: little else is worth study.' Some years later, in commenting on Tennyson's *The Holy Grail*, he indicated what he would have done with Gawain: 'I should judge the conflict in the knight's soul the proper subject to describe ...'[1] The 'development of a soul' is the shaping of identity through the success or failure of aspirations, the testing of beliefs, the making of choices, and all the other aspects of the moral and religious life. Browning knew that it was unsatisfactory simply to define and describe such a process. He wanted to do much more – to recreate the process in words, and to evoke in his readers his own insights into, and feeling for, the complexity of human development. In short, as he said in *Sordello*, he wanted to 'make' his readers 'see.'

As a 'Maker-see,' Browning has a place in the shift in critical and aesthetic theory that took place in the nineteenth century. Marshall McLuhan has called this shift 'the Copernican revolution in poetry': 'From Sir Philip Sidney in the sixteenth century to Alexander Pope, poetic art was typically directed to the shaping of the poetic object; from the pre-Romantics, Thomson, Gray, Collins, Akenside, and Chatterton, to the present, poetic art has consciously applied itself to the shaping of psychological effects in the reader.' Such a revolution, McLuhan continues, 'envisages art as a means of exploring and charting exactly discriminated mental states, on [the] one hand, and of evoking these newly discovered states in the reader, on the other hand, not indirectly, but by direct participation.'[2] Hence it was no longer possible to accept a poem passively. 'The reader must assume the poet's role. The poem is to be a do-it-yourself kit rather than a fully-processed consumer commodity.' McLuhan calls such poetry 'the poetry of suggestion rather than statement,' 'poetry in which the statements are themselves suggestions and in which the poetic form is the mode of the creative process itself, so that the reader is co-creator with the poet ...'[3] M.H. Abrams has described the shift somewhat more accurately as a movement away from the mimetic theory of Plato and Aristotle, through the 'pragmatic theories' and their concern with the poem as an artifact designed 'to achieve certain effects in an audience,' to the 'expressive theories' and their concern with the poem as an embodiment of 'the poet's perceptions, thoughts, and feelings.'[4] All three kinds of theories are applicable (in varying degrees) to Browning's work, and the last in particular raises once again the problem of the extent to which the poet revealed himself in his work. Whatever the views of this problem, and of Browning's attempts to affect his readers in various ways, it is clear that the 'pragmatic' and 'expressive' theories are closer to Browning's purposes as a poet than is the mimetic theory. Such purposes make Browning a part of the nineteenth-century revolution in poetry.

To say that Browning's art is the art of indirection, and that it went contrary to the demands of the nineteenth-century critics that the poet teach as directly and simply as possible, is not to say something new; it does emphasize the fact that the relations between the poet and his work, and between the poet and his readers, were matters of prime concern in the Victorian age. Critics spent much time trying to decide whether the poet was speaking with his own voice (if he were, the poem was often labelled, somewhat indiscriminately, a 'lyric' because it was 'personal') or with the voice of an assumed character (in which case the poem was called 'dramatic,' because it was 'impersonal'). Browning knew, of course, that the relation between the poet and his readers was much more complicated than that, especially if they were to 'see' what he himself had 'seen.' Nonetheless he explored all the possibilities of both the lyric and the drama, and from the beginning experimented with a combination of the two. In many ways, then, the relation between the lyric and the drama is, as Robert Langbaum has demonstrated, the central critical problem in dealing with Browning's testing of various genres.

Acknowledgments

This study developed out of a doctoral dissertation completed under the direction of Professor F.E.L. Priestley at the University of Toronto. The dissertation, in turn, grew out of Professor Priestley's graduate seminar in Victorian poetry, where the highly experimental Victorian approach to genre was one of the central topics of discussion. It is to Professor Priestley himself, however, that I am chiefly indebted. An outstanding teacher, he is unusually generous with new and exciting ideas. The work he himself has done with Tennyson's *The Princess* and *Idylls of the King* and his analyses of various poems by Browning in the graduate seminar provided the starting point and set the direction for this study, and his careful reading of the manuscript at various stages has been invaluable. I record my debt to him with profound gratitude, and hope that whatever is worthwhile in this study may honour him as that best of all teacher-scholars, the 'Maker-see.'

I am indebted to Miss Tina Vandermeer, Mrs Lori Cole, Mrs Sonia Bevan, and Mrs Jessie Abbott for typing and retyping the manuscript, and to Miss Jean C. Jamieson and Miss Prudence Tracy of University of Toronto Press, for their expert care of the work at every stage.

I am grateful to the University of Western Ontario for several research grants during the preparation of the manuscript. This book has been published with the help of a grant from the Humanities Research Council, using funds provided by the Canada Council, and of a grant from the Publications Fund of the University of Toronto Press.

BIBLIOGRAPHICAL NOTE

In chapters one, two, and four, all quotations from Browning's work are from the first editions of the poems and plays. The quotations from the shorter poems in chapter three are from the third edition of *The Poetical Works*, published in 1863. Full bibliographical information for all these editions may be found in the list of 'Browning's Works' in the Bibliography. Where these editions do not give line numbers, I have used the line numbers from the Centenary Edition, even though (given Browning's revisions) they may not always be applied to the first editions with absolute accuracy.

Browning's Experiments with Genre

1 The early poems

Browning's first three published poems – *Pauline, Paracelsus,* and *Sordello* – are experiments with the three primary literary kinds first distinguished by the Greeks: lyric, drama, and epic or narrative poetry respectively. 'Experiment,' rather than 'exercise,' is, I think, the proper word, because Browning was not simply practising, nor training himself for proficiency in the traditional genres, but was exploring the possibilities of each genre and testing each as a means of fulfilling his poetic purposes. In doing so he assumed, like most nineteenth-century poets, that genres may be treated with considerable freedom, and that they may be modified and combined according to the purposes of the poet and the effects he seeks.

The particular kinds of lyric, drama, and narrative that *Pauline, Paracelsus,* and *Sordello* most closely resemble help in defining Browning's experiments. *Pauline* clearly belongs in a continuing Romantic tradition, and foreshadows in both structure and style the Spasmodic poetry of the 1850s; *Paracelsus* is a 'dramatic poem' which belongs generically with works like *Philip Van Artevelde*; while *Sordello* is related to the narrative romances of Scott and Byron. A knowledge of these literary relations helps us to define both the extent to which Browning modified each genre to suit his special purposes as a poet – to trace 'incidents in the development of a soul' – and a problem with which Browning struggled throughout his career: the relation between the poet and his readers. *Pauline* was part of Browning's design (which he devised with youthful exuberance and confidence) to inspire admiration for the poet's versatility in creating various masks and assuming different voices. The poem asked primarily for praise of the poet. But Browning soon realized that poetry which served only to swell the self-esteem of the poet had little value, and that the true worth of poetry lay in the extent to which it could enlarge the reader's sympathy, stimulate his imagination, and contribute to his moral development. This was a major shift in the relation between the poet and his readers, a shift from the techniques of the virtuoso who would display himself through a variety of characters to the techniques of the more mature poet who would evoke in the reader his own insights and emotions.

Pauline

Critics usually approach *Pauline* as an autobiographical poem, embodying Browning's mental and emotional state at the age of twenty, and describing his mental and emotional development up to that time. The comments of John Stuart Mill, preserved in the copy of the poem which Browning kept as his own and later gave to Forster, provide a starting point for such a study, and the 'intense and morbid self-consciousness' that Mill speaks of is generally considered to be Browning's.

The problem of the extent to which the poem is autobiographical has taken precedence over attempts to study the form of the poem, or to relate it to a literary tradition. Yet literary relations are just as intriguing a critical problem as biographical ones, and the literary relations of *Pauline* are particularly interesting. The poem not only belongs to a continuing Romantic tradition in poetry, but also seems to anticipate the Spasmodic theory of the 1850s, a somewhat idiosyncratic view of the relation between lyric and drama, which provides clues toward an understanding of Browning's early poetic techniques.

The tendencies that produced Spasmodic poetry – a reliance on the imagination rather than on the intellect and will, an emphasis on the expression of feelings and the inner life rather than the imitation of 'real life,' an interest in a flood of images and imaginatively exciting passages rather than in the selection of images and the careful construction of a poem – were evident in the 1830s, largely in the critical theories

4

that made Romanticism a continuing tradition. The critics of the 1830s defined poetry first as an artifact, a structure of words and rhythms, and, secondly, as the state of mind which produces this artifact, on the one hand, and appreciates it, on the other. The reviews of the period make it clear that critics were more interested in poetic feeling and a poetic state of mind than they were in what was called 'metrical speech,' and they referred to the latter, often derisively, as 'art.' Newman's statements in his article on 'Poetry' for the *London Review* are typical: 'The art of composition is merely accessory to the poetical talent'; 'attention to the language *for its own sake* evidences not the true poet but the mere artist'[1]; his distinction between 'an exhibition of ingenious workmanship,' on the one hand, and 'a free and unfettered effusion of genius,'[2] on the other, runs throughout the whole article. Hallam's review of Tennyson's early poems reiterates Newman's Romantic point of view. Hallam distinguished between poets of reflection, who in composition were more likely to be guided by the careful consideration of discursive thought than by the generous outpouring of feeling, and poets of sensation, who revelled in the emotions aroused by their sensitive perception of nature, and whose delight in their perceptions 'tended to absorb their whole being into the energy of sense.'[3] Hallam labelled Tennyson a poet of sensation, and praised him, among other things, for two characteristics: 'his luxuriance of imagination, and at the same time his control over it,' and 'his power of embodying himself in ideal characters, or rather moods of character ...'[4]; characteristics that seem to indicate Tennyson's lyric and dramatic gifts. Mill made a similar distinction in his 1833 essay called 'The Two Kinds of Poetry.' In that essay he tells us that poetry delineates the inner life of the poet, and is itself 'but the thoughts and words in which emotion spontaneously embodies itself.'[5] Alexander Smith (the critic, not the Spasmodic poet) makes the same point in his essay on 'The Philosophy of Poetry.' He defines poetry as 'the language of emotion,' language which is 'generally figurative or imaginative,' argues that poetry does not convey information but rather transmits feeling, and describes the process of composition as the mind expressing 'its own feelings as excited by the object' and pouring forth 'the stream of its associations as they rise from their source.'[6] Newman, Hallam, Mill, and Smith bear witness to the strength of the Romantic tradition in the 1830s, and Taylor's reaction to the tradition (in the Preface to *Philip Van Artevelde*, 1834) is yet further evidence of the context of critical opinion in which *Pauline* appeared.

The Spasmodic school of the 1850s exaggerated certain tendencies of the Romantic tradition of the 1830s. Where Hallam praised Tennyson's control of a luxuriant imagination, the Spasmodics admired verse which was poured forth without any design or purpose other than the venting of the effusion itself. The 'convulsive throes in the soul of the writer'[7] were considered evidence of divine inspiration, and of the special genius of the poet. And the poem so created belonged in a natural rather than an artificial world. Sydney Dobell, for instance, insisted that a 'work of Art which in construction is strictly teleologic – in which every part is essential to the whole – is artificial not natural, architecture not Nature.'[8] This extreme shift of aesthetic values was accompanied by new definitions of the lyric and the drama. The lyric traditionally had been impersonal, and had expressed the feelings of the community rather than of the poet as an individual. And it had been distinguished by the formality and variety of its metrical and stanzaic patterns. More than earlier poets, the Romantics made the lyric the personal outpouring of feeling, though the feeling was still controlled by complicated metres and stanzaic forms. The Spasmodics rejected such control as artificial, and insisted that the poet's mind itself provided the unity of any poem. The definition of the drama underwent a similar change. An action carried forward by dialogue, the drama was traditionally impersonal, the poet being hidden behind the characters seen on stage. The Romantic poets tended to make the drama a reflection of events within their own souls, and the Spasmodics went even further by insisting that every character was an aspect of his creator. In short, the Spasmodics made the lyric and the drama ways of defining the relation between the poet and his work. Because this relation is one of the central critical problems in *Pauline*, and because the poem anticipates the poetry of the 1850s, particularly in its structure and manner of proceeding, we must consider at some length both Spasmodic theory and Spasmodic practice. Sydney Dobell's lecture on the 'Nature of Poetry' (1857) is a good starting point.

Since Dobell assumes that poetry is the product of an intense inner life, he is primarily concerned with the way in which the poet expresses, or (literally) 'carries out,' his mind. Expression is the discovery of some 'imaginative equivalent,' which Dobell defines as 'that product of an active mind, which being presented to the same mind when passive, would restore the former state of activity' (p 9). For the lyric, which is what Dobell calls a 'simple' expression, the 'imaginative equivalent' is simply the act of speech itself, 'as if, feeling Love, I should say, "I love"' (p 13). 'Indirect' or 'compound' expression is more complicated, and leads the poet into what Dobell calls the 'Epic': 'as if I should express the feeling of Love not by saying "I love", but by calling up in the imagination some beautiful object which is the equivalent of Love – that is, which would rouse my Love into activity – and finding for that object some equivalent in words – that is, such words as when the object has disappeared from my inward sight would make it reappear' (p 14). Robert Preyer, in his analysis of 'The Nature of Poetry,' relates this method of composition to Jung's theory of the collective unconscious, to Yeats' early ideas on rhythm, and to Eliot's concept of the 'objective correlative,' and by doing so emphasizes the close affinity of the Victorian 'epic' and the lyric.[9] Dobell himself writes that 'the two great forms of Poetic expression ... – the Epical and Lyrical – are governed by the same laws' (p 15). That the 'imaginative equivalent' may be an image or metaphor as suitable for the lyric as for the 'epic' seems sufficiently demonstrated.

The relation between the 'epic' and the drama, on the other hand, is by no means so clear. It is obvious, as Preyer points out, that Dobell has little sympathy with the drama proper: 'I do not mention the Drama among the great separate forms of Poetry, because the Drama is merely an Epic produced under compulsory external conditions that interfere with the natural laws of epical production' (p 15). Dobell seems to mean that the limitations imposed by writing for the stage restrict the poet's imagination, and force him to be concerned, not with himself, but with his audience; not with his own emotions, but with the demands for action and spectacle in the theatre.

In spite of his summary dismissal of drama, dramatic elements are not lacking in Dobell's concept of the 'epic.' Although it is not immediately clear from the discussion of the 'epic,' it seems entirely likely that the 'imaginative equivalent' may just as well be a dramatic character as an isolated image. The 'equivalent in words' of such a character would then be, not merely a description of actions and speeches, but a rendering of the actual speeches themselves. The poet would thus modify his own voice to suit that of his characters. It is this modification to which Dobell seems to be referring when he speaks of the poet's power of 'transfiguration.' 'The higher forms of this gift,' Dobell says, 'enable the possessor to re-construct (so to speak) his whole character into that of some other mind' (p 28). This 'transfiguration' is as much a matter of imaginative activity as is the calling up of a sequence of images.

It would seem, then, that what Dobell calls the 'epic' is actually a combination of the traditional literary modes, a combination achieved through the imaginative process which makes all parts of the poems, the characters and the images both, aspects of the poet's mind. On the one hand, the 'epic' poet approaches the lyric in calling up in his imagination images which express his feelings; on the other, he approaches the drama in modifying his voice to suit that of his characters. But the 'epic' stops short of the traditional lyric because it proceeds, not according to a carefully conceived, formal pattern, but in a loosely organized fashion; it stops short of the drama because the characters exist, not in their own right, but as different voices of the poet, so that he is maintaining as it were a dialogue with himself.

Because both the images and the characters reveal varied aspects of the poet, the poem as a whole is considered to be the 'imaginative equivalent' of the poet's mind. Hence its structure is determined, not by the formality of art, but by the nature of the mind itself. A Spasmodic poem is not a tightly unified pattern of words, but rather a loosely connected series of reflections that represent the stream of unselected associations passing through the poet's mind as he considers his subject. Preyer calls this structure 'an improvisation about a theme or a series of themes'[10] and suggests that unity is achieved through the recurrence of themes, as in music. The analogy with music is made by Dobell himself in a letter of 1856. There he speaks of the instinct of the song-writer 'to accustom the perceptions to an idea and phrase in one portion of a lyric, and then to repeat them in other parts, with slight variations, or under fresh conditions of context ...'[11] Such repetition of thought and phrase makes a certain appeal to the intellect, Dobell says, but the structure of the poem is determined, not by the intellect (to which he attributes such repetitions), but by feelings, emotional states. The emotional states the Spasmodic poet most prized occurred in moments of inspiration, when the poet's feelings rose to the point of frenzy, and images poured out, not according to the careful ordering of art, but with the unthinking abundance of nature. These moments produced the 'beauties' beloved by Victorian anthologists, passages where inspiration produced a flood of images revealing the overwrought passions and violent emotions of a great man at war with himself. The value placed on such lyric outbursts did not encourage the Spasmodic poet to give careful attention to the construction of his poem, or to its completeness in an Aristotelian sense. But his interest in assuming a dramatic mask provided a structure of a different sort.

In theory, the Spasmodics had a great range of characters into which they could enter, for they were convinced, like Sordello, that the poet by his very nature could be anyone he chose to be. 'A Poet,' Dobell writes,

8

'has ... an inexhaustible stock of men and women in the transmutable substance of his own character ...' (p 29). In practice, the range of characters is limited. The central figure of a Spasmodic poem is usually a poet, and he exists largely to reveal the mind of his creator. Marston's *Gerald* (1842) and Dobell's *Balder* (1853) bear the names of their poet-heroes, while both Smith's *A Life-Drama* (1853) and Bigg's *Night and the Soul* (1854) trace the fortunes of struggling poets. And in the second edition (1845) of Bailey's *Festus*, Festus is portrayed as a poet. Not one of these figures could resist giving examples of his own work, and hence he often became the means of achieving that variety and looseness of structure so typical of a Spasmodic poem. It was with considerable excitement that Dobell discovered how useful Balder could be if he were a poet: 'The hero of the drama is a student,' Dobell wrote to Gilfillan in 1851, 'the subject his inner life: so far I had advanced months ago; but now my student is *writing an epic*, of which passages and best points, introduced in various manners, come naturally into the more subjective matter of the piece.'[12]

It is paradoxical that this looseness should make possible another kind of structure which could be very subtle and complex. Balder's epic is entitled 'Genius,' and its central figure is an allegorical representation of this essential quality of the Spasmodic poet. Balder reminds us several times that this figure is an aspect of himself:

The hand that writes is part of what is writ,
And I, like the steeped roses of the east,
Become the necessary element
Of that which doth preserve me.   (p 19)

Dobell thus draws attention to the close connection between himself and his *persona* by showing the close connection between the *persona* and the characters he in turn creates. Smith uses a similar technique in his *A Life-Drama*. The poet, Walter, is so constantly telling tales whose central figures are thin disguises for himself that one of his friends characterizes him as 'a masker in a mask of glass': 'You've such transparent sides, each casual eye / May see the heaving heart.' This close connection between characters and the central figure of the poem, and between that central figure and his creator, compensates for the looseness of structure that is made possible by the use of a poet-hero. Instead of a series of more or less disconnected scenes and events (as we have in *Festus*), we tend to have poems within poems, tales within tales, each reinforcing and illuminating the themes and characters of the context within which it is enclosed. The structure of a Spasmodic poem is not unlike the Ptolemaic concept of the universe, a system of sphere within sphere, and a *primum mobile* – the poet – giving life and motion to all.

The extremes of Romanticism which would become evident in the work of the Spasmodics had already appeared in the work of the young Robert Browning. Indeed, W.J. Fox, in his review of *Pauline*, praised the poem on the basis of assumptions which, twenty years later, would have been classified as Spasmodic. The same attitudes toward the lyric and the drama, the same concept of the relation between the poet and his work, are clearly evident:

> The knowledge of the mind is the first of sciences; the records of its formation and workings are the most important of histories; and it is eminently a subject for poetical exhibition. The annals of a poet's mind are poetry. Nor has there ever been a genuine bard, who was not in himself more poetical than any of his productions. They are emanations of his essence. He himself is, or has been, all that he truly and touchingly, *i.e.* poetically, describes. Wordsworth, indeed, never carried a pedlar's pack, nor did Byron ever command a pirate ship, or Coleridge shoot an albatross; but there were times and moods in which their thoughts intently realized, and identified themselves with the reflective Wanderer, the impetuous Corsair, and the ancient Mariner. They felt *their* feelings, thought *their* thoughts, burned with *their* passions, dreamed *their* dreams, and lived their lives, or died their deaths. In relation to his creations, the poet is the omnific spirit in whom they have their being. All their vitality must exist in his life. He only, in them, displays to us fragments of himself. The poem, in which a great poet should reveal the whole of himself to mankind would be a study, a delight, and a power, for which there is yet no parallel; and around which the noblest creations of the noblest writers would range themselves as subsidiary luminaries.[13]

The prime purpose of the poet is to reveal himself; a self-revelatory poem is both lyric, insofar as it is an 'emanation' of the poet's 'essence,' and dramatic, insofar as the poet displays in all his various characters 'fragments of himself.' From what we know of the composition of *Pauline*, it is not too difficult to deduce that Browning shared Fox's assumptions about poetry.

Browning's comments on *Pauline* are late and characteristically restrained. But it is clear enough that in 1833 he anticipated the Spasmodic concept of the poet as capable of entering into any character he chooses – a concept he explains in a MS note (written at a much later date) in his own copy of *Pauline*:

> The following Poem was written in pursuance of a foolish plan which occupied me mightily for a time, and which had for its object the enabling me to assume & realize I know not how many different characters; – meanwhile the world was never to guess that 'Brown, Smith, Jones, & Robinson' (as the spelling books have it) the respective authors of this poem, the other novel, such an opera, such a speech, etc. etc. were no other than one and the same individual. The present abortion was the first work of the *Poet* of the batch, who would have been more legitimately *myself* than most of the others; but I surrounded him with all manner of (to my then notion) poetical accessories, and had planned quite a delightful life for him:
>
> Only this crab remains of the shapely Tree of Life in this Fool's Paradise of mine.[14]

Browning skirts the question of self-revelation ('The present abortion was the first work of the Poet of the batch, who would have been more legitimately *myself* than most of the others ...') and goes on to imply that he was portraying a poet as he should be (according to his youthful concept) and not as he himself was. The fact is that the 'poetical accessories' Browning planned for his character are the characteristics popularly assigned to a poet in the 1830s, the characteristics that came to be associated with the Spasmodic school: excessive self-consciousness, divine inspiration, and overwrought passions and emotions. Browning's statement of 1868 that the poem was 'my earliest attempt at "poetry always dramatic in principle, and so many utterances of so many imaginary persons, not mine" ' takes on new meaning in the context of Spasmodic practices, for, while Browning undoubtedly meant us to take the 'dramatic' as the impersonal, he may have been not unaware of the Spasmodic sense of the 'dramatic' as self-dramatization. It may have been for this reason that he suppressed the poem.

In his introductory note of 1868 Browning gave another reason for wanting to suppress the poem: 'good draughtsmanship ... and right handling were far beyond the artist at that time.' And in 1888 he referred to 'the helplessness of juvenile haste and heat.' Even in 1833 Browning was not unaware of the loose construction of the poem. One of **Pauline's** tasks is to edit and clarify ('mieux co-ordonner certaines parties') what her lover says, and her footnote assumes a patronizing attitude to this poem of 'songe et confusion.' Browning may have meant Pauline's comments to be ironic, for what we know of the circumstances of composition indicate that the young man was far more interested in being a poet than in being an artist; and that, like the Spasmodics who followed him, he valued 'songe et confusion' as a way of representing (in Fox's words) 'the annals of a poet's mind.' The poem is dated 22 October, 1832, the date not of the completion of the poem but of its conception. On that day, Browning tells us in yet another MS note in his own copy of *Pauline*, he saw Kean act in *Richard III* and was so fired by the performance that he planned a whole series of poems. 'I don't know whether I had not made up my mind to *act* as well as to make verses, music, and God knows what, – que de châteaux en Espagne.'[15] The dating of the poem reflects the ecstasy with which Browning conceived his plan and emphasizes the priority of conception over execution. Like Walter's poem in scene xii of Smith's *A Life-Drama*, *Pauline* may have been 'done at a dash,' before the excitement of his inspiration faded. Romanticism gave priority to the process rather than the product, to the inspiration rather than to the poem representing it. And in 1833 Browning was apparently no more ready to question such a scheme of aesthetic values than were the Spasmodics one or two decades later.

Browning's assumptions guide us in dealing with the poem itself. We should expect a lyric outpouring of images expressing the inner life of the poet, and at the same time a modification of the poet's voice to that of the *dramatis persona* speaking the poem. And it is just such a combination of the lyric and the dramatic that *Pauline* provides us with. Perhaps Browning's technique can best be described if we make a distinction between the poet and the speaker in the poem. For the poet, the interest centres in the principal character, the figure who contains what takes place in the poem. For the speaker, the interest centres in the progress from doubt to faith, and also in the poem which he is in fact composing as he is pouring forth his feelings in confession. It is primarily this poem, and not Browning's poem, which is the fragment, of which Pauline is to 'mieux co-ordonner certaines parties.' Once a distinction is made between the poet and the speaker, it becomes evident that the structure of *Pauline* is similar to that of many Spasmodic works: that is, a poem within a poem. There is the fragmentary poem improvised by the speaker, a loose conglomeration of images much interrupted by lengthy and rather arid sections of mental analysis; and there is the complete poem composed by Browning, of which both the images and the analytical sections combine to make up the dramatic speech which is the 'equivalent in words' of the assumed character.

Though the poem-within-a-poem technique anticipates the structure of many Spasmodic poems, Browning realizes his dramatic character in a way rather different from that of the Spasmodics. The speaker does interweave a number of themes by free association but his analysis of himself proceeds in quite a different way, in the planned and logical manner of a psychologist's report. Such an analysis seems to indicate a more thoughtful and objective attitude on the part of the poet, and suggests that *Pauline* is in fact Browning's first attempt to trace the 'development of a soul.' The distinction between these two ways of proceeding provides a basis for dividing the poem into three sections. T.J. Collins has commented on the changes in tense in the poem.[16] For the most part, the central portion of the poem is written in the past tense, while the beginning and end are in the present. The changes in tense help define the speaker's changing mental activities: from line 1 to line 259 the speaker proceeds imaginatively, and pours out his feelings in a rush of images. There follows a long section (lines 260 to 708) in which analysis predominates. Then a series of imaginative scenes (709–1031) leads to the final affirmation.

The first verse paragraph introduces the three major themes of the poem. The first deals with Pauline and her lover whom she encloses and protects, thus easing his fear and tension, and so creates the conditions under which he can confess. The second theme centres in the speaker's emotion. He feels guilty because he has experienced nature's enchantments and learned her secrets, but has not used such experience or knowledge. Rather, he 'departed, smiling like a fiend / Who has deceived God' (22–3). The purposes of the confession make up the third theme, one aspect of which is artistic (the confession will enable him to write poetry again) and the other religious (he will 'stand robed and crowned / Amid the faithful ...' (24–5). Since the poem moves toward a statement of faith, this beginning suggests the shape of the whole work.

Once the themes have been introduced, the interweaving begins. In the second verse paragraph (28–38) the speaker suggests a connection between Pauline and the faith he is seeking ('I had been spared this shame, if I had sate / By thee for ever, from the first ...' (28–9). The third verse paragraph (39–54) is an elaboration of the connection between love and faith: 'Thou lovest me, / And thou art to receive not love, but faith ...' (42–3). The fourth verse paragraph (55–88) deals

13

with the discrepancy between the beauty of the natural world and the ugliness of his own lack of faith. When he describes the spring landscape, the images he casts on nature reveal his own feelings of guilt. There is, for instance, the wind 'murmuring in the damp copse, / Like heavy breathings of some hidden thing / Betrayed by sleep ...' (66–8). As the full force of his guilty feelings comes rushing in upon him he moves from the discrepancy between himself and nature to the dichotomy between his better and worse selves. The speaker's self-centredness reveals itself as a conflict between his soul and the 'dim orb / Of self' (91–2), a conflict which, even though it brings about decay and ruin, arouses in him a 'strange delight' (98). This emotion finds its 'imaginative equivalents' in equally strange images: the fiend and the swan, and the young witch and the god. The grotesqueness of these images, and the suggestion of overwrought and perverse emotions, was to become typical of the Spasmodics.

By now the method by which this part of the poem proceeds is becoming clear. The speaker 'sings' his confession in the same way that the Spasmodic poet 'sings' his 'epic.' Strong feelings recreated by his memory embody themselves in images; these are perceived by the imagination and poured out in unpremeditated song. The images are related to one another not directly, but indirectly, through the emotion which bore them. Yet each image has its own shade of emotion which in turn leads to a new variation.

The ninth verse paragraph (230–59) functions as an interlude between the first and second sections of the poem. It is as if an aria full of coloratura passages had been sung, and were succeeded by a quieter passage of recitative that turns one's attention from the performer's virtuosity to the dramatic situation. For the speaker turns to the present and mentions the autumn landscape, Pauline's love, and the possible effect of his confession on her. And finally, at line 256, he gives us the key to the method by which the first section of the poem has proceeded:

I must not think – lest this new impulse die
In which I trust. I have no confidence,
So I will sing on – fast as fancies come
Rudely – the verse being as the mood it paints. (255–9)

It is clear from this passage that the speaker is creating a poem extemporaneously. He is inspired, yet must not analyse his impulse ('must not think') lest he destroy it. Since he sings 'fast as fancies come / Rudely ...' the images follow one another by association. Hence the poem

14

wanders as much as the speaker's thoughts. Finally, the verse is the 'imaginative equivalent' of the mood felt by the poet, and reflects in its imagery and rhythms his emotions.

Although the speaker promises to 'sing on,' he does not in fact do so. For, in describing his method of composition, he has begun to think about what he is doing; consequently his inspiration fades and he proceeds to analyse himself. This analysis of the mind of the poet is quite a different thing from the actual rendering of the act of composition. It is planned from the beginning, and proceeds in as strictly logical a fashion as the plan suggests:

> I strip my mind bare – whose first elements
> I shall unveil – not as they struggled forth
> In infancy, nor as they now exist,
> That I am grown above them, and can rule them,
> But in that middle stage, when they were full,
> Yet ere I had disposed them to my will;
> And then I shall show how these elements
> Produced my present state, and what it is.   (260–7)

John Stuart Mill objected to this passage. In the Forster copy of the poem Mill stroked out these lines and wrote, 'This only says "you shall see what you shall see" & is more prose than poetry' (p 21). Mill's comment calls attention to the awkward manner in which Browning introduces a new section of his poem, and the overly systematic way in which the speaker proceeds to set forth the 'first elements' of his mind: 'consciousness / Of self' (269–70), 'self-supremacy' (273), 'a principle of restlessness' (277), and 'imagination' (284), and 'a need, a trust, a yearning after God' (295). The poem is thus moving in quite a different manner. Interest lies, not in the speaker's production of images, but in the poet's analysis of his subject. The images are still there, of course, but they serve a different purpose. One has the sense of listening, not to the speaker displaying his powers of imagination, but to the poet exploring the nature of the speaker's mind. Thus, when the speaker's imagination is described as 'an angel to me' (285), the image not only conveys the speaker's emotion when he thinks of this faculty of his, but also indicates the function of this particular characteristic that the poet is analysing: it is 'beside me ever, / And never failing me ...' (286–7).

The speaker retraces in an analytical fashion the ground covered imaginatively in the first section, beginning with the feelings of guilt and moving through memories of youth to the discovery of Shelley,

Then he turns to 'real life' (440ff) and to a consideration of 'how best life's end might be attained ...' (445). But almost immediately his plan gives way to new inspiration when he remembers how he suddenly stood off from his life and saw it as a beautiful dream. The memory of the change recreates within him the emotions connected with it, and these in turn inspire in him the image of 'strange towers, and walled gardens' (451). The analysis, it is clear, is maturing into inspiration. The consideration of his new powers, 'wit, mockery, / And happiness' (463–4) leads to a major 'imaginative equivalent,' the image of the temple of the soul (469–88). Similarly, the consideration of his present state, which centres in the tension between the 'strange powers, and feelings, and desires' (595) of his soul and the limitations of his body, the 'clay prison' (594), leads to the most important 'imaginative equivalent,' the Andromeda passage which is the turning point of the poem. Although it is introduced as an escape from the speaker's present confusion, and is dismissed with 'Let it pass' (668), it is in fact a portrayal of the perfect faith that he has been seeking. In short, his imagination, his powers as a poet, are lifting him above the chaos of his present situation, and are presenting him with the 'imaginative equivalent' for the emotion of pure faith that his analytical and reasoning faculty could not alone induce. The sudden appearance of this emotion prepares the way for the final resolution, a resolution that is not possible from analysis alone: 'I feel I but explain to my own loss / These impulses – they live no less the same' (682–3). With line 708 the analysis comes to an end, and we turn now in a new direction.

Partly because the analysis has been completed, partly because the speaker turns again to Pauline, his song itself becomes once more important. He compares Pauline to a winter flower, and goes on to identify himself imaginatively with all natural life. The identification brings a new rush of inspiration ('I am inspired – come with me, Pauline!' 731), and he pictures 'a home for us, out of the world: in thought ...' (730). There follows a description of a retreat to nature (732–97), a retreat which brings regeneration and renewal of purpose. As he floats in the air, in the 'clear, dear breath of God, that loveth us ...' (789), he feels an exhilarating sense of freedom. This emotion continues when he returns to the world of ordinary men, until he realizes that the same nature that brought about his regeneration is also a barrier beyond which the soul cannot see: 'I cannot be immortal, nor taste all' (810).

In spite of the constant lapses, the recognition of limitations, there has been, ever since the Andromeda passage, a steady if nonrational

16

progression towards faith. In fact, his analysis has proved nothing but the need for faith, and it is this need which constantly presses the speaker on. Hence, lines 811 to 859 are in the main addressed to God, and consolidate his faith. Lines 811 to 821 analyse his need for faith; the lines following are actually a prayer in which the speaker recognizes that ' "there is that in me / which turns to thee ..." ' (829–30). The next section (831–54) proceeds in the manner of a church service: there is the recognition of sin ('I am knit round / As with a charm, by sin and lust and pride ...' 846–7), the realization of the finitude of his reason and the desire for the grace and salvation that goes beyond reason, and the resulting vision of Christ the Saviour. This vision leads to commitment:

A mortal, sin's familiar friend doth here
Avow that he will give all earth's reward,
But to believe and humbly teach the faith,
In suffering, and poverty, and shame,
Only believing he is not unloved ...   (855–9)

Having reached such a position, the speaker realizes that both Pauline's love and the process of putting his emotions into words have been responsible for the renewal of his faith. Thus the end of the poem looks back to the themes and techniques introduced at the beginning.

This final section of the poem includes some comments on the nature of poetry which help us to define further the kind of poem we are dealing with:

Thou know'st, dear friend, I could not think all calm,
For wild dreams followed me, and bore me off,
And all was indistinct. Ere one was caught
Another glanced; so dazzled by my wealth,
Knowing not which to leave nor which to choose,
For all my thoughts so floated, nought was fixed –
And then thou said'st a perfect bard was one
Who shadowed out the stages of all life,
And so thou badest me tell this my first stage –
'Tis done: and even now I feel all dim the shift
Of thought.   (877–87)

Pauline's definition of the perfect poet and her advice to the speaker both seem to foreshadow what was to become Spasmodic doctrine. The speaker is clearly concerned about his method of composition, and feels (or has felt) that a poet must control his imagination, must choose his images with care, and must mould and shape his poem. Pauline emphasizes, not the art of poetry, but the ability of the poet to enter imaginatively into 'the stages of all life.' She makes it clear that the immediacy and the richness of such experiences can never be fully conveyed in poetry, and that the poem must always be an imperfect and obscure representation of the poet's concept. 'To represent imperfectly' is one of the meanings of the verb 'to shadow' in Johnson's Dictionary, and that is apparently the meaning of the verb here. The Dictionary also lists the meaning, 'to represent typically,' and types are of course suggested through images and symbols. If 'shadowing' refers to the poet's imaginative involvement in all aspects of life, and to his ability to express that involvement in images, then his word for the representation of 'this my first stage' – to 'tell' – seems curiously flat and matter-of-fact. In 1888 Browning replaced 'tell' with 'shadow,' perhaps to indicate his feeling that the poem was indeed imperfect; he also substituted 'chronicled' for 'shadowed out' (884), and by doing so shifted the emphasis in Pauline's definition of the perfect poet from the genius whose imagination enters into all experience to the observer who provides an objective record of what he sees. But in 1833 Pauline seems to be identifying 'the stages of all life' with the poet's life, and to be encouraging him to provide what Fox was to call 'the annals of a poet's mind.'

Pauline's advice that her lover capitalize on his wealth of 'wild dreams' and floating images may have encouraged him to begin the poem, but it is not much help in ending it. For the 'wild dreams' and the floating images go on, and a poem cannot. And, moreover, an end implies shape, and shape in turn requires careful selection and construction. The speaker in Pauline is thus faced with an almost impossible task: to bring to an end a poem about experience which has no end. It is this difficulty that makes the final lines of Pauline so unsatisfactory. Most critics have found them full of unresolved contradictions: protestations of faith and the nagging doubts of 'a soul half-saved' (990); 'an end in perfect joy' (994) and a sinking toward death: 'For I seem dying, as one going in the dark / To fight a giant ...' (1026–7). T.J. Collins has summed up these 'unresolved problems' by emphasizing 'the young poet's ambiguous attitude toward Shelley' and 'the unconvincing tone of the religious resolution and the rejection of selfishness which occurs in the final stages of the poem.'[17] Part of Browning's difficulty was certainly artistic. He had not yet learned that a poem was artifice rather than nature, and that a poem may represent mental confusion without itself being confused.

Pauline thus emerges as a curious experiment. In its 'poetical acces-sories' – the outpouring of images and emotions – it resembles a Spas-modic poem. In structure too it foreshadows the poem-within-a-poem technique of Dobell, Smith, and others. But, even when writing most like his contemporaries, Browning's characteristic purposes and methods are evident. In making the confession not his own utterance but that of an assumed character, and in attempting, rather crudely, an analysis of that character's mind and emotions, Browning presents his first account of 'the development of a soul.'

Paracelsus

While *Pauline* tends to be an effusion of youthful enthusiasm, *Paracelsus* is a highly experimental poem, the first in which Browning freely modi-fies the generally accepted concept of a genre to suit his own purposes.

In the original preface to *Paracelsus* Browning gives us some indica-tion of the nature of his experiment. His first concern is to make it clear to his readers that the poem is not governed by the traditional concept of the drama: 'I am anxious that the reader should not, at the very outset – mistaking my performance for one of a class with which it has nothing in common – judge it by principles on which it was never moulded, and subject it to a standard to which it was never meant to conform.' These principles, Browning goes on to explain, 'have immediate regard to stage representation,' but can only be 'restrictions' for the kind of poem he is about to present.

Browning seems to be referring to the demand for action on the stage, the necessity of a well-contrived plot, interesting characters, and some observance of the unities. To do away with such 'restrictions' precludes certain reactions on the part of the audience. With little or no action and no stage representation, love of spectacle is neither aroused nor satisfied. Nor is the intellect pleased by a plot which is wound and unwound logically and consistently. The kind of curiosity that asks, 'How is this story going to turn out?' will find little pleasure in *Paracel-sus*, and anyone who tries to reconstruct the events of Paracelsus' life has clearly missed the import of Browning's treatment. For Browning wants the reader to ask, not, 'How did Paracelsus live his life?' (a ques-tion answered by the *Biographie universelle*) but 'What is the point of Paracelsus' life?' Browning tries to satisfy what he calls the 'co-operating fancy' (ie, the imagination): 'It is certain ... that a work like mine depends more immediately on the intelligence and sympathy of the reader for its success – indeed were my scenes stars it must be his co-operating fancy which, supplying all chasms, shall connect the scattered lights into one constellation – a Lyre or a Crown.' The 'chasms' are not the historical parts of Paracelsus' life; they are its moral and spiritual aspects, the significance of which cannot be fully conveyed by direct statement. The reader is therefore invited to regard the poem in much the same manner as the poet regarded his original materials. Whatever the poet's fancy has done in shaping the material is yet one more fact for the 'co-operating fancy' of the reader. He is asked to attempt to understand Paracelsus' existence, to find in it a pattern (the Lyre or Crown). It is thus evident that Browning is for the first time concerned, not with the relation between himself and his poem (as he apparently was when writing *Pauline*), but with the relation between the poem and its readers; not with revealing or hiding himself, but with the problem of awakening in his readers insights similar to his own.

Although Browning was writing 'a poem, not a drama,' he nevertheless chose a dramatic form. He emphasized that his choice did not in any way restrict him, as such a choice often did when poets wrote what was called a 'dramatic poem,' and he would have disagreed heartily with J.A. Heraud, a critic who had argued that the 'dramatic poem' ('a modern species of composition, which has sprung up amongst us in consequence of the degraded state of our theatre ...'), though written for the closet and not the stage, must, nevertheless, not 'violate all the proprieties of the theatre ...'[18] The extent of Browning's innovations in this form becomes evident when we compare *Paracelsus* with the most famous 'dramatic poem' of the day, Henry Taylor's *Philip Van Arte-velde*. Published in June 1834 (fourteen months before *Paracelsus*), it was an immediate success. Taylor was hailed as a 'brilliant originator of something novel and startling in poetry,' and the poem itself was discussed as 'an experimental work.'[19] Taylor describes in the preface to the poem the kind of experiment he was trying: 'As this work, consisting of two Plays and an Interlude, is equal in length to about six such plays as are adapted to representation, it is almost unnecessary to say that it was not intended for the stage. It is properly an Historical Romance, cast in a dramatic and rhythmical form.' In thus dramatising a mode made popular by Sir Walter Scott, but at the same time rejecting the condensation and concentration necessary for the stage, Taylor apparently hoped to combine what he called a 'bald strength in character and incident'[20] with variety of action and a comprehensive view of an

20

heroic life. The poem traces all of Van Artevelde's long career, from the time when he becomes ruler in Ghent, until his death in battle at Oudenarde. Yet the complexity of his motives is never fully explored, and the dialogue is primarily a means for advancing the action. The poem is, first and foremost, a tale of love, war, and politics, with plenty of action and intrigue – this in spite of the fact that in April of 1834 Taylor drew the attention of Lockhart (whose review appeared in the *Quarterly* in June 1834) to the characterization of Van Artevelde rather than the action and the handling of the plot[21] (which, he told Southey, 'is the great difficulty with me').[22]

Because the work is largely a tale of action, it seemed to at least one reviewer, T.H. Lister, that Taylor did not gain a great deal by using the form of the 'dramatic poem': 'In the dramatic form, with its exclusion of all save dialogue and soliloquy, and its division into acts and scenes, we see no advantage ...'[23] The fault, the reviewer goes on to say, lies in the fact that Taylor is still bound by the conventions of the drama, even though he is no longer writing for the stage:

> The original intention with which the dramatic poem was devised, had reference solely to the stage. Among the ancients, and in our Elizabethan age, plays were no more composed for mere perusal, than essays are written to be acted. It is only in these later times, when the spectacle-loving public of the seventeenth century has been succeeded by a reading public, that the drama has been not unfrequently accommodated to the altered habits of the community. But the authors of such works, influenced, we suppose, by association, and reverence for precedent, have omitted to disenthral them from forms, of which, when the destination was altered, the utility ceased. (p 4)

The reviewer goes on to quote Taylor's motto from Bacon (*Dramatica Poesis est veluti Historia spectabilis*) and to point out that 'with no propriety could the epithet "*spectabilis*" be applied to a work ... "not intended for the stage" ' (pp 4–5). And yet Taylor's stage directions indicate that he visualizes his sets, and even the groupings of the actors. The reviewer also points out that 'when action is introduced, the words which accompany it are short, strong, and appropriate, suitable to the situation, and equally to the character of the speaker' (p 7). Dialogue is thus used in the traditional way. It becomes evident, then, that Taylor's work was not as experimental as he thought it was. Aside from the fact that he dispensed with stage presentation, he wrote a fairly conventional drama.

21

It is possible that Browning is referring to *Philip Van Artevelde* when he writes in the preface to *Paracelsus*: 'I do not very well understand what is called a Dramatic Poem, wherein all those restrictions only submitted to on account of compensating good in the original scheme are scrupulously retained, as though for some special fitness in themselves – and all new facilities placed at an author's disposal by the vehicle he selects, as pertinaciously rejected.' The 'new facilities' that Browning discovered in the drama are hinted at in his description of the kind of experiment he tried in *Paracelsus*:

> It is an attempt, probably more novel than happy, to reverse the method usually adopted by writers whose aim it is to set forth any phenomenon of the mind or the passions, by the operation of persons and events; and ... instead of having recourse to an external machinery of incidents to create and evolve the crisis I desire to produce, I have ventured to display somewhat minutely the mood itself in its rise and progress, and have suffered the agency by which it is influenced and determined, to be generally discernible in its effects alone, and subordinate throughout, if not altogether excluded ...

He disposes of action and of characterization that results in action ('the operation of persons and events'), and of plot ('an external machinery of incidents'). Instead he shows the 'rise and progress' of 'the mood' through dialogue, and requires of the reader a keen and lively awareness of the patterns of imagery and the irony of shifting relationships.

The ironic pattern of *Paracelsus* has been described by F.E.L. Priestley[24] who points out that we must not expect 'the irony of external drama, in which we watch characters misjudging an external situation' but rather 'the irony of the wrong thought or the wrong emotion, an intellectual or mental illusion set against the reality of truth.' Such irony operates, he continues,

> when a character is obviously and firmly in error. But it can also operate when a character is right without knowing it, or arrives at a right conclusion from the wrong premises, or the wrong conclusion from the right premises, or when he is right but not in the way he thinks he is, or when he arrives momentarily at a truth and then dismisses it, and so on. All these modes are at work in *Paracelsus* ...

For Paracelsus aspires to infinite knowledge, the kind of knowledge that can only be God's. His failure to attain his goal, and his developing insight into the meaning of his failure, provide the ironic pattern.

The poem, like a traditional drama, is divided into five acts. Each of the five 'moments' from Paracelsus' life is chosen, not because it has the dramatic potentialities of action or striking event, but because it is the point at which Paracelsus is best shown trying to make sense of his situation. The reader is given, not the facts of Paracelsus' life, but a dramatic portrayal of the way in which he approaches the truth of his existence. Hence the interest lies in the aspirations, the values, and the beliefs that make Paracelsus what he is, and that show his developing understanding of the proper relation of the infinite and the finite. The movement of his thoughts and emotions is indicated in a sometimes ironic fashion by the titles Browning gave to each of the five acts: Paracelsus Aspires, Paracelsus Attains, Paracelsus, Paracelsus Aspires, Paracelsus Attains. Priestley defines the pattern of these acts: 'true aspiration and ironic attainment followed by ironic or false aspiration and true attainment.'

The first act, entitled in a straightforward manner 'Paracelsus Aspires,' centres on Paracelsus' plan

> to comprehend the works of God,
> And God himself, and all God's intercourse
> With our own mind ... (I 533–5)

Although act II is entitled 'Paracelsus Attains,' it is only too evident that Paracelsus has failed to carry out his original plan, and that he has attained only 'half-gains, and conjectures, and crude hopes ...' (II 18). He does, of course, attain love through meeting Aprile, but is only half aware that by love Aprile refers to the beautiful, the ' "loveliness of life" ' (II 485) (as Priestley was the first to point out). The irony is heightened by Paracelsus' failure to understand the meaning of Aprile's death. Having aspired infinitely in the manner of Paracelsus, and having failed too as Paracelsus has done, Aprile reached the moment of death only to discover that 'God is the PERFECT POET, / Who in his person acts his own creations' (II 648–9), and that man cannot attain the perfection of God. At the end, to his surprise, Aprile is crowned: the life which he judged a failure through his inability to attain to infinite beauty is not judged so by God. Paracelsus, however, thinks that Aprile has succeeded through love, and determines to follow his course.

The ironic pattern is supported and enriched by the pattern of imagery. Paracelsus is associated with a star (I 527), a gier-eagle (I 347), and a bright light (I 376–80), images that indicate in different ways his superhuman God-like aspirations, his striving after infinite knowledge. Michal, by way of contrast, has an intuitive understanding

23

of the relation between infinite and finite. The images associated with her are not things far above and beyond ordinary life, but things that suggest a close link between heaven and earth. She is closely connected with nature, and particularly with the garden at Würzburg, as 'the lady of this / Sequester'd nest!' (I 35–6). (The *hortus conclusus* image derived from the Song of Songs seems relevant here.) Paracelsus thinks of Michal in connection with flowers, particularly violets (III 127–9); he also thinks of her as an angel (v 213–17) with a halo of 'quiet and peculiar light' (III 23–5). Michal's affinities with the natural and supernatural world come together in the image of the bird (III 28–35) whose song provides insight into the love and harmony that govern the created universe. The perfect love of Festus and Michal is one aspect of this God-ordained harmony, while Paracelsus' sense of self-sufficiency, his desire to serve mankind, but on his own terms, is really pride, the primary sin.

In act III we learn that Paracelsus has tried Aprile's way of love, and has failed once more: 'I cannot feed on beauty, for the sake / Of beauty only ...' (III 701–2). He is led to consider the nature of his failure:

> I know as little
> Why I deserve to fail, as why I hoped
> Better things in my youth.   (III 523–5)

Festus suggests a new meaning for the term love:

> Love is never blind; but rather
> Alive to every the minutest spot
> That mars its object ...   (III 833–5)

Love, it is clear, is closely identified with acceptance of the finite. It is the faculty by which one not only recognizes the limitations and imperfections of this world, but also values such an existence as a 'vale of Soul-making,' to use Keats' phrase. Festus explains that within the heart of each loving individual grows the 'giant image of Perfection' (III 857) that gives life its meaning and purpose, and that this image grows, not by scorning but by accepting the limitations of life, by stooping to the finite. Some such concept of love appears to be already working in Paracelsus' life. Because of Aprile's influence, Paracelsus has been moved to become a teacher, to give his gains, 'imperfect as they were,' to men.

In spite of such a slight advance, Paracelsus' aspirations in act IV are basically the same as those in act I, with this difference: that he will now accept any help, and will seek both to know and to enjoy at once. His songs help in pointing up the irony of these aspirations, for they are songs, not of imagined success – as one might expect when an individual aspires – but of all-too-possible failure. The first song, 'Heap cassia,' describes the passing of his fancies, his youthful aspirations. It is the song of a funereal ritual, sung so 'that fitting dignity might be preserved ...' (iv 210). Like most rituals, it expresses and directs emotion, controlling it while letting it run its course. The function of the second song, 'Over the sea our galleys went ...' (iv 450–522), is somewhat different. Paracelsus describes it as a 'tale' or 'parable' and indicates that it refers obliquely to his own situation. The song is one of partial failure, of aims only half achieved. Like the voyagers, Paracelsus has gone ashore and set out his work too soon; he has settled for immediate results rather than the long-term struggle dictated by his aspirations. His sense of the discrepancy between his desires and his achievement prepares for the intuition which he has at the end of this act. Such a vision is hardly possible when pride and a sense of self-sufficiency blind a man. It is only when one has admitted that life is a mystery and that the human understanding is finite that the way is open for non-discursive insight. In Paracelsus' case, the vision is evoked by news of Michal's death. His statement, 'I believe we do not wholly die' (iv 676), is very different from his angry complaint at the end of act iii:

Another world!
And why this world, this common world to be
A make-shift, a mere foil, how fair soever,
To some fine life to-come? (iii 1011–14)

For the first time he modifies his demand that this life should be totally explicable.

In the final act, Paracelsus attains the only end that human beings can attain. He recognizes that the real meaning of his existence lies in its finiteness (v 541ff), and that man, while being the consummation and 'completion of this sphere / Of life' (v 684–5), must still struggle on:

When all mankind is perfected alike,
Equal in full-blown powers – then, not till then,
Begins the general infancy of man ... (v 750–2)

'Paracelsus presents a vision,' writes Priestley, 'not of a static, complete, perfect world, but of a vast, joyous, striving world of becoming, the infinite world of the imperfect, dynamic because never finished.' In the light of this vision, Paracelsus concludes that his career may not be the failure he had considered it. He realizes 'that his own life, by revealing a measure of truth through the process of striving, defeat, and error, has in fact carried out its real purpose.'[25]

The movement of Paracelsus' understanding is supported by the light-darkness imagery. The poem is pervaded by physical darkness, symbolizing the limitations of man's understanding. In act I the sun sets soon after Paracelsus begins speaking (I 59–60); similarly, act II takes place after sunset, and the night complements the physical darkness Aprile experiences in death (II 628); in act III the night dominates the scene, and gives way only at the end to the cold and cheerless light of morning; act IV takes place during an evening in an inn and act V in the darkness of a hospital cell. Contrasting with the physical darkness are the glimpses of spiritual light. Aprile has a radiant vision at his death, while Paracelsus on his own death-bed speaks of the 'splendour' of 'God's lamp' (V 901–2). The light-dark contrast is related to the star image, which, since it is a physical phenomenon, links physical and spiritual light, and to the angel image, by which Michal is associated with the radiance of God's harmony.

Browning referred to *Paracelsus* as 'an experiment I am in no case likely to repeat,' yet this 'experiment' was the most successful of his early poems. For he learned how to develop 'new facilities' in the genre he chose, not just for the sake of novelty, but to trace what he was chiefly interested in: 'the development of a soul.' He learned too that if he were to convey to his readers his own insights with all the force and immediacy with which they came to him, he must use techniques which would stimulate the reader's 'co-operating fancy.' Irony is a particularly good technique for this purpose, since the reader then may take no statement at face value, and is forced, like Paracelsus, to an awareness of a world where no knowledge seems certain. Imagery is equally difficult to fix, since an image never means one thing only, but finds its meaning in a pattern of relations that shift as the poem moves along. Browning asked for readers with 'intelligence and sympathy,' and asked them to construct patterns from the patterns he himself provided in the poem. This construction of patterns – his own, his characters', his readers' – was to become a major concern of *The Ring and the Book*.

Sordello

In the preface to *Paracelsus* Browning spoke of 'other productions which may follow in a more popular, and perhaps less difficult form.' And on page vi of the first edition of *Strafford* appeared the words, 'Nearly ready. *Sordello*, in Six Books.' These two comments, 'popular' and 'in Six Books,' give us the key to the literary kind to which *Sordello* belongs: the narrative poetry which was immensely popular in the early nineteenth century, of which the best examples are the metrical romances of Scott and the Turkish tales of Byron. These poems were imitated by many less important writers, including Mrs William Busk, whose own *Sordello* (1837) has some part to play in the history of Browning's poem.

The characteristics of these narrative romances are simply speed and colour. It is the task of the narrative poet, one reviewer said, 'to embellish striking incidents by splendid descriptions,'[26] and certainly the rapidity of the action, and the vivid descriptions of unfamiliar scenes, manners, and customs, account for much of the popularity of these poems. While the reviewers might criticise Scott and Byron for the construction of the story, they rarely failed to praise the gusto, energy, and passion of their narratives. And while they might quibble about some of the diction, they admired the wide and accurate knowledge these poets had of far-off ages and far-away places. Byron's descriptions owe less to literary sources than they do to first-hand knowledge gained in his travels through the countries of the eastern Mediterranean.[27] And Scott was so steeped in the lore of the Middle Ages that, as he tells us in the preface to *The Lay of the Last Minstrel*, 'the description of scenery and manners was more the object of the author than a combined and regular narrative ...' The 'striking incidents' and the 'splendid descriptions' were, in the minds of reviewers and readers both, the essential ingredients in narrative romances. The term 'romance' meant other things as well, as we shall see in chapter three, but these were the characteristics of the popular tradition within which Browning was working.

It was the same tradition that Mrs Busk worked in. Following the example of Scott, she tells us that her purpose is to illustrate customs and manners, to give 'a picture of what a Troubadour was, or, in early times, was supposed to be.' The troubadour's triple role as knight, lover, and bard not only gave him a place in several representative parts of his society, but also made him a highly suitable hero for a poem of action and adventure. Mrs Busk's story moves along rapidly, but lacks the energy of Scott's work. Scott was capable of conveying, through the quality of his verse, the excitement of heroic action. Mrs Busk, on the other hand, hurries through events – both heroic and otherwise – with the grim persistence of a chronicler.

Of particular importance in these narrative poems is the role of the narrator. Sometimes the narrator is a shadowy figure who calls his audience together at the beginning and disperses it at the end, as in Mrs Busk's *Sordello*. But sometimes he is carefully delineated, as in Scott's *Lay of the Last Minstrel*, where the minstrel is himself a representative of the age he sings about. The minstrel-narrator is the *persona* of the poet. His function is to tell a story, to describe manners and customs, and to comment on the action, where necessary, by making general observations or by explaining motives and feelings. Some reviewers thought that the narrator ought to go further, and describe in detail his characters' mental and emotional life. Francis Jeffrey, for instance, praised Byron for his 'delineation of the stronger and deeper passions,' and for doing what all modern narrative poets should do: 'The passion itself must now be pourtrayed – and all its fearful workings displayed in detail before us. The minds of the great agents must be unmasked for us – and all the anatomy of their throbbing bosoms laid open to our gaze.'[28] The *Quarterly Review* disagreed: 'The writer, who seeks to excite any emotion, will never effect this by attempting to analyse its nature and origin, but must content himself with describing its effects ...'[29] Most critics agreed that the narrator deals primarily with externals: with events rather than character, with appearances rather than states of mind.

It seems curious that Browning should choose the narrative mode to deal with 'the development of a soul.' The 'historical decoration' – which for Scott is an essential part of the narrative – is, for Browning, 'of no more importance than a background requires ...' His emphasis is on the inner growth of his central character and it is not surprising that he had to modify considerably the conventions available to him. Browning's experiment can best be defined by examining the poem itself.

Browning begins *Sordello* with the narrator speaking to a select group of poets 'Summoned together from the world's four ends' (i 32):

Who will, may hear Sordello's story told:
His story? Who believes me shall behold
The man, pursue his fortunes to the end
Like me ... (i 1–4)

The manner of presentation resembles – initially – that of the conventional narrative poem. Browning, however, goes on to tell us that he chose the narrative mode ('not the worst / Yet not the best expedient' i 12–13) for purposes quite different from those of his predecessors. His chief reason becomes evident when he contrasts narrative with the drama. The dramatist, he says, is hindered by the conventional manner of presentation: he is hidden behind his characters, and can give no clue to the interpretation of the piece: his is, he says,

A story I could body forth so well
By making speak, myself kept out of view,
The very man as he was wont to do,
And leaving you to say the rest for him ... (ɪ 14–17)

But Browning is very conscious that in tracing 'the development of a soul' he is a 'setter-forth of unexampled themes' (ɪ 26). The novelty of his concerns as a poet, he thought, made it necessary for him to choose a genre in which he could comment on the actions and characters:

It seems
Your setters-forth of unexampled themes,
Makers of quite new men, producing them
Had best chalk broadly on each vesture's hem
The wearer's quality, or take his stand
Motley on back and pointing-pole in hand
Beside them; so for once I face ye, friends ... (ɪ 25–31)

The speaker, then, not only tells the story, but discusses characters and explains the significance of events. These two aspects of the poet's voice I refer to as the narrator and the commentator.

The narrator's function is that of the traditional minstrel. He tells his story in a straightforward manner, and, aside from the beginning *in medias res*, moves from event to event in the proper chronological sequence. In producing his characters and in telling his story, the narrator gives a vivid description of externals. In fact, as a recent critic has pointed out, he introduces each stage of his story in the manner of a diorama.[30]

Lo, the Past is hurled
In twain: upthrust, out-staggering on the world,
Subsiding into shape, a darkness rears
Its outline, kindles at the core, appears
Verona. (ɪ 72–5)

He goes on to present a vivid picture of Verona during the Guelf-Ghibelline struggle, and uses both descriptive details and scraps of conversation to portray 'the time's aspect and peculiar woe' (ɪ 188). Browning outdoes both Scott and Mrs Busk in his descriptions which are colourful and realistic. He emphasizes not so much the romance of a distant age (that is, the features of the age that make it distinct from his own) as the common characteristics of humanity in all ages. Nevertheless, his historical settings constitute, like the entertainment in the palace at Verona, a 'voluptuous pageant' (1 326).

The commentator interprets the descriptions presented by the narrator. He proceeds, not in a straight line, but by turning the action over and over in his mind. Miss Barrett's criticism of the poem may be taken as a description of the commentator's method: 'I think that the principle of association is too subtly in movement throughout [*Sordello*] – so that *while* you are going straight forward you go at the same time round & round, until the progress involved in the motion is lost sight of by the lookers on.'[31] As Miss Barrett's disapproval indicates, the commentary is worked out in a very complex way. In the opening part of Book 1, for instance, the narrator presents the essential details of the situation in Verona (1 72–187). His is an account of the way in which hate worked, as he tells us (1 93–4), and he recounts events and snatches of conversation to explain the situation. Although the narrator vividly recreates 'the time's aspect and peculiar woe' (1 188), the commentator reminds us that what has been told is no more than what is already in the history books: 'Yourselves may spell it yet in chronicles' (1 189). Browning was to call this material, in his later work, the 'facts.' The commentator must interpret these 'facts,' and so give the significance of the events. He does so by developing the imagery which he finds in the narrator's account. He deals first with the effect of the war on Italy. The Guelf-Ghibelline struggle originated in Germany, and the commentator is anxious to show the adverse effect of a foreign quarrel on both the Italian people and their leaders. The image of the vine has already been suggested by the imagery associated with fear and hate ('root' 1 91; 'wine' 1 93). This vine becomes the chokeweed (1 212–37) – an image whose importance is emphasized by the parenthetical 'conceive' which immediately precedes it (for Browning often uses parentheses for emphasis, or to set off a highly significant comment). In this elaborately developed image, the cliffs represent the Italian leaders; the 'shoal and shelf' the people; the chokeweed the vast web of hatred, inspired by a foreign quarrel, but capable of 'some growth / Unfancied yet' (1 231–2); that is, the growth of Italian nationalism that would eventually thrust the Germans out of Italy.

At first the commentator seems limited to the material provided for him by the narrator. As the story proceeds, however, he plays an increasingly important role. Rather than rearranging, analysing, and explaining the material presented to him, he provides the essential insights that give the poem shape, and the facts meaning. His function is best seen when he deals with Sordello himself. The narrator describes Sordello's features, and can only suggest, through his appearance, that he is a gifted youth:

> Yourselves shall trace
> (The delicate nostril swerving wide and fine,
> A sharp and restless lip, so well combine
> With that calm brow) a soul fit to receive
> Delight at every sense ... (1 462–6)

The commentator goes beyond appearance, and makes clear the nature of Sordello's gifts by distinguishing two classes of poets: that 'regal class' (1 467) who locate the source of their vision outside themselves, and hence feel 'A need to blend with each external charm' (1 507); and that 'gentler crew' (1 524) who find the source of their vision within themselves. Both classes worship loveliness or beauty as the revelation of the infinite. To the first class the commentator poses a question: 'How can such love?' (1 483). He is asking not how this class shows an appreciation of loveliness, but how it can work some good for that towards which its feelings are directed. The commentator distinguishes two faults that prevent such men from loving: an unwillingness to stoop to the imperfections of the world (1 538–61) and an attempt to force an imperfect world to contain the perfection of heaven ('Thrusting in time eternity's concern' 1 566). As soon as the commentator mentions the second fault, one of the audience immediately identifies it as Sordello's flaw, his 'mark / Of Leprosy' (1 567–8). Having thus revealed one of the essential features in the development of Sordello's soul, the commentator feels some concern lest such knowledge should vitiate the enjoyment of his listeners in hearing Sordello's life told. And so he addresses them directly, and instructs them on the proper use of such insight:

> Go back to the beginning rather; blend
> It gently with Sordello's life; the end
> Is piteous, you shall see, but much between
> Pleasant enough ... (1 587–90)

The complexity of the method by which the poem proceeds is evident. Browning deliberately slows the narrative, so that instead of the conventional velocity and gusto that carry the reader rapidly through the course of the story, there are elaborately developed patterns that force the reader to consider the significance of each part in relation to the whole. Indeed, what Naddo quotes Squarcialupe as saying about Sordello may be said about Browning as well:

> the man can't stoop
> To sing us out, quoth he, a mere romance;
> He'd fain do better than the best, enhance
> The subjects' rarity, work problems out
> Therewith ... (II 784–8)

Browning's answer to this kind of criticism would be that his purpose was not simply to tell a story or to write 'a mere romance' in the manner of Scott or Byron, but to trace 'the development of a soul.' Indeed, he could not touch on any part of a character's life without exploring all aspects of it. Browning would certainly share Sordello's aims as summed up in the 'pompion-twine' image:

> Observe a pompion-twine afloat;
> Pluck me one cup from off the castle-moat –
> Along with cup you raise leaf, stalk and root,
> The entire surface of the pool to boot.
> So could I pluck a cup, put in one song
> A single sight, did not my hand, too strong,
> Twitch in the least the root-strings of the whole.
> How should externals satisfy my soul?   (II 775–82)

Although Browning thus modified considerably the conventions of the narrative poetry of his day, he was far from satisfied with the results. His dissatisfaction is evident in the middle of book III, where he suddenly breaks off his story to discuss again his narrative techniques.

Browning's dissatisfaction rests upon his feeling that his narrative has not had the desired effect upon his audience. The purpose of the narrator-commentator device, the proceeding not only in a straight line but round and round as well, was to give his audience insight into Sordello's situation by revealing the poet's knowledge of the total pattern of Sordello's life. But now Browning begins to realize that a poet cannot by discursive statement 'give' anyone insight, just as Lazarus with his knowledge of immortality cannot 'give' Karshish faith. Insight, like faith, is something that the individual must work out for himself. The poet may provide the materials for such insight, and impose on them a certain artistic pattern, but these patterns are complete only when they become living truth in the mind of the reader.

These ideas Browning works out through the image of the 'transcendental platan' (iii 596). The platan (that is, the poem) is a glittering artifice fashioned by the consummate art of a master magician. Complete in itself, it is at best an amusing contrivance. While the listener (in this case the 'novice-queen') may feel 'uncontrolled delight' (iii 606), the magician becomes 'decrepit, stark' (iii 605). His fate seems to represent that of the poet whose art is made not for life's sake, but for its own sake. There is a parallel between the platan image and Browning's comments on *Pauline*, in which he describes his portrayal of the speaker as a 'shapely Tree of Life in this Fool's paradise of mine.' In each case, the tree image stands for the wealth of the poet's fancies, fancies that have not yet been brought to bear upon life itself.

Browning rejects such self-sufficient fancies in favour of the kind of poem which finds its completeness only in the imaginative response of the reader. He describes this new type of poetry by distinguishing three kinds of poets:

> The office of ourselves nor blind nor dumb
> And seeing somewhat of man's state, has been,
> The worst of us, to say they so have seen;
> The better, what it was they saw; the best,
> Impart the gift of seeing to the rest ...   (iii 864–8)

Browning is striving to be the third kind of poet, the 'Maker-see' (iii 928), but he is not yet sure how well the various genres suit his purpose. For this reason, then, he considers in turn each of the three principal genres, and tries to describe the effect of each on the audience.

First of all, he gives the speech of a young man imprisoned in the Piombi. The speech, insofar as it is an accurate representation of what a youth would say in such circumstances, is dramatic. In judging the 'truth' of it, the audience recognizes the appropriateness or fitness of the speech to the circumstances ('the incarcerated youth / Would say that!' iii 880–1), and hence has gained an insight into this particular situation. In the second example – this time a narrative – Browning tells about Plara the Bard, who, in a grimy town, wrote sonnets celebrating the country. The kind of insight conveyed here is somewhat different: the audience recognizes the accuracy of the description ('Exact the town, the minster and the street!' iii 901). In the third example, Browning presents Lucio the lover. But, instead of describing Lucio, or presenting one of his speeches, he discusses love and lust in relation to happiness and sadness. The aphoristic tone, the sense of universal truth, marks the passage as a lyric:

As all mirth triumphs, sadness means defeat:
Lust triumphs and is gay, Love's triumphed o'er
And sad ... (III 902–4)

These truths, however universal, lead to an insight into the exact nature of Lucio's mood: ' 'Tis of the mood itself I speak, what tinge / Determines it, else colourless ...' (III 908–9). And the audience agrees: ' " 'Ay, that's the variation's gist!' " ' (III 911). With this agreement, Browning goes on:

Thus far advanced in safety then, proceed!
And having seen too what I saw, be bold
Enough encounter what I do behold
(That's sure) but you must take on trust! (III 912–15)

In other words, the next step is the audience's. If they would arrive at the insights and understanding of the poet, they must do so themselves, by turning his account of what he has seen over and over in their minds, until all its complex significance becomes evident. Through the use of various generic patterns, the poet must dissolve, diffuse, dissipate, in order that the audience may recreate.

In book v Sordello explains his poetic purposes in terms that seem to be Browning's comments on his own poem:

Leave the mere rude
Explicit details, 'tis but brother's speech
We need, speech where an accent's change gives each
The other's soul – no speech to understand
By former audience – need was then expand,
Expatiate – hardly were they brothers! true –
Nor I lament my less remove from you,
Nor reconstruct what stands already: ends
Accomplished turn to means: my art intends
New structure from the ancient ... (v 634–43)

If we take these words to be Browning's, the 'mere rude / Explicit details' would refer to the material provided by the narrator: the account of historical events, and the description of 'the time's aspect and peculiar woe' (I 188). The need to 'expand, / Expatiate' would refer to the function of the commentator, who showed the significance of the material provided by the narrator. Although Browning will not 'reconstruct what stands already' he is clearly dissatisfied with his modifications of the narrative conventions established by Scott. He turns, as Sordello does, to 'brother's speech': 'speech where an accent's change gives each / The other's soul.' Browning is apparently referring, not to a conscious revelation of self, but to the materials that give insight into motives, moods, and passions that prompt a character to act.

Books IV, V, and VI reflect Browning's new effort to provide insights into his characters. The most noticeable change is perhaps in the number and length of the direct speeches. In book IV, for instance, we learn from Taurello's lengthy meditation a good deal about the warrior himself: his stifled ambition, his feelings about his lost son, his sense of being deserted by Ecelin. All these thoughts, presented seemingly at random, give us insight into Taurello's curious actions in book V: when he makes Sordello head of the Ghibelline faction by throwing the badge around his neck; when, even after recognizing the minstrel as his son, he does not embrace him, but rather swears allegiance to him. An important parenthesis makes the pattern of thoughts and acts clear: 'So like a nature made to serve, excel / In serving, only feel by service well!' (V 729–30). Thus, instead of recounting events and then commenting on them, Browning presents his characters in such a way that the event simply completes a pattern and confirms our understanding of motives and passions.

In spite of this change in narrative technique, many parts of the last three books of the poem are narrated in Browning's earlier manner. Although we cannot date any part of the poem, it seems likely that some of the final sections were written before Browning's 1838 Italian journey – the occasion of the digression in book III. At any rate, the poet himself still appears from time to time as a commentator who summarizes and clarifies ('I labour to extract the pith / Of this and more' VI 322–3). And when Sordello fails to realize how divine purpose can be revealed in ordinary life, Browning supplies the missing insight ('I this once befriend / And speak for you' VI 590–1) and gives us the elaborate concept of the out-soul.

Browning's account of Sordello's poetic development parallels his own artistic problems. Sordello's first public effort – in the tournament of troubadours at Mantua – is a narrative poem based on the tale of Apollo sung by Eglamor. In spite of the fact that Sordello's song fills up the framework provided by his predecessor ('his own task was to fill / The frame-work up, sing well what he sang ill ...' 133–4), the song is not contrived or made by conscious effort. Rather, it is a product of pure inspiration, a 'fit / Of rapture' (ii 139–40) which unlocks 'many a hoard / Of fancies' (ii 144–5). Like the Spasmodics of the 1850s, Sordello is totally dependent on inspiration. The commentator, in his discussion of Sordello's experience at Mantua, emphasizes the necessity for art to shape inspiration:

> Had he ever turned, in fact,
> From Elys, to sing Elys? – from each fit
> Of rapture, to contrive a song of it?   (ii 138–40)

Such inspiration, the commentator continues, should not be applauded as specially admirable, since it is assumed that all men have similar fancies. But art (which the commentator calls 'song,' ii 167) connects 'each floating part,' making it 'palpable, distinct' (ii 167–8). It is the artist's task to find a pattern that clarifies and intensifies the significance of ordinary experience. Hence Browning disapproves of Sordello's expectation that he should be worshipped for his 'mere consciousness' (ii 429): 'All that is right enough: but why want us / To know that you yourself know thus and thus?' (ii 423–4).

Much that Browning was reacting against seems represented by Eglamor, who, had he appeared in the 1850s, would have been labelled a Spasmodic for he is typically shown composing verse as a spontaneous reaction to nature. The commentator speaks of 'the April woods he cast / Conceits upon in plenty as he past ...' (ii 233–4) and, in fact, begins book ii with an example of one such conceit:

> The woods were long austere with snow: at last
> Pink leaflets budded on the beech, and fast
> Larches, scattered through pine-tree solitudes,
> Brightened, 'as in the slumbrous heart o' the woods
> 'Our buried year, a witch, grew young again
> 'To placid incantations, and that stain
> 'About were from her caldron, green smoke blent
> 'With those black pines' – so Eglamor gave vent
> To a chance fancy ...   (ii 1–9)

Later on, the mourning of nature over the death of Eglamor is described with another of Eglamor's conceits:

You saw each half-shut downcast violet
Flutter – a Roman bride, when they dispart
Her unbound tresses with the Sabine dart,
Holding that famous rape in memory still,
Felt creep into her curls the iron chill,
And looked thus, Eglamor would say ...   (II 176–81)

Eglamor's conceits are similar to those Walter calls up for Violet in scene ix of Smith's *A Life-Drama*. They have the same sensational quality, the same suggestions of violence, of overwrought emotions. Like the Spasmodics, Eglamor is a proud and persistent worshipper of inspiration. For him verse is 'a temple-worship vague and vast' (II 197), a ritual yielding one or two insights which are 'mixed / With his own life' (II 206–7). And because he is so concerned with his own insights, he is proud, selfish, and lacking in human sympathy: 'one not to care, take counsel for / Cold hearts, comfortless faces ...' (II 221–2).

Although the commentator discusses Sordello as Eglamor's 'opposite' (II 195), he is clearly in danger of becoming like Eglamor. Like his predecessor, he is proud and lacks human sympathy. Styling himself 'Monarch of the World' (II 355), he spurns the suggestion that he has 'hopes and cares / And interests' (II 369–70) common to all people. According to his concept, the poet can be all people, but he is never limited by any of the characters he assumes. Each serves simply to reveal a different aspect of himself to be wondered at and worshipped. This sense of 'mastery' (II 430) leads Sordello to voice what might be taken as the first principle of Spasmodic poetry: 'So, range, my soul! Who by self-consciousness / The last drop of all beauty dost express ...' (II 405–6).

When Sordello is invited back to Mantua by Naddo (II 473ff) he begins to discover the limitations of such an extreme Romantic aesthetic. ' 'Twas the song's effect / He cared for, scarce the song itself' (II 485–6), the narrator tells us. In thus seeking to be worshipped for his inspired self-consciousness, Sordello begins to realize that the song itself must be carefully wrought if it is to have the desired effect. With this realization begins his growth as a poet.

As Sordello develops, he moves through the chief genres in the historical sequence described by Aristotle in the *Poetics*, and, in the Victorian period, by George Grote in his *History of Greece* (I xvi). Inspired tales of the gods and goddesses were the earliest form of Greek literature. In what Grote calls the 'age of faith,' these myths were accorded spontaneous belief, largely because of the 'holy and all-sufficient authority of the Muse.'[32] 'The poet – like the prophet, whom he so much resembles – sings under heavenly guidance, inspired by the goddess to whom he has prayed for her assisting impulse. She puts the word into his mouth and the incidents into his mind: he is a privileged man, chosen as her organ and speaking from her revelations' (I 344). Sordello's first major effort as poet is similar to these ancient Greek epics. It is a myth, a tale of Apollo, and it is inspired, sung in a 'fit / Of rapture' (II 139–40). The narrative is apparently as rapid and exciting as any by Homer (who was admired for the impetuosity of his verses) or Scott or Byron:

> On flew the song, a giddy race,
> After the flying story; word made leap
> Out word; rhyme – rhyme; the lay could barely keep
> Pace with the action visibly rushing past ...   (II 84–7)

As Greek civilization developed, Grote tells us, there was a tendency in Greek poetry towards 'the present and the positive' (I 351). New metres were invented. 'The iambic, elegiac, choric, and lyric poetry from Archilochus downwards, all indicate purposes in the poet, and impressibilities of the hearers, very different from those of the ancient epic. In all of them the personal feeling of the poet and the specialities of present time and place, are brought prominently forward ...' (I 351). So too Sordello moves from narrative to lyric. In the 'toilsome process' (II 489) of composing poetry he becomes familiar with a great variety of intricate metres and forms: 'Rondels, Tenzons, Virlai or Sirvent' (II 516). His lyrics are concerned with the present ('As from the welter of their time he drew / Its elements successively to view ...' II 521–2) and they are taken as expressing his own feelings ('"You love Bianca, surely, from your song ..."' II 541).

The drama was the last genre to develop. 'The Grecian drama, comic as well as tragic, of the fifth century B.C.,' Grote writes, 'combined the lyric and choric song with the living action of iambic dialogue – thus constituting the last ascending movement in the poetical genius of the race' (IV i). So too the drama is the last of the genres Sordello tries. His chief difficulty is with characterization. At first his characters are 'mere loves and hates / Made flesh' (II 567–8), an 'unreal pageantry / Of essences' (II 564–5). His characters are, to use E.M. Forster's term, 'flat,' and lack complexity. But then Sordello begins to conceive characters in the round, and he himself becomes hidden in his creatures:

> He took
> An action with its actors, quite forsook
> Himself to live in each, returned anon
> With the result – a creature ...   (II 581–4)

As Sordello moves from genre to genre, so his powers of expression develop. At first he imitates: 'the rhymes ... were Eglamor's ...' (II 493). Then he begins to mould contemporary speech to his poetic purposes:

> He left imagining, to try the stuff
> That held the imaged thing and, let it writhe
> Never so fiercely, scarce allowed a tithe
> To reach the light – his Language. How he sought
> The cause, conceived a cure, and slow re-wrought
> That Language, welding words into the crude
> Mass from the new speech round him, till a rude
> Armour was hammered out, in time to be
> Approved beyond the Roman panoply
> Melted to make it, boots not.   (II 570–9)

Once Sordello reaches this stage of technical accomplishment, he begins to discover the limitations of his art. For up to this point he had assumed that language was capable of conveying the wholeness, the unity of perception. But now he discovers that such unity can exist only in the mind, and hence it is his purpose as poet to provide the materials, properly organized, for his readers to reach such insights:

> Perceptions whole, like that he sought
> To clothe, reject so pure a work of thought
> As language: Thought may take Perception's place
> But hardly co-exist in any case,
> Being its mere presentment – of the Whole
> By Parts, the Simultaneous and the Sole
> By the Successive and the Many. Lacks
> The crowd perceptions? painfully it tacks
> Together thoughts Sordello, needing such,
> Has rent perception into: it's to clutch
> And reconstruct – his office to diffuse,
> Destroy ...   (II 589–600)

Here is the true poet's task: his 'perceptions whole,' the products of his imagination, cannot be presented directly by analysis or 'thought,' but can be so broken into parts by language as to enable the poet's audience to reconstruct his imaginative vision. Wordsworth insisted that 'we murder to dissect'; Sordello realizes that the poet must murder, must dissect, in order to communicate. The degree to which the listeners' perceptions approximate those of the poet depends upon the poet's skill in using language.

It seems evident that Sordello has reached the point where he could become a 'Maker-see.' But, faced with such difficult work, Sordello (unlike Browning) falters, and settles back content with the 'old verse' and the 'old praise' (II 609–10). What he goes back to is narrative: 'He set to celebrating the exploits / Of Montfort o'er the Mountaineers' (II 616–17), in what Browning calls in later editions 'ballad-rhyme' (II 622). Sordello's development as a poet has thus come full circle, and he is back where he started.

Browning's review of his poetic techniques in book III is paralleled by Sordello's speech on the poet as 'earth's essential king' (V 505–665). Sordello speaks of himself as a 'Maker-see,' even though he has failed to become one, and he asks the question that Browning has already asked himself: 'How much can mortals see / Of life?' (V 582–3). By this time Sordello knows that the infinite cannot be totally revealed to finite minds, but at the same time he would have man see to the limit of his ability. Like Browning, Sordello distinguishes three kinds of poetry, or, at least, three kinds of moral insight. First there is 'Life's elemental Masque' (V 584):

I covet the first task
And marshal yon Life's elemental Masque
Of Men, on evil or on good lay stress,
This light, this shade make prominent, suppress
All ordinary hues that softening blend
Such natures with the level: apprehend
Which evil is, which good ... (V 583–9)

Sordello is referring to the function of the narrative poet (whom Browning in his page-heading of 1863 calls the 'epoist'), for he goes on to discuss some of the conventional methods of characterization that we find in the epic or ballad: Friedrich, for instance, is associated with hell, Matilda with Venus. Here moral insight is a simple matter of indicating character by conventional literary images, symbols, and allusions. The next step is to set the characters in motion, so that each fully reveals his own nature:

The men and women stationed hitherto
Will I unstation, good and bad, conduct
Each nature to its farthest or obstruct
At soonest in the world ...   (v 602–5)

The poet no longer comments ('shrink or smile / At my own showing!'
v 600–1) but stands apart, 'Superior now' (v 612). Such a method of
presentation makes it evident that Sordello is talking about the drama.
In the final stage, the poet displays 'Man's life' (v 617; later editions
read ' "man's inmost life" ') rather than 'external things' (v 618):

Man's life shall have yet freer play:
Once more I cast external things away
And Natures, varied now, so decompose
That ... but enough!   (v 617–20)

(In later editions, 'but enough!' is replaced with ' "Why, he writes
Sordello!" ') In decomposing 'Natures, varied now' the poet not only
reveals the exact condition of the inner life of his characters, but provides insight into the attributes that make up all human beings. This
sense of universal truth is one of the marks of the lyric. It is difficult,
however, to label this final stage of the poet's progression. Browning
himself, in his heading of 1863, supplies the term 'synthetist' for the
poet who has reached this point, and 'synthesis' suggests, not the cast-
ing away of external things, but the treatment of them as an extension
of man's inner condition. In short, this final stage may not be a purely
lyrical one, but may take up and transform the two earlier stages as
well. The same difficulty appears in trying to define what Sordello
means by 'brother's speech.' On the one hand, it seems to be lyric, since
there is an attempt to condense, and to get at the essence of things. On
the other hand, the poet retains what he has already written, and it is
apparently the task of the audience to fuse the various generic patterns
into which his insights have been dissolved, and so recreate his perception of the work as a whole. These difficulties are not resolved in the
poem, and for this reason the words 'Once more' in the line 'Once
more I cast external things away' (v 618) are crucial.[33] They suggest
that the poet himself has not yet reconciled his desire to get at the
essentials of the human soul and the necessity of conveying such insights by using the concreteness of our finite world – hence the tension
in the poem between the abstractions (like the out-soul), on the one
hand, and the particulars of Sordello's life, on the other.

In itself *Sordello* is not a successful poem, marred as it is by Browning's shifting intentions. But in Browning's development as a poet it is an extremely important step. For, through his experiments with the narrative mode, Browning consolidated what he had learned from working with the dramatic mode in *Paracelsus*: that the artist's insights cannot be fully conveyed by assertion and explanation; and that the poet must somehow stimulate the reader's 'co-operating fancy' through the concreteness of images and characters, and through the patterns derived from the various genres, so that he may discover the meaning that lies beyond the facts. *Sordello* is, among other things, a poem about poetry, and in particular about the various kinds of poetry. By exploring the nature of the genres, their relations and combinations, and their suitability for his purposes, Browning came to realize fully his problems as an artist. The solutions were yet to come.

2 The plays

Browning's experiments in the drama began with a suggestion of Macready's in 1836 and ended with the publishing of the last number of the *Bells and Pomegranates* series in 1846. The conventions of the genre were, initially at least, as appealing to the young poet as Macready's request at Talfourd's dinner party was inspiring. Far from feeling the requirements of stage presentation as restrictions, as he had when considering a suitable genre for *Paracelsus*, Browning seems to have welcomed them. Drama has always demanded the modification of the poet's voice to that of his characters; the poet rarely speaks *in propria persona*. Browning, whose avowedly dramatic *Pauline* had been criticised as morbidly subjective, and whose characteristic conflict between speaking of himself and concealing himself was already developing, was undoubtedly attracted to a genre which was often defined by its impersonal nature.

Aside from the characteristics of the genre itself, Browning probably found a challenge in the condition of the theatre of his day. Macready recorded in his diary that he hoped he had awakened in Browning 'a spirit of poetry whose influence would elevate, ennoble, and adorn our degraded drama.'[1] and it seems probable that this sentiment was not confided to the pages of the diary alone. Being ambitious, Browning accepted the challenge, but he was soon to discover that the theatre was being pulled apart by the conflicting demands of the audience, the managers, and the dramatists themselves, and that his own ideas for the drama satisfied none of these groups.

The chief conflict in the Victorian drama existed between the 'patent' or 'legitimate' theatres and the 'illegitimate' theatres. The 'patent' theatres thought of themselves as the home of the national drama and of the cultural tradition it represented. The 'illegitimate' theatres presented the kind of popular entertainment that was sneered at by such critics as Herman Merivale in *The Edinburgh Review*: 'Adaptations from the French farces, occasional pieces to suit the talents of particular actors, and those lowest specimens of what the human intellect can do, the *libretti* of comic operas – these are the commodities in which they chiefly deal.'[2] The men who wrote for these theatres, men like Edward Fitzball (who has left us a fascinating account of his career), wrote only to please the taste of the day, and, in accounting for his success, Fitzball boasts: 'I possessed the felicitous art of suiting myself to my audience.'[3]

Browning greatly disapproved of dramatists who wrote only to please an audience. His selection of mottoes for the chapter on drama in R.H. Horne's *A New Spirit of the Age* (1844) indicates his intense dislike of the dramatist who would 'popularize and degrade his style and matter *ad captand. vulg.* ...'[4] The first motto is taken from Bishop Hall's fourth satire:

Too popular is Tragic Poesy,
Straining his tip-toes for a farthing fee.
Painters and Poets hold your ancient right!
Write what you will, and write not what you might.
Their limits be their list – their reason, *will!*

The second motto is from one of Goethe's prologues, in which a theatre manager is portrayed as saying, 'But above all things action must abound; / Men come to look – they crave shows for the eye.' The Poet answers: 'Thou feel'st not how this handicraft is base; / How little it befits an artist true!' The true artist, in Browning's view, writes according to his own purposes, and is not bound by popular theatrical conventions.

By criticising the 'illegitimate' theatres, Browning placed himself on the side of the 'legitimate' houses, but he soon found that their concept of the drama was not his. For, while these theatres considered themselves the guardians of an important artistic form, they could not exist without some measure of financial success. These two considerations

44

constantly plagued the managers of the major theatres, so that Macready, for instance, could beg Browning to improve the national drama, on the one hand, and invite Fitzball to write a financially successful play, on the other.

Those playwrights who satisfied both demands often did so by producing two versions, one to be acted, and one to be read. The former, with its provisions for action and spectacle, came closer to the techniques of Fitzball than many of the 'patent' theatre managers would care to admit. The latter concerned itself with what may be described in Aristotelian terms as 'character' and 'thought,' and contained passages 'which,' as Bulwer Lytton pointed out in the preface to *Richelieu* (1839), 'without being absolutely essential to the business of the stage, contain either the subtler strokes of character, or the more poetical embellishments of description.'[5] Lytton's statement indicates his keen awareness of the limitations of the theatrical conventions of his day. Popular entertainment tended to be melodramatic; structure was provided by an action which moved along swiftly rather than by the slower and more subtle interaction of characters; characters tended to be types rather than individuals with mixed motives; and the effect sought was openly moral and emotional, a simplified version of the more subtle appeal to one's sense of life's complexities. Browning faced the same popular demands that Lytton did. And, like Lytton, he sometimes turned to the reader of plays rather than the spectator in the theatre, because it was easier to convey to the reader his special interests as a writer.

It was chiefly in the matter of characterization that Browning's aims in writing plays clashed with those of his contemporaries. His primary interest in the drama was no different from that in *Sordello*: 'my stress lay on incidents in the development of a soul.' For Browning these incidents are usually moments of choice when the individual determines or significantly alters the course of his life. The portrayal of the alternatives, of all the factors he must take into consideration, of all the subtle pressures put upon him, could not be hurried. At the same time, however, Browning wanted to satisfy Macready, and to make such a portrayal suitable for the stage, which demanded an uncomplicated swiftness in the unfolding of the drama. For nearly ten years Browning believed he could reconcile his interests with those of Macready, and the plays reflect his struggle to do so.

This conflict in intention was especially acute when Browning tried to realize, in words and deeds, the 'development of a soul.' In the first place, the inexperienced playwright usually has some difficulty in setting his characters before the audience in such a way as to reveal what is essential to their natures without parading it in a patently artificial manner. In a letter postmarked 10 August 1845, Browning complained to Miss Barrett:

And what easy work these novelists have of it! a Dramatic poet has to *make* you love or admire his men and women, – they must *do* and *say* all that you are to see and hear – really do it in your face, say it in your ears, and it is wholly for *you*, in *your* power, to *name*, characterize and so praise or blame, *what* is so said and done ... if you don't perceive of yourself, there is no standing by, for the Author, and telling you: but with these novelists, a scrape of the pen – out blurting of a phrase, and the miracle is achieved – 'Consuelo possessed to perfection this and the other gift' – what would you more?[6]

This difficulty in characterization was multiplied when Browning tried to portray the movement of subtle thoughts and emotions that constitute the pattern of an individual's life. Such development is scarcely noticeable in ordinary life, primarily because it is not conveyed by actions. For this reason, too, it could not be readily portrayed on the stage. Finding the techniques of his contemporaries unsatisfactory for his purposes, Browning turned from action to dialogue, to the kind of dialogue which, rather than carrying the plot forward, reveals the inner life of the character himself: the long speech, the aside, and particularly the soliloquy. As Browning wrote to Miss Barrett: 'Whatever comes of [*Luria*], the "aside," the bye-play, the digression, will be the best, and only true business of the piece.'[7]There is always the danger, of course, that the play will become nothing but a number of set pieces strung along a thin line of action. Browning's solution was simple in principle if difficult in execution: he turned the play inside out, and had all the essential action take place within the characters themselves. He wrote to Miss Barrett: '[the effect] is all in long speeches – the *action, proper*, is in them – they are no descriptions, or amplifications – but here ... in a drama of this kind, all the *events*, (and interest,) take place in the *minds* of the actors ...'[8] What takes place in the minds of the audience is equally interesting. Each member must constantly compare speeches, weigh them, and judge them. He must become aware of the discrepancies among different points of view, and of the gap between illusions and reality. He must, in short, sense the irony that is frequently the chief aspect of the kind of play Browning was trying to write.

In the sections that follow I concentrate on those plays that seem to represent best both the range of Browning's experiments in the drama, and his difficulties with the theatre.

Strafford

With the letters about *Luria* in mind, we can better understand what Browning meant when he described his first play, *Strafford* (1837), as one 'of Action in Character rather than Character in Action.' It should be noted, in the first place, that Browning does not dispense completely with 'Character in Action.' The play is, after all, a tragedy, and the action, based on a more or less historical sequence of events, has the traditional tragic shape, beginning as it does with Strafford in a high position, and ending with his defeat and execution. 'Action in Character' complements the traditional shape of tragedy by emphasizing, not the suffering and the final disaster, but the reaction of the tragic hero and his struggles to understand his lot. 'Action in Character' does not mean that the basic personality of the hero undergoes striking changes, for that would destroy probability or consistency of character. Rather, it is composed of a series of insights leading steadily if intermittently to the kind of perception that has always been part of the tragic hero's experience: an awareness of the inexorable mystery of the human lot, the sense that he has come close to the ultimate scheme of things.

Strafford's struggle to understand his lot is particularly difficult, largely because of the complex political situation. Who is friend, and who is foe, is never clear. In the first act, Vane denounces Strafford as the supporter of a tyrannous king; Pym, on the other hand, speaks of Strafford as a friend for whom the good of England is all important. Strafford himself can never be sure that the king trusts him, and finally declares in act III: 'God put it [in] my mind to love, serve, die / For Charles – but never to obey him more!' (III ii 218–19). Strafford is thus caught in a complex web of human relations, a web woven of mixed motives and uncertain loyalties.

Faced with such a situation, he reacts in a way that precipitates his tragedy: he tries to simplify the pattern of his life by serving England through unquestioning loyalty to the king. Throughout the play, his powers of action are bound up with the king's attitude. When Charles trusts Strafford, his soul is 'well and happy, now' (I ii 523); when the king betrays him he is 'old' again (II ii 293).

In spite of this attempt at simplification, Strafford is constantly aware of the discrepancy between his ideal view of the king and the weak nature of Charles himself. In literary terms, this awareness corresponds to the difference between romance and irony. Romance presents us with a simplified view of the world, where motives are relatively unmixed, and friends and foes clearly distinguishable. Irony, on the other hand, makes the most of complexities and shifting ambiguities, and delights in the discrepancy between illusion and reality. Strafford himself makes this literary analogy:

> I shall make a sorry soldier, Lucy!
> All Knights begin their enterprise, you know,
> Under the best of auspices; 'tis morn –
> The Lady girds his sword upon the Youth –
> (He's always very young) – the trumpets sound –
> Cups pledge him, and ... and ... the King blesses him –
> You need not turn a page of the Romance
> To learn the Dreadful Giant's fate! Indeed
> We've the fair Lady here; but she apart, –
> A poor man, rarely having handled lance,
> And rather old, weary, and far from sure
> His Squires are not the Giant's friends ... (II ii 283–94)

Strafford, then, is fully aware of his situation, and has no illusions about himself or the king. At the same time he orders the whole of his life around his loyalty to Charles. Such loyalty is Strafford's tragic flaw. Indeed, he recognizes it as such when, as Lady Carlisle describes her love for Strafford as 'a weakness, but most precious, – like a flaw / I' the diamond ...' (II ii 350–1), he thinks of his own admiration for the king.

The other characters – and particularly Lady Carlisle – assume that Strafford is deluded about the nature of the king, and direct most of their efforts to disillusioning him. But Strafford's loyalty is not blind devotion. When Lady Carlisle says, 'Charles never loved you!' Strafford answers quickly, 'And he will not, now ...' (II ii 329). Similarly, Pym and his friends expect Strafford to recognize the true nature of the king when, contrary to Strafford's advice, Charles dissolves parliament. Instead, Strafford takes the responsibility himself ('Strafford, guilty too / Of counselling the measure' II ii 256–7) and defends the king. Efforts to disillusion Strafford are misdirected, for Strafford is fully aware of his situation, and fully responsible for his actions. The choice that he makes determines again and again the final stages of his life.

'Action in Character,' then, is not a matter of disillusion. It is rather a strengthening of Strafford's determination to die for the king. Initially Strafford hopes to save Charles (and himself) with 'damning proof (III ii 227) of the treachery of his enemies. The impeachment destroys Strafford's plan, and the question, as Hollis points out to Lady Carlisle,

> takes
> Another shape, to-day: 'tis not if Charles
> Or England shall succumb, – but which shall pay
> The forfeit, Strafford or his Master ...   (IV i 91–4)

It is Strafford who pays, and willingly. When Lady Carlisle gives him an opportunity to escape, Strafford refuses to flee: 'Die, and forsake the King? / I'll not draw back from the last service' (v ii 293–4). His determination points to the curious ambivalence that surrounds the death of the tragic hero. On the one hand he can take comfort from the thought that he has remained loyal to the end; on the other hand, he now knows that the choice he has consistently made could have no other outcome: 'Be witness, he [Charles] could not prevent / My death!' (v ii 256–7). Even to escape, Strafford realizes, would lead to 'something ominous and dark, / Fatal, inevitable ...' (v ii 304–5). Strafford's understanding, his responsibility for his actions, and the inevitability of his fate, arc all necessary to the tragic effect.

Though Browning's chief interest lay in the development of a soul, he nevertheless provided some elements which he must have hoped would make up for the theatrical disadvantages of such a subject. Frequent entrances and exits give the impression of action, while spectacle is provided by the settings and the crowd scenes, the stage directions for which, as Park Honan points out, often suggest 'a tableau or even a large painted portrait in the heroic manner.'9 Moreover, the domestic sentiment provided by Strafford's children in act v scene ii was a direct appeal to popular taste. Macready, we know, proposed 'the children's voices being heard in the pause following the announcement of Strafford's death.'10 The use of such domestic sentiment may have been suggested by Sheridan Knowles' *Virginius* (1820), one of Macready's favourite plays. Knowles treated Livy's story, not as a noble and tragic struggle for individual freedom (as Vittorio Alfieri had done earlier) but as a family disaster where pathos is the principal tragic effect. Macready's suggestion was not altogether successful, for the domestic sentiment tends to diffuse a tragic effect of a more heroic kind than that attempted by Knowles. For, although Browning is concerned with the pathos of Strafford's career, he does not treat Strafford as a family man until the king draws attention to that aspect of his life late in the fourth act (IV iii

380–4). It is only when Strafford examines his motives in act v that he mentions for the first time his love for his children as well as for Charles when refusing to escape from prison (v ii 165), and makes it clear that his heroic self-sacrifice is also a father's proud and rather stubborn attempt to leave to his children a reputation for honour.

This confusion of effect is not the only weakness of the play. Because Browning was concerned with character, he paid little attention to plot, and yet 'an external machinery of incidents' was necessary for the stage. Macready recognized as much when he was producing *Strafford*: 'I had been too much carried away by the truth of character to observe the meanness of plot, and occasional obscurity.'[11] Moreover, Browning's analysis of Strafford's heroic determination is so thorough that it often seems a portrayal of weakness, and Strafford's loyalty to the crown is sometimes indistinguishable from an obsession with the person of the king, 'The man with the mild voice and mournful eyes ...' (II ii 408). These may have been some of the reasons, then, that Browning grew to be dissatisfied with the play. It was not included in the collected edition of 1849, and reappeared only in the general collection of 1863.

This dissatisfaction with *Strafford* may have led Browning to try a similar experiment in *The Return of the Druses* (1843). Again he dealt with a hero who, in spite of his admirable motives, is caught up in circumstances that are largely of his own making, and is led inevitably toward death. The play goes beyond *Strafford* in exploring more fully the hero's conflicting motives, illusions, and insights in lengthy soliloquies and asides, and hence his problems in compensating for the theatrical disadvantages of such techniques were even more acute. The crowd scenes, the frequent exits and entrances, the occasional outbursts of violent action, and the display of exotic costumes, were all attempts to make the play suitable for the stage. In addition, Browning attempted to differentiate the speech of the Europeans from that of the Druses, and to combine the two styles in Djabal's speeches.[12] In spite of these efforts, Browning's conflicting intentions are just as evident as they are in *Strafford*, and the uneasy combination of various techniques represents little progress in solving his problems as a playwright.

Pippa Passes

In *Pippa Passes* (1841), Browning made a considerable advance in the dramatic realization of the 'development of a soul.' In each of the four scenes he concentrated on the moment of choice, and, through the characters and events that influence the decision, he suggested the complexity of human motives and the uncertain nature of moral insight. Initially, the scenes may simply have been exercises, for Browning seems to have conceived at least one or two of them as separate and complete in themselves. We know from one of his letters to Miss Haworth that he wrote a brief dramatic sketch while sailing through the Straits of Gibraltar on his way to Italy in 1838.[13]

Browning's handling of the short dramatic scene has some affinity with the dramatic technique of Walter Savage Landor, whose works Browning admired. Landor was not interested in shaping a drama 'of a certain magnitude' (he once remarked, 'What is *plot* but *trick?*'),[14] but did his most characteristic work in brief discrete scenes like *Ines de Castro* and *Ippolito di Este*. Two phrases that Landor used to describe his work help in determining the characteristics of this particular dramatic mode. In 1828 Landor wrote, in a note to *Ines de Castro*, 'Character is the business of the Dialogue.'[15] Later, in the edition of 1846, Landor spoke of his dramatic scenes as 'Imaginary Conversations in metre.'[16] Now, a conversation (as one gathers from Landor's better-known prose works) is a free-flowing dialogue; interest depends partly on the points of view of the different characters and partly on the total shape that the dialogue takes. From these various points of view or modes of thought arises a decision, a principle, or a theme, which gives the whole conversation direction and purpose.

So, too, in Browning's play. In each of the scenes of *Pippa Passes* the situation is resolved by the moment of insight evoked by Pippa's song. Once the song is reached it may be seen that all the imagery and thought in the preceding dialogue is caught up in the simple lyric, and turned so as to present a totally new view of the situation. In this respect, then, *Pippa Passes* represents an advance over *Strafford*, insofar as Browning concentrates on the moment of choice, and not only makes clear all the alternatives, but also indicates how the decision changes the pattern of each character's life. In the earlier play, Strafford had in effect made his choice long before the play began, and his reiteration of it simply confirmed the course of his life.

It is not merely Browning's handling of the short scene that makes *Pippa Passes* an important work. The structure of the work in its entirety is experimental, and is Browning's solution to the problem of linking the scenes. Just when Browning made this decision we do not know, but it resulted in a play which (considered as a whole) was to be read rather than produced. Such a shift in intention carried Browning away from the constricting demands of the theatre, and made it possible for him to experiment with dramatic form as freely as he had done when writing *Paracelsus*. And, as in *Paracelsus*, he worked out a complex pattern of irony that depends less on the outward structure of the play (the four scenes linked by the wanderings of Pippa herself) than it does on the choice which is the central concern of each scene. Choice, it must be remembered, depends upon limited knowledge; if man had God's omniscience, alternatives would not seem equally advantageous, and the moral consequences of any course of action would be clear. But Browning believes that the purpose of man's life on earth is moral growth, and such growth can come about only when man acts on a choice he has made, and learns through trial and error. Incomplete knowledge, then, is a condition of moral growth. When these ethical concerns are translated into literary terms, we have the materials of irony which, like the making of choices, depends upon limited knowledge. It is from such irony, from the discrepancies, both moral and factual, among different points of view, that the structure of *Pippa Passes* evolves.

The chief aspect of the ironic pattern of *Pippa Passes* has been defined by Eleanor (Glen) Cook as 'the irony of God's ways when regarded from man's point of view.'[17] This pattern is particularly evident in Pippa herself who, as Mrs Cook points out, is the 'unifying factor' in the poem (p 411). Through her we become aware of the discrepancy between the actual working out of God's purposes, and man's limited understanding of his ways. Pippa feels, for instance, that what 'Asolo's Four Happiest Ones' (the phrase is from a later edition) are and what they do are important, while what she is and what she does are unimportant. But God's point of view is presented in Pippa's New Year's hymn, which provides the theme of the whole poem. In Mrs Cook's words, 'God is working out His purposes as He wills through men whether they strive for or against these purposes. Men are in the hands of God, be they conscious or unconscious of it ... Every event would prove as significant as another, as complex and as influential, if we looked at life not from our limited viewpoint but from God's' (p 412). Through her songs Pippa conveys, unconsciously, something of God's point of view, so that the moment when she sings is, for those who hear her, a moment of insight or, to use Joyce's term, 'epiphany.' Yet Pippa herself is unaware of her influence, and in the epilogue feels some disappointment that the significance of her day has apparently been so slight.

The irony of Pippa's point of view is not confined to her understanding of her influence. The four people of Asolo she is chiefly interested in she calls 'Happiest Ones,' and yet it gradually becomes apparent that these four are not happy at all, but are in fact facing crises that change the patterns of their lives. Similarly, Pippa is mistaken in her understanding of the nature of happiness itself. Without giving much thought to what she is saying, she tells us that her happiness depends upon external circumstances (the weather, the nature of her holiday) while the happiness of the Four depends upon internal conditions (love, serenity, a contented state of mind). And yet, ironically, Pippa's good-natured shrewdness is just the outlook that ensures her happiness. Finally, Pippa's game of fancy (she is going to pretend to be each of 'Asolo's Four Happiest Ones' in turn) provides irony of a different kind. There is, of course, the obvious discrepancy between her daydreaming and reality, but the discrepancy becomes less obvious when she describes the Four in terms of an ascending scale of love: adulterous love, married love, parental love, and finally love of God. Pippa realizes, not only that this last is 'The greatest love of all,' but that in fact she shares in it. The irony here is central to all Browning's thought: what starts out as a fantasy becomes reality.

Each of the four scenes not only has a place in the broader ironic pattern (in which God works out his purposes through men whether they strive for or against him), but presents other kinds of irony that vary the general pattern and diversify the dramatic effect.

The chief irony in the scene entitled 'Morning' is the discrepancy between the lovers' view of their affair, and the reality that keeps intruding. Ottima and Sebald think of themselves as the heroic lovers of romance, struggling to enjoy their love against almost impossible odds. Their point of view, however, is really an inversion of the conventional romance. In romance, moral categories are clearly defined; black is always clearly distinguished from white; lovers are good and virtuous, and struggle against evil circumstances. But Ottima and Sebald look upon themselves as 'magnificent in sin' (I 218), as guilty lovers struggling against a universe full of wrath, and constantly threatening to punish them. Their account of their meeting in the woods during a storm best illustrates what they think of as their heroic defiance. The lightning is like 'God's messenger' who

> thro' the close wood screen
> Plunged and replunged his weapon at a venture,
> Feeling for guilty thee and me ...   (I 194–6)

Reality keeps challenging this romantic point of view, the corpse of Luca Gaddi, Ottima's husband, being the chief obstacle to their love in the present, just as his living presence was the chief obstacle to their love in the past. He was scarcely the kind of figure to provide strong opposition in an heroic conflict: he was old, obtuse, affectionate to Ottima, and kind and generous to Sebald when he was starving. With such opposition, Sebald in particular finds it difficult to maintain the illusion of romance.

Ottima has almost succeeded in restoring their former point of view when Pippa sings the song ending with the famous lines, 'God's in his heaven – / All's right with the world!' (I 227–8). These lines are far more important as part of the ironic pattern of the play than they are as an indication of Browning's thought, or of the Victorian world picture. The discrepancy between Pippa's statement and actual circumstances is obvious. A murder has just been committed and all is not right with the world. Though Pippa's words do not fit the situation, they are, in another broader sense, true, for (as we know from Pippa's New Year's hymn) God works out his purposes through all things. Pippa's song, then, reminds Ottima and Sebald that there is a universal moral order which cannot be defied.

The song changes the outlook of both. Sebald simply reinverts the romantic view, sees sin for what it is (he no longer exalts it as heroic), hates Ottima, and would gladly undergo punishment to save himself. Ottima's change is far greater. She too recognizes her sin as a sin, but shows true love in her willingness to sacrifice herself for Sebald. These two, who had tried to avoid the reality of Luca's death, ironically must now face the reality of their own deaths.

The students' scene, like the other interludes, provides the necessary information for the scene that follows, and gives us the context, not only in which the vital choice is made, but out of which the ironic pattern grows. Here we learn of the plot of Lutwyche and the other students against Jules. The students are, as Gottlieb says, heartless. For them the tenderer human feelings – love, pity, sympathy – are a joke, and only hate and envy are real.

Irony of various sorts is at work in the scene between Jules and Phene. There is, of course, the obvious discrepancy between Jules' concept of his courtship and marriage, and what it really is – a plot of the students. But this irony is complicated by other factors. The students do not really know Jules (Lutwyche says that when the trick is discovered 'Jules must not be suffered to hurt his bride' I 288–9) and neither the students nor Jules know Phene. For the students Phene is nothing more than the instrument of their plot, a girl of the commonest sort. But Phene is in fact a human being who feels love and concern for Jules. From Jules' point of view, Phene is 'Hippolyta, / Naked upon her bright Numidian horse' (II 54–5), an Amazon whose attractiveness is linked with war and hatred. In reality, Phene's attractiveness lies partly in her fragile beauty, partly in her tender feelings of love.

On learning of the plot, Jules' first reaction is to take revenge by killing Lutwyche and his fellows. But then Pippa sings her song, 'Give her but a least excuse to love me!' and reminds Jules of the proper point of view. By taking revenge, he would be destroying, not only Lutwyche, but his own new-found feelings of love and inspiration. And so the broader irony of the scene becomes evident: the plot turns out in a way the students did not expect. When the students tried to use Jules and Phene, God used them for his own purposes.

The pattern of irony in the scene entitled 'Evening' is different yet again. We know that Luigi has made the right decision in choosing to leave Asolo, for through Bluphocks we have already learned that if Luigi remains in Asolo he will be arrested, while, if he leaves on his dangerous mission, he will, for the time being, be safe. But although Luigi has made the right decision, he has made it for the wrong reasons, while his mother reaches the wrong decision (that he should stay in Asolo) for the right reasons. Luigi explains to his mother that he is going to assassinate the Austrian emperor to free Italy from foreign domination. And yet when he tries to explain the issues involved, he has to admit that he does not understand them. His attitude is a fatalistic one (he has no thought of escaping after the planned assassination) and his motives, as his mother is shrewd enough to realize, are largely selfish: 'If patriotism were not / The easiest virtue for a selfish man / To acquire!' (III 124–6). The mother's motives, on the other hand, are as admirable as Luigi's are mean and narrow. She shows genuine love for her son and concern for his safety, and is concerned too about his fatalistic attitude when life is meant to be enjoyed.

Under the influence of his mother Luigi's determination to leave Asolo is weakening when Pippa sings her song. She sings of an ideal king whose rule is characterized by both justice and mercy. With a clearer understanding of political ideals, and with motives far less selfish, Luigi immediately leaves Asolo. The pattern of irony, then, is resolved through the insights that come with an examination of motives.

In the final scene there is no question but that the Monsignor's motives are good. Sprung from a wealthy but wicked family, he hopes to redress their wrongs by gaining control of his brother's estates, and by using the wealth for good purposes. The one obstacle, as the Intendant tells him, is Pippa who, as we have already learned from the previous interlude, is the true heir. And hence the Intendant offers to do away with Pippa. Such, then, is the pattern of irony: the Monsignor plans to act from the right motives, but is tempted to use the wrong means. Pippa's song about the innocence of childhood enables the Monsignor to reject temptation and to have the Intendant arrested.

Pippa Passes has generally been judged favourably by critics. Its success is due in part to the fact that Browning was not writing specifically for the stage, and was therefore free to develop all the possibilities of the dramatic genre. He had already learned from writing *Sordello* that assertion and explanation were not adequate means for conveying his insights, and hence he sought devices that actively engaged the 'co-operating fancy' of the reader. For this purpose irony is particularly appropriate. As with *Paracelsus*, the reader or spectator gradually becomes aware that he cannot take any speech at face value, but rather that he must seek the full meaning of any assertion in its context. In this way a complex web of relationships gradually comes alive in the reader's mind, and the patterns that the poet constructs are charged with the significance of a living experience.

When Browning tried to portray on the stage ironic patterns similar to those of *Pippa Passes*, he was faced with the by now familiar problem of satisfying popular expectations in the theatre. In *King Victor and King Charles* he made a valiant effort. The irony is of the same kind as that in *Pippa Passes*, since it has an ethical basis (in the making of choices) and a metaphysical significance (in the working out of divine purposes), but its effect is different. For Browning does not explore a series of complex and interwoven relationships among a wide range of characters, but concentrates rather on the relation between his two principal characters. King Charles is concerned primarily with the human relation of father and son, while King Victor thinks in political terms of a king and his heir. As the play proceeds, the concerns of each are reversed. Charles discovers that he has political abilities, while Victor discovers that his son loves him. By the end of the play the pattern of irony is clear: Charles and Victor both began with a limited understanding of their relationship, and with a limited understanding of themselves; each corrects such narrowness by reacting to the other and by developing some of the qualities of the other; and each discovers that such growth gives meaning to lives that had seemed to be failures. Browning deals with this complex pattern of irony in a concentrated and rather austere manner. He may have modelled his play on the tragedies of Vittorio Alfieri (whose works he was studying at the time[18]), for he limits his characters to four, has the action take place in a single setting, and, in each part, observes strict unity of time. By thus concentrating his materials, and eliminating anything which might diffuse the ironic effect, Browning may have hoped to succeed in the theatre, and to do so on his own terms. But Macready rejected the play (it was, he wrote in his diary, a 'great mistake'[19]), and, when it was published, Browning thought of it as 'a very indifferent substitute'[20] for a play he deliberately designed to be popular: A Blot in the 'Scutcheon.

A Blot in the 'Scutcheon

After the rejection of both *King Victor and King Charles* and *The Return of the Druses*, Browning made a determined effort to adapt his own concepts of the drama to the demands of the Victorian theatre. The result was *A Blot in the 'Scutcheon* (1843). Browning described the play as 'quiet, generally-intelligible, and (for me!) a popular sort of thing,'[21] and told Macready that it was 'a sort of compromise between my own notion and yours.' 'There is *action* in it,' Browning continued, 'drabbing, stabbing, et autres gentillesses ...'[22]

The part of the play that owes most to Macready's 'notion' is undoubtedly the Mildred-Mertoun plot, which is popular not only in its subject matter (a clandestine love affair that results in a duel and the death of both lovers) but in its melodramatic treatment. The techniques of melodrama are nowhere more evident than in the characterization, for the *dramatis personae* tend to be types rather than individuals. In the opening scene the retainers characterize Mertoun as 'young rich bountiful / Handsome' (i i 10–11) and again as 'So young, and yet / So tall and shapely!' (i i 62–63). Mildred is the typical heroine of melodrama:

> You cannot know the good and tender heart,
> Its girl's trust, and its woman's constancy,
> How pure yet passionate, how calm yet kind,
> How grave yet joyous, how reserved yet free
> As light where friends are – how embued with lore
> The world most prizes, yet the simplest ... (i ii 176–81)

Such a portrayal is partially rescued from stereotyping by the fact that it is spoken by Tresham, who loves his sister and is naturally extravagant in praising her.

The tone of melodrama is usually a sensational one, and is evident in this play in the term by which Browning describes the love affair: 'drab-bing' or whoring. The term seems a strong one, especially when applied to such an innocent child as Mildred, but its full significance becomes clear when we compare Browning's treatment of Mildred with Mrs Gas-kell's treatment of Esther in *Mary Barton*, and more especially with Dick-ens' treatment of Little Em'ly in *David Copperfield*.[23] Browning, in fact, characterizes Mildred in much the same way that the fallen woman is usually characterized in Victorian literature – as a child-like creature, who falls because she is 'pure yet passionate,' who suffers agonies of guilt and is to be both punished and pitied. The pity is, of course, aroused by the lines that Dickens admired so much: 'I was so young – I loved him so – I had / No mother – God forgot me – and I fell' (i iii 508–9). The stern melodramatic morality, which necessitates the fallen woman's re-morse and guilt, makes itself felt in Mildred's suffering:

> Have I received in presence of them all
> The partner of my guilty love, – with brow
> Trying to seem a maiden's brow – with lips
> Which make believe that when they strive to form
> Replies to you and tremble as they strive,
> It is the nearest ever they approached
> A stranger's ...   (i iii 406–12)

When Mildred dies, it is because of the strength of her remorse over her relationship with Mertoun, a relationship she calls a 'planned piece of deliberate wickedness' (i iii 415). Like other melodramatic heroines of the period, she is carried off by her emotions, unable to sustain the con-flict between the 'pure' (her rigid sense of morality) and the 'passionate' (her love for Mertoun).

It is characteristic of melodrama to emphasize action and plot at the expense of characterization. Such an emphasis results in a certain lack of verisimilitude or probability – charges levelled against *A Blot in the 'Scutcheon* by both H.B. Charlton and Thomas Lounsbury. Charlton finds the actions of the characters 'unintelligible' and 'arbitrary' because of the play's moral chaos, and because of the failure of 'honour as the code which will provide an unequivocal standard of moral compulsion for his audience, and therefore, a sense of natural obligation for his characters, the dramatic inevitability which Aristotle called necessity.'[24] Lounsbury concentrates on 'the untruthfulness of the play as a represen-tation of real life.'[25] The motives are not believable: why should not the hero 'from the outset have wooed the heroine in the way of honourable marriage as he is represented as doing at the time the play opens'? Why should the heroine 'cast aside maidenly reserve and virginal modesty on a slight pretext'? Incidents in the plot are equally unbelievable. When Mertoun is accepted by Tresham, 'it would seem,' Lounsbury argues, 'that during this brief interval they [Mertoun and Mildred] might refrain for the sake of their common future from doing the slightest act that would tend to bring about the revelation of their secret.' Yet the Earl visits Mildred in her chamber, and he does not steal in but comes singing a song.[26] Such comments emphasize how unrealistic – and hence how conventional – Browning's treatment of the story is. It is easy enough to make the play look ridiculous by refusing to accept its conventions. It is more difficult to accept the fact that the lack of plausibility allowed Browning to provide the rapid succession of sensational incidents which is one of the requirements of melodrama. The simplified action of melodrama makes more of characters reacting to a given situation than it does of the chain of cause and effect that leads to the situation itself. This characteristic of melodrama gave Browning the opportunity to develop other – and, for him, more interesting – aspects of the play.

In spite of the melodramatic techniques and effects, Browning calls the play a 'tragedy.' Now Browning, as we have seen from the earlier plays, had a high concept of tragedy, and hence it is unlikely that the melodramatic deaths of Mildred and Mertoun could alone make the play worthy of such a name. Tragedy, for Browning, usually involves some character who is caught in a web of circumstances from which he cannot escape; who, as he is inevitably drawn towards the final catastrophe, struggles to make sense of all the beliefs and emotions that have made him what he is. The only character in this play who is capable of such insights, of such suffering, is Tresham. The first clue to his general elevation is given by the retainer who characterizes him as 'older, graver, loftier' (i i 65), and certainly gravity and dignity pervade the measured phrases with which he welcomes Mertoun in the second scene of the first act. In spite of such dignity, his nature is not a cold one. His extravagant praise of his sister, his warm welcome for Mertoun, his easy intimacy with Guendolen and Austen – all indicate the warmth and affability of an admirable personality. It is, in fact, his very lack of secretiveness and suspicion that constitutes much of what Guendolen describes as the 'perfect spirit of honour' (i iii 308). For Tresham, the tragedy lies, partly in the guilty love affair, but more particularly in the deception involved. He is convinced that Mildred is not only concealing her lover from him, but also from Mertoun, and he cannot condone the continued dissimulation, the 'planned piece of deliberate wickedness.'

His judgment of the affair, however, is more complex than one might expect in melodrama. Tresham is painfully aware of lapses in understanding which he considers deception by his own mind. He cannot reconcile Gerard's tale with what he knows of Mildred, nor can he reconcile his cherished family honour with his love for his sister: 'I ... yield my reason up, inadequate / To reconcile what yet I do behold – / Blasting my sense!' (ɪɪ i 84–8). The complexities of Tresham's reactions to the situation are particularly evident in his conflicting feelings: on the one hand he has high ideals of the love between brother and sister; on the other, he describes their day-to-day relations as 'slender threads' that have eventually composed a 'web' hiding Mildred's real nature (ɪɪ i 195–203). It is this conflict within Tresham himself that leads him to destroy his family by denouncing Mildred and murdering Mertoun. The melodramatic plot thus gave Browning the opportunity to explore incidents in the development of Tresham's soul, and to portray a character imprisoned by irreconcilable feelings and loyalties and eventually destroyed by them.

Tresham's passionate action is succeeded by a calmness that leads to insight. He is able to forgive Mertoun and to realize that 'haste / And anger have undone us' (ɪɪɪ i 125–6). He begins to understand the conflict in himself, and his responsibility for what has happened:

What have I done that, like some fabled crime
Of yore, lets loose a fury – free to lead
Her miserable dance amidst you all?   (ɪɪɪ i 220–2)

The 'dance' has whirled Tresham round to a point where he can recognize clearly a 'depth of purity immovable!' (ɪɪɪ ii 326) in the love of Mildred and Mertoun. Like many tragic heroes, Tresham thus seems to intuit a more comprehensive moral order, a moral order which (for him) goes beyond family honour; at the same time he realizes that he has destroyed his own place in the ordinary scheme of things. The world has become for him, as it has for so many tragic heroes, only an illusory pageant:

The life out of all life was gone from me!
There are blind ways provided, the foredone
Heart-weary player in this pageant-world
Drops out by, letting the main masque defile
By the conspicuous Portal: – I am thro' –
Just through! –   (ɪɪɪ ii 362–7)

Browning described the play to Macready as 'a sort of compromise between my own notion and yours.' It seems evident now that the story of the lovers belongs to Macready's 'notion' and the characterization of Tresham to Browning's. The linking of the two is only partially successful, principally because the sensational tone of the melodramatic parts detracts from the loftier tragic effect. The combination is made smoother, however, by the presence of Guendolen and Austin, who represent the norm of conduct and attitude in the play. Though they never disparage family honour, they regard it with some sense of humour. And, in contrast to the adolescent passion of Mildred and Mertoun, their love is sensible and mature, easily carried yet deeply felt. They are fitting successors to the Tresham name, and seem likely to erase the blot that Mildred and her brother have left in the family escutcheon.

Up to this point I have been dealing with the published version of the play, and with what it shows about the conflicting intentions of Browning himself. The production of the play caused other problems. Although Browning devised the Mildred-Mertoun plot with the hope that it would make the work the popular success that Macready the theatre manager wanted, it seems likely that he created the part of Tresham for Macready the actor. When Macready assigned the part to Phelps Browning was not so much offended as he was disillusioned that Macready failed to admire a serious attempt to delineate a tragic hero. The extent of Macready's lack of sympathy with Browning's aims as a dramatist is nowhere more evident than in the cuts and revisions he proposed for the play as it was to be acted. These changes are fortunately preserved for us in the Yale manuscript of the play,[27] and give us a fairly clear indication of Macready's 'notions' as to plot, characterization, and general tone. Browning tells us in a note which he prefixed to the manuscript in 1884 that very few of the excisions were restored for the actual performance, and hence we are dealing with the acting version of the play.

Macready's principal concern seems to have been to simplify and speed up the play. In act i scene i, for instance, where Browning leads us into the story by showing the retainers watching the arrival of Tresham and Mertoun, Macready cuts out everything which does not either describe the two noblemen, or direct our attention to the unaccountable gloom of Gerard. The description of the pageantry of the arrival is done away with – Macready would probably have preferred such pageantry to be shown rather than described – and the scene is reduced to such flat factual statements as 'The Earl descends' (i i 58). Removed also is the boisterous drinking of health (i i 75–81); Macready substitutes the line,

'Here Gerard, see, they are coming this way' and so prepares us for
Gerard's sullen exit. And for the general exit at the end of the scene Macready condenses Browning's seven lines to the single line, 'Hush! they're
here, quick, to our posts – to our posts.' The scene is thus speeded up
considerably, and more emphasis is placed on Gerard's melancholy. For
it is of course Gerard's attitude that rouses interest, and leads to the
unfolding plot.

In act I scene ii Macready's cuts are less frequent for here we are introduced to the principal characters, and shown Mertoun's application to
Tresham for the hand of his sister. This piece of action is both interesting
and necessary to the plot, and Macready retains most of it. He does cut
what must have seemed to him some unnecessary poetical embellishments: a parenthetical simile that interrupts the flow of Tresham's opening speech (I ii 5–8); an impassioned utterance of Mertoun about his
visible and true selves (I ii 33–8); and a comment on faith and fraud
that is not immediately comprehensible in the action of departure (I ii
127–9). Aside from these few changes, Macready seems to have approved of the scene, and it is not too difficult to see why. The proposal
moves forward swiftly; Tresham appears simply as a grave but affable
nobleman, Mertoun as the conventional stammering lover, and Guendolen and Austin as somewhat amused observers. Characterization is thus
restricted to the simple outlines necessary for the plot.

Macready tries not only to simplify the play but to attenuate the 'drab-
bing' aspects of the plot, and to surround the lovers with a rosy glow of
sentiment. He changes Mildred's age from fourteen to eighteen, in spite
of the Shakespearean precedent, and so makes the legal aspects of the
affair less sensational. He cuts out, particularly in act I scene iii, all the
references to sin and guilt, and thus softens the stern moral sense that
pervades Mildred's speeches. At I iii 79–80 he removes the reference to
sin as the snake of the Eden story; at I iii 120–1 he cuts out the discussion of sin and punishment, and at I iii 136 the word 'guilty.' He does
away with Mildred's consciousness of guilt – the speech about her pre-
tending to maidenly innocence (I iii 137–42) – changes the word 'wickedness' to 'feigning' (I iii 144), and substitutes for a long discussion of
shame (I iii 145–6, 148–64) the line, 'Oh Henry — Will you not despise
me?' He even changes the word 'God,' with its implication of a single
divine will roused to wrath, to the more general 'Heaven' with its overtones of composite angelic pity (I iii 143 and thereafter). With no reference to a guilty conscience the tone of Mildred's remarks moves towards
the sentimental axiom that the course of true love never runs smoothly,

and that deception is a lover's prerogative. Macready's excisions emphasize the deception rather than the sin, the woman's concern with the
course of her love affair rather than the girl's shame. Such an effect is
clear when we construct Macready's version from I iii 132–64 of Browning's manuscript:

> MER. It will soon be over.
> MIL.   Over?
> Oh, what is over? what must I live thro'
> And say, ' 'tis over?' Is our meeting over?
> Have I received in presence of them all
> The partner of my love, – with brow, with lips –
> Ah, Heaven! some prodigy of thine will stop
> This planned piece of deliberate feigning
> In its birth even – I
> Shall murmur no smooth speeches got by heart,
> But – O Henry – Will you not despise me?
> MER. Mildred, break it if you choose,
> A heart the love of you uplifted – still
> Uplifts, thro' this protracted agony,
> To Heaven!

Macready thus condenses thirty-two lines to fourteen, speeds up the
play, and changes its tone completely. Similarly, at the end of the act,
Macready stroked out the lines Dickens admired, 'I was so young – I
loved him so – I had / No mother – God forgot me – and I fell,' and had
Browning substitute an innocuous description of Mertoun's departure:

> His foot is on the yew-tree bough – the turf
> Receives him – now the moonlight as he runs
> Embraces him – but he must go – is gone –
> Ah, once again he turns – thanks, thanks, my love!
> He's gone – Oh, I'll believe him every word!

Browning incorporated both versions in the printed play.

In act II Macready made relatively few excisions, principally because
most of the dialogue is necessary for the plot: Gerard's revelation to
Tresham, Tresham's confrontation with Mildred, and Guendolen's discovery of Mildred's secret. The cuts he did make conform to the pattern
already established. He omits an unnecessary simile (II i 19–20), speeds
up Tresham's long speech on a brother's love by cutting over half of it
(II i 166–85), and shortens other lengthy speeches with the omission of

lines 284–9, and 337–46. He also leaves out some implications of lust (II i 262–6) and cuts both repetitions of the lines Dickens admired (II i 361–6, 400–4). Similarly, in the sword play in act III Macready dispenses with much of Browning's dialogue (III i 74–6, 78–83, 84–5, 86–7, 93, 95–9, 102–6) and lets the swift action alone maintain the interest.

Aside from these predictable cuts, there are several significant changes that reduce the status of Tresham as a tragic hero, and direct our attention towards Mertoun as a melodramatic hero. Of these changes, the most important is the delay of Tresham's recognition of Mertoun until after the fight. In the published version Tresham recognizes Mertoun, pauses, then challenges him to fight. In the acting version Tresham recognizes Mertoun only after the young man falls, and the recognition immediately dispels his anger. Macready thus changes Tresham's wilful passion to blind haste and eliminates the tragic hero's responsibility for his fate. Tresham becomes only an instrument of the plot, the kind of nemesis that true love sometimes encounters. Mertoun's refusal either to reveal his name or to put up an effective defence is, under the circumstances, the forbearance of a hero, and most of our attention is directed to him.

Macready also cuts the reconciliation scene drastically. Having prevented Tresham from becoming a tragic hero, he is forced to cut the moment of Tresham's tragic insight, when he recognizes that 'haste / And anger have undone us' (III i 123–8). He dispenses with Mertoun's long speech on his admiration for Tresham (III i 130–47) and shortens Mertoun's dying speeches by omitting lines 149–55 and 162–76. The audience is left, not with the tragic sense of pity and terror, but with the melodramatic sense of pathos amidst general forgiveness and pardon. The scene, to which Browning devoted fifty-six lines (III i 121–77), is condensed by Macready to fifteen:

> MER. I must wring a partial – dare I say,
> Forgiveness from you, ere I die?
> TRESH.   I do
> Forgive you.
> Be but your pardon ample as my own!
> MER. Ah, Mildred! What will Mildred do?
> Tresham, her life is bound up in the life
> That's bleeding fast away! We've sinned and die:
> Never you sin, Lord Tresham! – for you'll die,
> And Heaven will judge you.

TRESH.   Yes, be satisfied –
That process is begun.
MER.   And she sits there
Waiting for me. Now, say you this to her –
You – not another – say, I saw him die
As he breathed this – 'I love her' – (you don't know
What those three small words mean).
TRESH. Ho, Gerard!

Mertoun's admission of sin and his reference to death and judgment have
a certain effect here after being so rigorously excluded from previous
speeches, but that effect is largely mitigated by the general willingness
to forgive all.

The final scene between Mildred and Tresham is cut by Macready to
bring the play to a swift conclusion, particularly after Mildred's death.
Most of the excisions up to this point only shorten and simplify the long
speeches (III ii 11–14, 20–4, 41–2, 96–103), for Macready seems to have
been generally satisfied with the meeting between Mildred and her
brother, and with the melodramatic manner of Mildred's death. Thereafter he quickly ended the drama. Of the thirty-six lines with which
Browning brought the play to a close, he cut about half. And, rather
than have Tresham die, he suggested that he be despatched to a monastery with the lines 'within a convent's shade in stranger lands / Penance
and prayer shall wear my life away.' Browning objected strenuously to
this change. 'The above,' he wrote on the manuscript in 1884, 'was the
substitution ... to avoid giving the piece the dignity of a Tragedy, and
Mr. Phelps the distinction of playing in one!' In Macready's view, Tresham's death would only diffuse the pathos he wanted concentrated on
the lovers. Browning, of course, wanted the melodrama balanced by the
profounder tragic effect.

This manuscript makes it evident, then, that Browning and Macready had quite different notions of plot and characterization. Where
Macready wanted a plot that was swift and consistently interesting,
Browning wanted situations that revealed the individual's struggle to
understand his life. And while Macready wanted the kind of simple and
powerful characterization that best served the interests of the plot,
Browning preferred to dwell on the complexities of an individual soul.
In A Blot Browning made his greatest effort to satisfy Macready. When
he failed to do so, he turned from Covent Garden, and went to one of
Macready's rivals, Charles Kean.

In spite of the break with Macready, the published version of *A Blot in the 'Scutcheon* sold better than most other numbers of the *Bells and Pomegranates* series. Its modest success led Browning to consider 'something as likely to be popular this present season,'[28] and accordingly *Colombe's Birthday* appeared early in March of 1844. Browning's avowed intention of keeping his hold on what he called '*my* public' led him to choose once again a popular form; his special interests led him again to an extensive revision of that form, but with happier results.

In portraying a love affair between persons of different rank, Browning chose a popular subject, a subject which lent itself to the kind of romantic comedy whose broad appeal had been proved by the success of Lytton's *Lady of Lyons* (1838). Lytton treated the situation in the conventional manner. His is a play of intrigue and adventure leading up to the point where obstacles (both the differences in rank and the lady's pride) are overcome and a happy marriage is at last possible. Browning, on the other hand, was less interested in a conventional plot than he was in the conflict taking place within Colombe herself. For Colombe must choose a husband, and consequently struggles to understand fully the basis of her choice. The obstacles she faces are not social or familial, as in a conventional comedy, but epistemological. The play moves forward only when Colombe gains a clearer understanding of her situation, and reaches its climax when she intuits the true nature of the choice she must make: between loving and not loving at all. Thereafter the affair with Valence simply completes a pattern, the essential significance of which has already been made clear. Tresham had destroyed himself; Colombe in effect recreates herself, and her birthday is really the birth of vital purposes in her life. In a more conventional comedy the marriage at the end would satisfy the erotic motive propelling the plot, and represent the creation of a new social unit; Browning shifts the emphasis, so that the incidents in the development of Colombe's soul are brought about by her attempts to understand her situation, and the marriage is not so much a social event as it is a moral and spiritual achievement in Colombe herself.

Browning was satisfied with the play, and told Alfred Domett: 'I feel myself so much stronger, if flattery not deceive, that I shall stop some things that were meant to follow, and begin again. I really seem to have something fresh to say.'[29] The 'things that were meant to follow' were apparently more plays designed for the stage. But Browning had, in writing *Colombe's Birthday*, discovered once again that the stage held less interest for him than the delineation of the moral and spiritual problem in which Colombe was involved. Because the writing of the play enabled him to understand where his interests as a poet lay, and helped him to conceive these interests more clearly, he felt he had indeed made some gain. Although he continued to write in the dramatic mode, he wrote 'for a purely imaginary Stage.'[30] Elated by his new insight, and freed from the tyrannous demands of the theatre, he did indeed have 'something fresh to say.'

Luria

The 'something fresh' found expression in the eighth and last pamphlet of the *Bells and Pomegranates* series, a pamphlet containing both *Luria* and *A Soul's Tragedy*. *Luria* is the more ambitious play, since the hero 'is a Moor, of Othello's country,'[31] and Browning therefore considered it a proper ending for the series. In spite of Browning's reference to *Othello*, *Luria* has no more than a superficial resemblance to Shakespeare's tragedy; in structure and theme it is similar to *Colombe's Birthday*.

Like *Colombe's Birthday*, the play concentrates on one all-important choice. Luria may on the one hand act on selfish motives, as do Braccio ('Man seeks his own good at the whole world's cost' i 133) and his secretary ('' 'Tis in self-interest I speak ...' i 62). Instead, he is entirely devoted to the service of Florence, in much the same way that Strafford is entirely devoted to Charles. In fact, it seems that Browning is returning to a tragic subject similar to that of *Strafford*, but treating it in the manner of *Colombe's Birthday* and thus avoiding the defects of his first play. Luria is portrayed, not as the weak victim of a tragic obsession, but as a strong sensitive figure who makes a choice and then stands by his decision. The choice is not one between the Tweedledum of Florence and the Tweedledee of Pisa, but the more basic one between placing one's faith in a cause or not having faith at all. Such a choice is the import of the scene in which Luria refuses to read the letter offered him by Tiburzio. The point is not that the contents of the letter would destroy his faith in Florence, but that the very reading of the letter itself would constitute an act of faithlessness. And Luria chooses to remain loyal. His choice is a continuing one, and bears evidence to the strength of his faith, which is no 'wild belief' (ii 289). His decision is tested in act iii when he reaches what he describes as 'this instant ... / like the turning moment of a dream' (iii 104–5), the moment when he realizes that Braccio and the Florentines have been plotting against him. But even in the bitterness of his disillusion he chooses to remain faithful, and, in fact, his suicide is in itself a triumph of faith. 'His aim,' Browning explains in a letter to Miss Barrett, 'is to prevent the harm she [Florence] will do herself by striking – so he moves aside from the blow ...'[32] If Luria had done anything other than kill himself, he would have destroyed the faith that was the entire basis of his life. His death is, in fact, an heroic sacrifice. It is true that, like Browning's other tragic heroes, Luria is caught up in circumstances from which he cannot escape. Through his faith, however, he rises above his situation, so that his death is a victory and his final status the elevated one that has traditionally belonged to the tragic hero.

Browning described the way in which he presented the drama to his readers as 'high fantastical.'[33] The phrase is an interesting one, since it suggests not only the method of handling the structure and theme, but something of the poet's attitude to his central character. The fantastical is, according to ordinary usage, synonymous with the whimsical, the irrational, the arbitrary, the capricious. These terms point to the central meaning of the word; that is, a deviation from the ordinary scheme of things. Though it appears irrational and arbitrary, this deviation is in fact governed by laws of its own, laws that are determined by the imaginative wish-fulfilment that is the basis of all fantasy.[34]

The fantastic elements in *Luria* become evident when one begins to consider why Luria's decision to commit suicide is made and carried out at the end of the fourth act, thus leaving an entire act in which the hero does nothing but await death. Browning tells us that 'the last act throws light back on all, I hope,'[35] and it seems therefore that it is the key to the play. Thematically the act is concerned with the mental, moral, and spiritual progress of man, and consequently with the teleological operation of the universe. Such a vision is 'fantastic,' especially when placed over against the 'brute-force world' (I 94) of the first act, where the situation gives no evidence of progress of any kind. But, as with Pippa's discussion of love, the fantasy becomes a reality. Luria is portrayed as a type or prefiguration of the more perfect man to come. Tiburzio says to him:

A people is but the attempt of many
To rise to the completer life of one –
And those who live as models for the mass
Are singly of more value than they all.
Such man are you ... (v 299–303)

68

Luria so influences those around him that, in spite of 'their worldly-wisdom and Tuscan shrewd ways,'[36] they become better men, and so contribute to the moral and spiritual progress of man. The greatest change is perhaps in Puccio, who, in yet another example of the first-firm-step image, insists that his place is as a soldier under Luria. The least change is in Jacopo, who always had faith in Luria, but was more often moved by self-interest. The other characters change in varying degrees. Domizia realizes that 'there's another world!' (v 193), Braccio recognizes Luria's honesty and good faith, while Tiburzio, who has always been an admirable figure anyway, is the spokesman for the change that is taking place. In effect, each character loses his selfish purposes and practical self-regard, and 'old memories reappear ...' (v 277). In time, Luria insists, 'all men become good creatures ...' (v 181), and hence the progress in act v is a partial fulfilment of Luria's wishes.

The fantasy in the play, then, brings into relief the gap between things as they are (the circumstances of the first four acts) and things as they might be (the progress in the fifth act). Fantasy is thus closely related to irony, which presents a gap between fact and illusion. Irony and fantasy go hand in hand throughout the play, especially in Luria's speeches, which can be considered on the one hand as a wilful disregard of facts, or on the other as an imaginative representation of things as they might be.

Browning's use of the word 'fantastical' also suggests something of his own attitude to the play. Fantasy may either be presented entirely for its own sake (as in some fairy tales), or to serve a didactic intention, like the fantastic elements in allegory and romance. If fantasy is presented entirely for its own sake, it is free from moral instruction, or is at least morally neutral. If fantasy is used for a didactic purpose, the poet is anything but neutral. It can be shown, I think, that Browning tried to have it both ways; that as an artist he used fantasy with a didactic intention, but that as a man he remained uncommitted to his own conceptions. This discrepancy between the artist and the man reflects the uncertainty of Browning's beliefs in 1845, and in particular the uncertainty of his attitude toward Christianity. The first part of *Saul* was, we know, written about the same time as *Luria*. The course of that poem demands a vision of Christ as a conclusion, but the poem was not finished until 1855 simply because Browning was not sure that he believed in the ending he had conceived. Something of the same problem has, I think, affected *Luria*. Browning's imagination was sufficiently involved in his subject that he did not wish to leave the play incomplete, but at the same time he could not honestly say that he believed in what he was creating. He portrayed Luria, then, in a 'high fantastical' manner, which allowed him to characterize Luria as a Christ-like figure while he himself remained morally neutral.

That Luria is a Christ figure becomes evident in act ɪɪ when he speaks of 'Florence, who to me stands for Mankind ...' (ɪɪ 242). Luria's entire life is devoted to saving Florence, and therefore, metaphorically, to saving mankind. The fact that he is ready to die for Florence (and in fact does so) strengthens the Christian overtones. Other passages in the play parallel the Christian story. Jacopo, the secretary, voices Pilate's thought: 'If Luria, that's to perish sure as fate, / Should have been really guiltless after all?' (ɪ 95–6). And again, he says, 'That man believes in Florence as the Saint / Tied to the wheel believes in God!' (ɪ 108–109). At the end of the act he describes Luria speaking of Florence 'as the Mage Negro king to Christ the Babe' (ɪ 383). Moreover, Luria is from the East, and even refers to himself once as a 'descended Deity':

Do you forget there was my own Far East
I might have given away myself to, once,
As now to Florence, and for such a gift,
Stood there like a descended Deity? (ɪɪ 312–15)

By sacrificing himself, and so preventing Florence from harming herself by striking him, Luria metaphorically takes upon himself the sins of mankind (the cruel motives of the Florentines), and thus makes possible the change of heart, the regeneration that takes place in the fifth act. The characterization is thus very complex, involving on the one hand all the interior action leading up to Luria's decision to remain faithful, and on the other all the fantasy that heightens Luria and makes him a type of the perfect man.

Browning's use of fantasy and his discussion of the play with Miss Barrett clarify the central problem of the dramatist who is also a moralist. Browning apparently discussed with Miss Barrett the indirect way in which the drama teaches men, for we find her urging Browning to 'teach what you have learnt, in the directest & most impressive way, the mask thrown / away)off / however moist with the breath. And it is not, I believe, by the dramatic medium, that poets teach most impressively ... it is too difficult for the common reader to analyze, and to discern between the vivid & the earnest.'[37] Browning evidently did not think that a dramatist, qua dramatist, should be morally neutral. Certainly he was worried about the initial moral effect of *A Soul's Tragedy*, and felt that the 'main drift' of the play might not be understood.[38] On the other hand, Browning, like Miss Barrett, recognized that the dramatist enters into all his characters, and he admitted that he sympathized with the Florentines as much as with Luria.[39] Dramatic composition, he had learned from experience, demands moral neutrality. Thus is clarified the problem facing Browning as dramatist and moralist: to realize all characters with equal vividness, so that the audience may sympathize with them, and at the same time to present the characters in such a way that the audience may distinguish good from bad, and in so judging make the play a step in their own moral growth. Browning solved the problem in the dramatic monologues. He did not do so in this play (with which he remained dissatisfied), partly (as he explained) because of his failure with Domizia, and partly because his original concept of the play had disappeared and he was left with a 'clever attempted reproduction of what was conceived by another faculty, and foolishly let pass away.'[40]

The year 1846 marked a turning point in Browning's career. On 13 July he wrote a curious letter to Alfred Domett in which he estimated the value of his years of experimentation with the drama:

Here is, without affectation, the reason why I have gone on so far although succeeding so indifferently: I felt so instinctively from the beginning that unless I tumbled out the dozen more or less of conceptions, I should bear them about forever, and year by year get straiter and stiffer in those horrible cross-bones with a long name, and at last parturition would be the curse indeed. Mine was the better way, I do calmly believe, for at this moment I feel as everybody does who has worked – 'in vain'? no matter, if the work was real. It seems disinspiriting for a man to hack away at trees in a wood, and at the end of his clearing come to rocks or the sea or whatever disappoints him as leading to nothing; but still, turn the man's face, point him to new trees and the new direction, and who will compare the power arising from experience with that of another who has been confirming himself all the time in the belief that chopping wood is incredible labour, and that the first blow he strikes will be sure to jar his arm to the shoulder without shaking a leaf on the lowest bough? I stand at present and wait like such a fellow as the first of these; if the real work should present itself to be done, I shall begin at once and in earnest ... not having to learn first of all how to keep the axe-head from flying back into my face; and if I stop in the middle, let the bad business of other years show that I was not idle nor altogether incompetent.[41]

It is clear that Browning is dissatisfied with what he has done, and that he is not quite sure where to turn next. At the same time he is certain of the value of attempting to express his 'dozen more or less of conceptions,' for in the attempt itself he clarified his intentions as a poet, and mastered the techniques of his craft. Although he had always been concerned with the development of a soul, with the moral problems an individual faces and the choices he must consequently make, he learned through the drama to portray this development more effectively. By 1846 Browning better understood how to realize character, how to show different characters approaching truth in different ways, and different individuals forging truth out of the complexity of their lives. More especially, he learned how to portray, through human relationships, the insights that mark the real turning points of an individual's life. And he learned, too, that the neutrality of the dramatist (who must enter into all his characters and realize them with equal vividness) is not incompatible with the commitment of the moralist (who must try to convey his judgment not by direct statement but by devices – especially irony – that evoke in the reader the poet's insights). These advances reflect Browning's clearer understanding of those aspects of drama suitable for his purposes as a poet, and indicate too a movement toward dramatic literature and away from the theatre. The conflict of intentions which characterizes all of Browning's attempts to write for the stage was never resolved, largely because Browning realized that the demands of the stage, for action, a swiftly moving plot, and simple characterization, placed intolerable restrictions on him, and made it all but impossible for him to portray the inner action in which he was chiefly interested. If he were to use the dramatic mode, he could be no more conventional than he had been in *Paracelsus*.

It was with mixed emotions, then, that Browning summed up his dramatic career to Miss Barrett: 'I have lost, of late, interest in dramatic writing, as you know – and, perhaps, occasion. And, dearest, I mean to take your advice and be quiet awhile and let my mind get used to its new medium of sight – , seeing all things, as it does, thro' you: and then, let all I have done be the prelude and the real work begin ...'[42]

72

3   Poems 1842–64

Between 1842 and 1864 Browning published four collections of shorter poems: *Dramatic Lyrics* (1842), *Dramatic Romances and Lyrics* (1845), *Men and Women* (1855), and *Dramatis Personae* (1864). At least two (and perhaps three) of the titles provide clues about the genres to which the poems belong. This evidence, however, is complicated by the fact that Browning later regrouped the poems under their original titles for collected editions. The poems from the volumes of 1842 and 1845 were combined for the collected edition of 1849; and the poems from the volumes of 1842, 1845, and 1855 were distributed in yet a different way for the collected edition of 1863. The grouping and regrouping of the shorter poems suggest that Browning's concepts of genres were changing and developing over the twenty-one years between 1842 and 1863. And while the poems themselves (with few exceptions) undergo no major revisions in that time, the shuffling and reshuffling of the groups indicate Browning's changing understanding of the common characteristics of the poems within each group, and perhaps indicate as well his attempt to emphasize, now this, now that, aspect of each poem.

Although it is likely that Browning's concepts of genres changed between 1842 and 1863, the nature of that change must be carefully defined. It could be argued that the regrouping of poems indicates, not a change in the poet's concept of a particular genre, but a change in his understanding of its potential, and of the flexibility with which it could be treated. Clearly, the groupings are not a precise classification of the poems; and it seems evident, too, that Browning's concept of genre was never prescriptive, and hence that he would be unlikely to base his grouping of the poems on a definition of a particular literary kind. It seems to me more likely that the groupings suggest the richness and range of each genre, and indicate the extent to which Browning modified and adapted each to his particular purposes. Browning probably did not attach much importance to labelling and classifying poems, but he was vitally interested in testing the flexibility of a genre, and in extending it until it broke the boundaries separating it from other literary kinds.

In the sections that follow I will discuss both the characteristics generally associated with the genres Browning names in his titles, and the range of Browning's experiments with them. I have not tried to retrace the steps by which Browning extended the range of his experiments (to do so would require a detailed study of the letters and other documents written between 1842 and 1863, as well as much speculation on the reasons for the reassignment of specific poems), but have concentrated, rather, on the groupings of 1863 as a representative stage of Browning's development.

Romance

When the Victorians spoke of romance in a general way, they nearly always had in mind something exotic and exciting, something that provided relief from the dull round of their own far too ordinary lives. Colourful descriptions of far-off places and of unfamiliar manners and customs – so much a part of the metrical romances of Scott and Byron – provided the exotic elements, while the excitement lay in the action and the swiftly moving plot (for romance was primarily a narrative mode). 'It is the end and object of romantic poetry,' one reviewer wrote, 'that, through its medium, this rude world may appear more interesting than it actually is. The romantic poet seeks to astonish his readers by marvellous adventures, by human characters which range above mortality, by chivalrous exploits, by excessive tenderness and heroism ... '[1]

Reviewers who dealt with romance in more specific terms rarely defined it by verse form, though Scott had made octosyllabic couplets the most widely used style in narrative poetry. More frequently romance was thought of as dealing with incident rather than character, and hence its shape depended upon the sequence of actions. Sir Walter Scott, for instance, spoke of 'wild adventures' as an 'absolutely essential ingredient' in romance: 'We would be ... inclined to describe a *Romance* as "a fictitious narrative in prose or verse; the interest of which turns upon marvellous and uncommon incident ..."'[2] Reviewers sometimes discussed too the manner of presentation, and talked about the narrator (who might or might not be the poet) and the various tropes that were a conventional part of his narrative (the wise comments, proverbs, and reflections, his formal invitation at the beginning and leave-taking at the end – devices very much in evidence in *Sordello*).* Although some or all of these characteristics usually had a place in any discussion of romance, it was primarily the mode of composition that, for the Victorians, distinguished romance from other literary kinds. Romance, most reviewers pointed out, is a product of the imagination, and depends upon the poet's shaping power rather than accurate observation. Hence, romance is poetic and 'ideal' rather than mimetic and 'real':

> The poet [who, in this review, is the writer of romance] does not sit down as a limner to a model, in all the drudgery of imitation; his models are in his mind, wherein he discovers a world that is as real in its own way as the world around us. True poetic genius reflects nature by a plastic operation, analogous in all respects to the processes of nature herself – in the same manner as the vital sap of the tree is nourished by the shower and the dew, but puts forth bud and blossom; thus converting all outward influences to its own ends, by the activity of inherent vigour.[3]

In prose fiction, the romance was usually contrasted with the novel, the distinction between them lying in the degree of probability. A novel is realistic because, in Scott's words, ' "the events are accommodated to the ordinary train of human events, and the modern state of society" '[4]: its events are plausible when measured by the empirical criteria of cause and effect. By these same criteria the events of romance seem improbable, exaggerated, and even absurd. They seem so because the romance is limited, not by actual experience, but by what is conceivable

---

* It should be noted that when Browning calls his romances 'dramatic,' it means that the speaker is not the poet himself, but rather a character who is a modification of the romancer's *persona*, the narrator.

within the imaginative process itself. It is this process, not the world around us, which gives romance its validity. The events reflect man's inner life, and hence the conventions of romance represent 'the order or pattern imposed on experience by the human imagination.'[5]

Romance, thus characterized, would seem to have afforded Browning a particularly good opportunity to deal with his special interest, the development of a soul. Here was a literary kind which, by its very nature, reflected man's inner experience. Moreover, romance dealt with such experience indirectly, through action, setting and character, and thus stirred the imagination of the reader to recreate typical experiences as they were reflected in the shaping power of the poet. But, suitable as romance seemed in essence, in practice Browning probably found it highly unsatisfactory. Popular taste sought action and excitement in romance, and expected heroes who would be, in Westland Marston's words, 'Warrior, Lover, Sage.'[6] Browning, as we already know from *Sordello*, was not interested in merely telling a story, and avoided such treatment of the hero, leaving tales of Sordello as 'Knight, Bard, Gallant' to the 'Chroniclers of Mantua' (vi 819–32). His modification of the romance mode in the shorter poems is as varied and extensive as his modification of the same mode in *Sordello*.

Browning's chief problem was to shift the emphasis in romance from 'Character in Action' to 'Action in Character.' He did so by retaining the essential shape of the action while modifying its nature to show forth inner experience. The adventures in romance fall into one major pattern, the quest, which is best illustrated by the old gipsy's tale in *The Flight of the Duchess*, and best defined by Northrop Frye: 'The complete form of romance is clearly the successful quest, and such a completed form has three main stages: the stage of the perilous journey and the preliminary minor adventures; the crucial struggle, usually some kind of battle in which either the hero or his foe, or both, must die; and the exaltation of the hero.'[7] Browning retained this threefold structure, but transformed its character. The basis of his transformation is the pattern the human imagination imposes on experience. Man imagines the kind of world he would like to live in, a world better than his own, a world that reflects the perfection of heaven. He also imagines the kind of world he would not like to live in, a world which reflects the perverted order of hell. In struggling to realize the one and avoid the other, man discovers that his success or failure depends to a large extent on his way of viewing the world around him. This process, like the quest, has three stages: an uncomfortable awareness of the meaningless complexity of ordinary life, a glimpse of ultimate reality that leads to a choice affecting the whole pattern of an individual's existence, and an attempt to realize that vision in an ideally human world. In dealing with these themes, Browning demonstrated the flexibility with which romance could be treated: it could, on the one hand, be extended toward 'realism,' and treat ironically the shifting ambiguities of life; it could, on the other, deal with a visionary or dreamlike world intuited by the imagination, a world characterized by exciting adventures and symbolized by remote and exotic landscapes; and, finally, it could deal with the quest to avoid the frustrations of ordinary life, and to make one's dreams come true.

John Westland Marston's *The Old Tower* (1842) provides a precise parallel to the range of Browning's interests in romance:

> THE SAGE. – What seest thou?
> FIRST SPECTATOR. – A pile decayed,
> Bricks in cunning fashion laid,
> Ruined buttress, moss-clad stone,
> Arch with ivy overgrown,
> Stairs round which the lichens creep, –
> The whole, a desolated heap:
> THE SAGE. – What seest thou?
> SECOND SPECTATOR. – Memorial of olden time.
> Telling of the feudal prime,
> And the glorious pageantry,
> Waking heart, and kindling eye;
> And the deep and solemn lore
> Learned by hearts that beat no more;
> Vows of faith, and high emprise,
> Knightly valour, love-lit eyes,
> Woman's whisper, trumpet's breath,
> Noble daring, valiant death; –
> More than History can give
> With this ruined tower doth live:
> THE SAGE. – Thus it is that vacant air
> MIND informs with visions fair,
> Hears its voice's potent sound,
> E'en in Silence's self resound,
> And all space an echo makes
> To the music it awakes!

What are Earth, and Air, and Sea?
Even what thou mak'st them be.
To the Soul whence beauties flow,
Flowers in every desert grow.
Ever signs of sympathy
Meet the sympathetic eye.
To the ear attuned to song
Ceaseless melodies belong.
To a Universal Love
Earth reflects the World above.[8]

The first spectator is wholly lacking in imagination, and can see only the complexities of the material world. The second spectator imagines the idealized and exciting world of the middle ages, a fiction which the sage interprets as a vision of heaven. These contrasting modes of perception correspond to the dialectic of traditional romance, but where, in earlier poems, the emphasis fell on varying powers of action, here the emphasis falls on varying degrees of insight and understanding. Browning's interests are strikingly similar. In the grouping of 1863, his *Dramatic Romances* extend all the way from more or less 'realistic' poems dealing with unimaginative involvement in the complex ironies of ordinary life, to highly 'unrealistic' poems where the order is that of a dream world. We must now examine the range of his *Dramatic Romances* in some detail.

Unimaginative involvement in the highly civilized, highly complex society of Victorian England is a common situation in the poems labelled romances in 1863, and is usually a situation from which the speaker wishes to escape. In such poems – *Time's Revenges* and *A Light Woman*, for instance – the story (which in popular romance would be the centre of interest) is only inferred, and the poems focus on the involved social relations and complex emotions of the speaker. In *Time's Revenges* the poet is bedevilled, on the one hand, by an overly eager friend whose belligerent defence of his poetry silences the critics, and, on the other, by a lovely but self-centred lady whose only interest at the moment lies in attending a famous ball. In each case the speaker would gladly exchange the real situation for a romantic one. From his friend he longs for the faithful care that would enable him to recover from a vein snapping in his brain – a romantic exaggeration of his very real headache. He longs to show his love for the lady by killing a threatening monster and proving himself a 'sea / Of passion' – an idealized version

78

of the foolish love that is destroying his well-being. The poem ends on a sardonic note, with the speaker reminding us both of the contraries appropriate to romance, and of the extent to which the real situation represents everything he wishes, unsuccessfully, to avoid: 'There may be heaven; there must be hell; / Meantime, there is our Earth here – well!' In *A Light Woman* the same three figures appear, this time in a love triangle. Here the romantic action is not wished for but rather completed. The speaker was determined to save his friend from a light woman by proving her untrue, and he did so by causing her to fall in love with himself. The act, however, saved no one, and may destroy all three. The moral worth of each character, and the rightness or wrongness of his attitudes and actions – usually clear in romance – are by no means clear here. In capturing the woman's fancy the speaker is, he admits, 'no hero' (44), and he knows, at least, that 'to play with souls' is 'an awkward thing' (45). In the end he appeals to the poet to give the situation imaginative shape: 'Robert Browning, you writer of plays, / Here's a subject made to your hand!' (55–6).

In *Waring* Browning describes a man who has rejected ordinary life in favour of travel and adventure. The poem is 'a fancy portrait of a very dear friend,' Alfred Domett, and, although the tone is one of friendly banter, Browning presents Waring as a hero of romance: he is a poet, a lover (though not a very successful one), and a military figure. Nor can the tone detract from the significance of Waring's escape from the formal social life of London with its 'indoor visits, outdoor greetings' (25) to the free life of the traveller who moves on whenever the mood strikes him. Waring is probably as close as Browning ever came to portraying a Byronic hero, for, while he lacks the blacker Byronic moods, his wild whims and his pride ('He was prouder than the Devil ... ' 22) place him in the line of heroes that can be traced to Childe Harold. Particularly Byronic is the last wild glimpse we have of Waring at Trieste, a striking figure on the deck of a swift ship that turns and flees much as Arnold's Tyrian trader was to turn and flee from the 'merry Grecian coaster.' The analogy with Arnold is not far-fetched, for in the middle of the sixth section the poet imagines Waring as a kind of scholar-gipsy. Like Arnold, too, Browning makes it clear that this hero's life is somehow more real than his own, and his plea to Waring is the plea of all lovers of romance: 'Bring the real times back ...' (207).

Waring discovers a 'real' life through travel and adventure, conventional aspects of romance. Though Browning was primarily interested in 'Action in Character,' he did not entirely discard the exciting events and the description of far-off lands that made the works of Scott and Byron so popular. The adventures of *The Italian in England* and the boyish heroism of *Incident of the French Camp*, for instance, have all the excitement and pathos that the ordinary round of one's life does not provide. And *In a Gondola* is probably included among the romances partly because the first stanza, written to illustrate Maclise's picture *The Serenade*, presents a romanticised description of Venice. As Browning wrote in 1841 to Miss Haworth: 'Singing and stars and night and Venice streets in depths of shade and space are "properties," do you please to see.'[9] In *The Englishman in Italy* a description of the Neapolitan autumn is juxtaposed with the corn-laws debate, with the implication that the poet's 'trifles' are more important than economic questions. The speaker's claim is borne out by the central part of the poem, where the Englishman diverts his companion, Fortù, from the storm outside by describing a ride over the mountains. This ride, it becomes clear, is not only a physical, but a mental and spiritual, ascent, and the changing landscape corresponds to the speaker's inner experience. The lower reaches of the mountain are wild and forbidding, and the reference to the archetypal Leviathan ('some monster, which climbed there to die / From the ocean beneath') suggests that the scene reflects hell. As if he were retracing Dante's journey, the speaker climbs to the top; there, he has a mysterious vision of the 'infinite movement' of the mountains, and, turning seaward, he sees the 'isles of the siren.' These islands (like Arthur's Avilion in *Idylls of the King*) are associated with paradise, and the surrounding landscape too suggests a paradise Browning mentions in a letter describing Italy, a paradise 'I have seen in my soul only, fruits, flowers, birds and all.'[10] The vision is not, however, entirely an ecstatic one, for, like Childe Roland, the speaker sees a 'strange square black turret' which is, for him as for the knight-to-be, a place of trial, a place where he is to learn 'life's secret.' Browning has transformed a conventional description of Italy, giving an unfamiliar scene universal significance.

Browning's treatment of material from the Middle Ages is equally unconventional. Scott had made such material the stock-in-trade of the romancer, and Browning himself had lived through what W.C. DeVane calls the 'curious fashion' of the early forties, 'the desire to recreate antiquity, to follow the sports and the manners of the Middle Ages.'[11] The prevailing view was that which the huntsman who narrates *The Flight of the Duchess* attributes to the Duke: 'The Mid-Age was the Heroic Time ...' (106). Browning treated the Middle Ages in quite a different way. He avoided the descriptions of manners, customs, and scenery which Scott had thought indispensable, and the accounts of exciting deeds demanded by popular taste. And he concentrated instead on the irony and moral ambiguity which arises from mixed motives and a complex inner life; which arises, too, when the particular is considered in a wider context. In *A Grammarian's Funeral*, for instance, there is, first of all, the obvious discrepancy between the lofty aspirations of the grammarian ('Let me know all!' 61) and the small amount he has actually been able to achieve. That irony takes on new significance, however, in the context of Browning's philosophy of the imperfect. 'Imperfection means perfection hid' (the phrase is Cleon's), incomplete knowledge implies perfect knowledge, and hence the grammarian's failure is a witness to his ultimate success, though not in this world. As far as civilization is concerned, the achievements of the grammarian, limited as they seemed in his time, were tremendously significant in preparing the way for the Renaissance. The many facets of this irony Browning presents in the context of a symbolic quest, the funeral procession up the mountain. The journey takes place in the last hours of night, just before dawn, and the mountain top, the goal of the quest, is 'citied to the top, / Crowded with culture!' – details that suggest the achievements of the early Renaissance. The 'sepulture' is on the topmost peak, and when it is reached, the meteors, lightnings, and stars that Browning usually associates with a vision of the infinite are seen. The journey, then, symbolizes the true significance of the grammarian's life.

Such ironic treatment is evident in other poems as well. In *Protus*, for instance, the speaker contemplates the chaotic politics of the late Roman Empire in the east, and meditates on the ironic discrepancy between promise and achievement. In *Holy-Cross Day* there is a more complex ironic discrepancy between the 'conversion' forced upon the Jews by the church, and their longing for the kind of salvation brought by the Messiah. *The Heretic's Tragedy* is full of mistaken motives and unrecognized virtues, both the basis of dramatic irony. *The Patriot* describes the gap between heroism and its reward, and *Instans Tyrannus* a tyrant's mistaken judgment of the subject he maliciously oppresses. In *The Boy and the Angel* and *The Twins*, poems based on moralized legends, an angel reminds Theocrite and the Abbot, respectively, of their misconception of the religious life.

When Browning does tell a story from the Middle Ages, he concentrates, not on action, but on point of view, motives, and moral growth.

Count Gismond, for instance, is a story of honour sullied, defended, and vindicated. But the point of view from which it is told – that of the woman about whom the action revolves – makes the poem much more than a conventional story of a tournament. David Shaw points out that 'the woman's image of the bloody sword which swings against her from Count Gismond's hip and her final statement to her husband, which we know to be a lie, compromise rather than confirm her innocence,'[12] and suggest that she may indeed be guilty. When the reliability of the narrator is thus called into question, the poem becomes an extended piece of irony. Browning's treatment of an old French story in *The Glove* is equally unconventional. The *Memoires* of the Marquis de Lassay, as DeVane points out,[13] suggested to the poet that the story might have a new meaning if only the characters' motives were fully understood. In the old version, the trial (a conventional part of romance) is ironically reversed, and the lady who tries DeLorge is herself tried and found wanting. In Browning's version, the speaker, Peter Ronsard, recognizes true worth and purpose in the lady whose challenge to her lover was supposedly so vain and whimsical. In trying DeLorge, she clarifies the choice she must make, and she and the youth who follows her away presumably attain a way of life far more vital and happy than that of the knight, who spends the rest of his life fetching his wife's gloves.

In Browning's treatment of the story, the physical trial, often the chief interest in the action of romance, is largely replaced by a difficult choice that affects the whole course of an individual's life. The choice is frequently the means of realizing an ideal existence. The speaker of *In a Gondola*, for instance, has apparently made the right choice, for he draws a contrast between his own happiness in love, and the unhappiness of those who inhabit the palaces they pass. In *The Last Ride Together* the woman has chosen not to continue the relationship, and yet the speaker experiences a curious satisfaction in the ride itself, and recognizes in it what is almost an 'instant made eternity' (108), a moment of quiet happiness that assures him that his quest has not been in vain. The lovers in *The Statue and the Bust*, on the other hand, miss happiness entirely. Convinced that 'the world and its ways have a certain worth' (138), they evade the choice that confronts them, and remain caught in social complexities. *Porphyria's Lover* varies the pattern in a grotesque fashion: he captures a moment of happiness only by strangling his mistress. The Duke of Ferrara too has apparently done away with his last Duchess, but unlike Porphyria's lover, he has failed to appreciate her natural joy, and can admire her only when she has become a work of art. Finally, the choice may be improperly realized, as it is in *Mesmerism*, where the method of the charm, and the steps leading up to the moment when 'the shadow and she are one' (100) are the principal concerns of the poem. The insight into the 'body and soul' of the woman the speaker loves is as guilty a knowledge as that gained by Poe's Roderick Usher.

The changes that Browning wrought in the romance mode are best seen in the longest poems in the group, *The Flight of the Duchess, The Pied Piper of Hamelin*, and '*Childe Roland to the Dark Tower Came*.'

According to one of his letters to Miss Barrett, Browning first conceived *The Flight of the Duchess* as a vision of an idealized world.

> As I conceived the poem, it consisted entirely of the gipsy's description of the life the Lady was to lead with her future gipsy lover – a *real* life, not an unreal one like that with the Duke – and as I meant to write it, all their wild adventures would have come out and the insignificance of the former vegetation have been deducible only – as the main subject has become now ...[14]

The main subject is the old gipsy's tale. The reason Browning found difficulty in the actual rendering of the tale is evident when one examines the way in which the hunter describes the narration. 'Was it singing, or was it saying?' (512) he asks. And again he says:

> And I kept time to the wondrous chime,
> Making out words and prose and rhyme,
> Till it seemed that the music furled
> Its wings like a task fulfilled, and dropped
> From under the words it first had propped,
> And left them midway in the world,
> And Word took work as hand takes hand,
> I could hear at last, and understand ... (557–64)

Here music represents the infinite, and hence the gipsy's tale provides a vision to anyone who listens properly. In effect she is doing what Browning tried to do in all his poetry: to put the infinite within the finite. Such a poem would have fitted particularly well into the *Bells and Pomegranates* series, for, when one remembers Browning's explanation of his general title ('an alternation, or mixture, of music with discoursing, sound with sense, poetry with thought'), it seems that the gipsy's tale was meant to be the perfect union of music and words, of infinite and finite. But Browning had long before learned that he could not deal with such insight directly. What is left is what Browning called 'the accessories in the story,' 'real though indirect reflexes of the original idea.' 'Of course,' Browning continued in the same letter, 'it comes to the same thing, for one would never show half by half like a cut orange.'[15] The reader, then, must recreate the gipsy's tale by inference.

The vegetable existence of the ordinary world is represented by the court of the present Duke, while the world of romance is represented by the life of his father, the old warrior-Duke. The present Duke maintains his father's customs, but they are for him more of an affectation than a way of life.

> 'Twas not for the joy's self, but the joy of his showing it,
> Not for the pride's self, but the pride of our seeing it ...   (114–15)

The Duchess, 'the smallest lady alive' (135), is, by contrast, full of 'life and gladness' (137) and as such is capable of ideally human happiness. As she appears in the sixth section, she is much like the Duke of Ferrara's last Duchess (compare, for instance, the huntsman's statement, 'she was not hard to please' 141, with Ferrara's 'She had /A heart ... how shall I say? ... too soon made glad, / Too easily impressed ...' 21–23) and is indeed placed in much the same position. But through the old gipsy she has a vision of what Browning calls 'a *real* life,' and, unlike the Duchess of Ferrara, she has the opportunity to pursue this paradisal existence. It is her choice, and the circumstances that lead her to make it, that are the central concerns of the poem, and the more conventional romantic elements – the flight, and the gipsy's account of the full quest (' "Our long and terrible journey," ' ' "the trials," ' ' "the thrill of the great deliverance" ' into love, light, and joy) can only be imagined.

The same themes are used much less seriously in *The Pied Piper of Hamelin; A Child's Story*. The setting of the story, Hamelin town, is not the stage for the 'Warrior, Lover, Sage' of the chronicles, but a domestic scene, where 'little boys and girls / With rosy cheeks and flaxen curls' (203–4) move in a world of cheeses, cooks' ladles, men's Sunday hats, and women's chats. Into this child's world the pied piper brings a vision of paradise. For the rats the piper pipes of the world ' " 'grown to one vast drysaltery!' " ' (138); for the children he promises ' " 'a joyous land" '

> 'Where waters gushed and fruit-trees grew,
> 'And flowers put forth a fairer hue,
> 'And everything was strange and new ...'   (242–4)

The exodus of the children, like the flight of the Duchess, is a quest, an attempt to realize the vision presented to them.

The quest is seen most clearly in the poem with which Browning ended his series of Dramatic Romances, 'Childe Roland to the Dark Tower Came.' Here Browning deals specifically with one aspect of the major adventure in romance, the perilous journey through a wasteland. In myth, the purpose of the journey was to bring about the revitalization of nature. Browning, however, treats the quest in his own characteristic way: the wasteland is not only a phenomenon of external nature, but a state of mind as well, and hence the quester seeks spiritual regeneration rather than the renewed fertility of the land. Childe Roland's state of mind is evident in the very first line of the poem: 'My first thought was, he lied in every word, / That hoary cripple ...' and yet it soon becomes evident that the cripple was not lying about the location of the young man's goal: the 'ominous tract ... all agree, / Hides the Dark Tower' (14-15). Childe Roland's distrust of the old man is but one aspect of the crippled understanding which characterizes his mental wasteland. He has no hope that his quest will be successful, and scarcely conceives of a renewal of life; instead, the end of his quest means simply the end of his present state, and his only concern is that he be fit to fail (41-2). This concern with his own fitness indicates to us the real direction of Childe Roland's quest: it is a journey into the self. What he meets in the wasteland are the horrors within his own soul. Of the 'stiff blind horse' (76), for instance, Childe Roland says, 'I never saw a brute I hated so – / He must be wicked to deserve such pain' (83-4). Yet his instinctive hatred for the horse's purported guilt is actually revulsion from his own guilt. As a member of 'The Band' of knights who sought the Dark Tower, Childe Roland represents all his compatriots, and consequently the sins of Cuthbert and Giles, which he goes on to describe, are also his sins, and it is his duty to expiate them. Childe Roland's attempt to escape from the sight of the 'stiff blind horse' to 'earlier, happier sights' marks the first point at which he tries to do something about his situation. Earlier he had shown only acquiescence and resignation, and had felt that everything he did was determined by his situation, that he could do nothing to help himself (note the words he attributes to nature: ' "It nothing skills: I cannot help my case ..." ' 64). Now he reacts by turning, significantly, within himself: 'I shut my eyes and turned them on my heart' (85). What he discovers in his memory, however, is not innocent happiness but rather sin and guilt, and these in turn force him to face up to the present ('Better this present than a past like that ...' 103). Childe Roland's awareness of the present becomes increasingly intense: the 'sudden little river' is described in such a way as to suggest the River Styx; the 'fell cirque' is associated with a mysterious battle; and the engine of torture is first seen as a 'wheel,' then as a 'brake,' and finally as 'Tophet's tool.'[16] Images of despair, horror, and torture give way to images of imprisonment when Childe Roland finds himself trapped by the mountains. The moment he realizes he cannot turn back, he also realizes, 'This was the place!' (176). Imprisoned within the self, he at last faces his own sin and guilt, symbolized by the Dark Tower. That the guilt is not just social but personal is made evident by the qualifying phrase, 'without a counterpart / In the whole world' (183–4), a phrase that also suggests that only Childe Roland can expiate such guilt; that he is at last aware of his own blindness is made evident by another qualifying phrase, 'blind as the fool's heart' (182). The discovery is a moment of self-knowledge and self-awareness that leads to regeneration. In the increasing noise, Childe Roland hears the names of all his predecessors, but now the names are linked, not with treason and disgrace (as they had been with Cuthbert and Giles), but with strength, boldness, and good fortune (196–7); and in a 'sheet of flame' (201) that is in effect a purgatorial fire Childe Roland sees the knights themselves. Like them, he may fail. But, even if he is killed in the crucial struggle, he has taken the first step toward spiritual regeneration by recognizing the enemy within. The outcome of the struggle itself is unimportant. Insofar as 'Action in Character' is concerned, the real quest has already been achieved.*

Lyric

Browning approached the lyric as he did romance – as an opportunity for wide-ranging experiment. The genre in itself was particularly suitable for such experimentation. In the classical tradition the lyric poet was the master of a wide variety of metrical and stanzaic patterns; traditionally, too, he spoke for the community rather than himself, and hence dealt with the community's relations with God and with other men, expressed its joys and sorrows, celebrated its triumphs, and mourned its losses. To

---

* This reading of the poem is not new (it is similar, in its chief points, to that of Robert Langbaum, who in turn was indebted to others: *The Poetry of Experience* 195); in the present context, however, I think it important to emphasize how Browning modified the traditional action of romance – the quest – and made it a journey into the self.

this other ages added the tradition of the lyric poet speaking of himself, and expressing his own feelings and emotions. Victorian reviewers, in speaking of the lyric spirit, defined it as insight into the general or the universal; most spoke of it as a quality of the poet or a reaction of the reader, but failed to define the features of the work which expressed the one and evoked the other. The genre was a very flexible one, and Browning made the most of its flexibility.

The lyric poet was usually expected to display special abilities in the technical aspects of poetry. Browning met this expectation by using a great variety of metrical and stanzaic patterns – patterns far more varied than those in the romances – and, with the facility of a virtuoso, proved himself the master of intricate metres and complicated rhymes. The best example is perhaps *A Lovers' Quarrel*. The seven-line stanza has a rhyme scheme which, with its many repetitions (AABBAAA) seems more appropriate to humorous verse than it does to a love lyric; yet Browning avoids the jingling effect of such repetitions, partly by run-on lines, and partly by an extremely complicated metrical pattern that is maintained, seemingly effortlessly, through twenty-two stanzas. The first two lines consist of three feet each, a trochee followed by two iambs, and an anapest followed by two iambs, respectively. There follow two dimeter lines, each consisting of one anapestic and one iambic foot. The fifth line lengthens to three feet, two anapests followed by one iamb, while the sixth line is a repetition of the first, and the seventh a repetition of the fifth. The very complexity of this metrical pattern keeps it unobtrusive, so that the general effect is far less formal than that of *Love Among the Ruins*, for instance. Browning's experiments with metre frequently led him to patterns that reinforce the feelings of the speaker. An extra beat at the end of the first and third lines of each stanza of *The Lost Mistress*, for instance, gives the metre a halting effect that conveys the stifled emotion of the poem. Not all of the *Dramatic Lyrics* share such formal metrical effects. In *The Laboratory* and the *Soliloquy of the Spanish Cloister*, the rhythms are close to those of ordinary speech, and consequently are more usually associated with drama than with lyric.

Browning insited that the mode of presentation in his lyrics was dramatic: his poetry is 'always dramatic in principle, and so many utterances of so many imaginary persons, not mine ...'* The statement goes

---

* Browning's statement must be attributed in part to the extra-literary considerations that F.R.G. Duckworth dealt with in *Browning: Background and Conflict*. The poet's characteristic reluctance to reveal his own feelings and point of view in the direct manner expected by the critics is the source of his statement.

directly against the general view of the lyric poet as revealing his own feelings, but is not wholly unsuited to the poems themselves. *The Laboratory* and *The Confessional,* for instance, are obviously 'utterances of ... imaginary persons.' On the other hand, the love lyrics, and particularly such poems as *By the Fire-Side,* are spoken by characters who often seem to be thin disguises for Browning himself. At any rate, his delineation of all the moods and variations of love inevitably reflects his own experience, and to that extent the lyrics are personal. Nevertheless, it is clear that Browning's intention was not to follow the nineteenth-century view of the lyric but to return to something akin to the classical concept of the lyric as an impersonal expression of community sentiment rather than a personal outpouring of intimate feelings. Such an intention (plus the fact that the lyric is traditionally associated with music) may account for the inclusion in the volume of the three *Cavalier Tunes* (*Marching Along, Give a Rouse,* and *Boot and Saddle*) and the drinking song, *Here's to Nelson's Memory!*

Browning himself, in one of his letters, provides some help (characteristically ambiguous) for the critic who is trying to deal with the range of his experiments. When Edmund Gosse asked him to pick "Four Poems, of moderate length, which represent their writer fairly,' Browning chose *Saul* and *Abt Vogler*.[17] These poems do not fit the ordinary concept of the lyric. Neither the rhyme nor the stanzaic structure is complicated. The long lines – pentameter in *Saul,* hexameter in *Abt Vogler* – seem more suited to heroic verse than they do to the lyric. The speaker in each case is clearly not the poet himself, and hence, so far as mode of presentation is concerned, the poems are dramatic. In spirit, however, the poems come closer to the Victorian concept of the lyric.

As in any composition, the spirit or 'inner form' is reflected in the theme. The theme, of course, is not just the subject – David's song or Abt Vogler's improvisation – but involves the poet's treatment as well. Browning is concerned primarily with the divine validation of human desires. In *Saul,* for instance, David's love for the king leads him to conceive of immortality; and, because Browning is constantly affirming that human love is a witness of divine love, David has a prophetic vision of Christ, through which God confirms the validity of his desire. Similarly, in *Abt Vogler,* the musician doubts the value of human concepts that cannot be immediately realized. His art, however, gives him insight into the divine inspiration that makes all things possible:

But here is the finger of God, a flash of the will that can,
Existent behind all laws, that made them and, lo, they are!

And I know not if, save in this, such gift be allowed to man,
That out of three sounds he frame, not a fourth sound, but a star.

(49–52)

Human desires, then, whether those of the artist or of anyone who feels love and sympathy, reveal divine truth, and provide insight into God's plan for the world.

This lyric spirit manifests itself in characterization as well as theme. When we compare *Saul* and *Abt Vogler* with *Fra Lippo Lippi* and *Andrea del Sarto*, it soon becomes evident that we have a far greater sense of the painters as individuals than we have of the musicians. The essay on Shelley helps us define the difference in treatment. There Browning makes it clear that the lyric poet is not concerned with the delineation of individual character, nor with 'the combination of humanity in action'; rather, it is 'with the primal elements of humanity [that] he has to do ...'[18] These 'primal elements' constitute the essence of individual character. But, in discovering the essence of the individual, the poet also discovers the characteristics of our common humanity, so that what at first seems highly personal and unique is gradually recognized as impersonal and universal. This paradox is summed up in book III of *Sordello*, where, when Browning defines the lyric, he speaks in terms of universals (love, lust, mirth, sadness), yet somehow indicates to the audience that he is defining the essence of a specific mood ('" "Ay, that's the variation's gist!" "' III 911). This passage helps explain why the lyric poet tends to speak in personal terms (as both David and Abt Vogler do about love and life) and yet at the same time manages to give the impression that he is conveying insights into the essential nature of human existence. For instance, in showing how David's personal love for Saul becomes a revelation of divine love Browning is giving the particular universal significance.

The lyric spirit also manifests itself in the presentation of time. In the conventional romance, the passing of time is a linear movement, and the narrative basis of the genre gives events a chronological sequence. In the lyric, however, sequence is linked with simultaneity, movement with stillness. As such, the lyric is closely related to the idyll and the epyllion as defined by Marshall McLuhan: 'Dramatic parallelism, multileveled implication, and symbolic analogy, rather than linear perspective or narrative, characterize the little epic at all times.'[19] When we look for these characteristics in *Saul*, we begin to realize that the poem sums up the whole of the Bible. For Browning is not simply retelling the Old Testament story, he is treating it in New Testament terms. The first dramatic appearance of Saul, leaning on the tent-prop, prefigures the Crucifixion, and, so far as the structure of the poem itself is concerned, looks forward to David's prophetic vision, which will give his dejected stance immense significance. Similarly, the king-serpent image, though derived from an incident in the history of the Israelites (see Numbers 21: 4–9), functions in this poem just as does in the Bible: as a foreshadowing of the Crucifixion, and as a promise of resurrection and eternal life. So, too, in *Abt Vogler*. The extemporization, the inspiration of a moment, sums up the aspirations of the musician's whole life. His personal desires become mingled with the desires of mankind when Vogler describes them in terms of a palace of art (an important image in Victorian poetry) and links the palace with the works of Solomon. Such a multiplicity of concern, concentrated in the moment that the poem itself deals with, is an important aspect of the lyric.

In the group called *Dramatic Lyrics*, Browning treats these characteristics in various ways, using different kinds of lyrics and different modes of composition. Some, such as the dream vision *Women and Roses*, depend upon the poet's imagination, while others, such as *The Laboratory*, depend more upon his sympathetic portrayal of dramatic characters. Browning refers to these modes of composition in *The Ring and the Book* when he describes the ' "special gift" ' of the poet as ' "More insight and more outsight" ' (1747) — terms that sum up the poet's vision of the infinite as well as his observation of the world around him. The poet's insight enables him to see the world in two ways: as a reflection of the order of heaven or the disorder of hell. For this reason, the range of themes and treatment of Browning's lyrics can best be described as a cyclic pattern. As the cycle moves downward, there is a feeling of loss, a concern with the ways of the world, and a growing sense of life as grotesque and horrible; as it moves upward, there is a feeling of gain, a concern with the ways of the imagination, and a growing sense of life as happy and even ecstatic. It is not too difficult to see that this pattern is really an extension of the pattern of themes in Browning's romances. On the one hand, Browning portrays a character's involvement in the complexities of worldly existence and his consequent loss of vision of an idealized world; on the other, he portrays characters who regain this vision and are able to transform ordinary existence.

Some of the *Dramatic Lyrics* are definitely expressions of the sentiments of society. I have already mentioned the drinking song, *Here's to Nelson's memory!* and the three *Cavalier Tunes*, all designed to inspire valour and courage. Closely related to these spirited partisan songs are the two poems, 'How They Brought the Good News from Ghent to Aix' and Through the Metidja to Abd-el-Kadr, both of which have a strong community reference, although the speaker in both cases is a single person. The galloping rhythm, and the sense of mission, of patriotic participation in an exciting cause, are the chief effects of the poems. A single person may, of course, speak for the community. Home-Thoughts, from Abroad is every Englishman's expression of love for his country, while Home-Thoughts, from the Sea is full of patriotic spirit.

Community songs may, of course, not only inspire, but express loss and disappointment. Such is The Lost Leader, which, whatever its value as Browning's opinion of Wordsworth, belongs generically with marching songs like the Cavalier Tunes. The connection is made explicit with these lines: 'We shall march prospering, – not thro' his presence; / Songs may inspirit us, – not from his lyre ...' (17–18). The poem may also be read as an inverted panegyrical ode which, in spite of the setback it records, ends on a note of encouragement: 'Best fight on well ...' (29).

As the sense of loss becomes greater, we move towards the elegy and the epitaph. Sometimes the loss is the impersonal passing of a way of life, as in Claret, the first of the Nationality in Drinks poems. The disappearance of 'some gay French lady' lurks behind Claret, and reminds us that the occasion of a sense of loss is usually death. And it is the death of a beautiful sixteen-year-old girl that is the subject of the elegy, Evelyn Hope. The poem follows the pattern of most elegies in that it moves from the speaker's grief to an affirmation of his belief in immortality, and it ends with a reconciliation to his present lot.

Evelyn Hope may also be read as a lament for a love affair that never happened ('It was not her time to love ...' 11). This theme leads us to the lament, the kind of poem which points, not to a specific person, but to the good things lost in the transitory and disappointing nature of life itself. Such a poem is Earth's Immortalities, which is a sardonic observation on two favourite Petrarchan themes, fame and love. The section called Fame describes the weathering of a poet's grave, while Love describes the passing of an affair in terms of the passing seasons. Browning said that he meant the refrain to be 'a mournful comment on the short duration of the conventional "For Ever." '[20]

A love affair (often the subject of the lament) is frequently the occasion for the neglect and cruelty that cause the poet to complain about his lot. A Serenade at the Villa, for instance, is a poem about rejected love, and, in the bitter manner of the lament, the poet concentrates on the love lost rather than on the lady who does not respond. The sense of loss is nostalgic in the poem *Misconceptions*, and is mitigated, in *The Lost Mistress*, by the agreement of the lovers to remain 'mere friends.' In *A Lovers' Quarrel* the joys of love during the winter are described with a whimsical amusement, an emotion that turns to passionate longing when the lovers are separated by 'a shaft from the Devil's bow' (82), a word. The feeling of isolation which lies at the centre of the lament is seen most clearly in *Two in the Campagna*. Here the speaker's concern is to share his thoughts and his feelings with his lady, but just when they achieve the desired unity, it eludes them:

> I yearn upward – touch you close,
> Then stand away. I kiss your cheek,
> Catch your soul's warmth, – I pluck the rose
> And love it more than tongue can speak –
> Then the good minute goes. (46–50)

There follows an expression of isolation worthy of Matthew Arnold:

> Where is the thread now? Off again!
> The old trick! Only I discern –
> Infinite passion and the pain
> Of finite hearts that yearn. (57–60)

When the theme shifts from what is lost to the causes for the loss, the lament becomes a complaint, and the reader's attention is directed towards the shortcomings of man and his society. The close connection between the complaint and the homily in early English literature[21] explains the tendency of the complaint to treat the errors of man categorically, and the poem typically centres on the abuse rather than on the abuser. In *A Lovers' Quarrel* the speaker has little to say about the ways of the world:

> Foul be the world or fair
> More or less, how can I care?
> 'Tis the world the same
> For my praise or blame,
> And endurance is easy there. (113–17)

But when we come to such poems as *One Way of Love* and *Another Way of Love* we are confronted with the imperfections of life in general. In *One Way of Love* the theme is the fortuitous nature of love; the poet complains that in spite of all his efforts Pauline has not chanced to fall in love with him. The note of acceptance is still prominent:

She will not give me heaven? 'Tis well!
Lose who may – I still can say,
Those who win heaven, blest are they!   (16–18)

Such a resigned attitude is not present in *Another Way of Love*, where
the lady speaks scornfully of her husband's boredom with her 'serene
deadness' (13), and by doing so voices every wife's reaction to every
man's desire for freedom in love. The same situation brings about 'love's
decay' (16) in *In a Year*, where the husband observes, ' "Love's so different with us men!" ' (67). *Any Wife to any Husband* is the fullest treatment of this theme. Here the 'one little hour' (48), the good moment of
love, is remembered bitterly by the wife because of the somewhat pro-
miscuous nature of her husband's attentions.

When the concern with the ways of the world develops from bitter
anxiety into repulsion, we have a grotesque and melodramatic situation
like that of *The Confessional*. Here the speaker is so moved by the fatal
result of her well-intentioned betrayal of her lover that she cries out:

It is a lie – their Priests, their Pope,
Their Saints, their ... all they fear or hope
Are lies, and lies – there!   (1–3)

As one moves closer to the point where human life reflects hell, the
confusing diversity of life becomes grotesque and inhuman, and the
sense of loss moves through disillusion to despair. In *A Toccata of Galuppi's*, for instance, Galuppi's 'cold music' (33), with its suggestions of
death, ' "dust and ashes" ' (35), is juxtaposed with the warm carnival atmosphere of Venice. The poem ends with Galuppi's audience of revellers
gone, and the poet feeling 'chilly and grown old' (45).

Galuppi is described as 'a ghostly cricket, creaking where a house was
burned' (34). The image has the grotesque overtones of a Gothic novel,
and indeed, the grotesque plays a large part in a world where men are
often as deformed as the nature of things is uncongenial to human happiness. *The Confessional* is a portrayal of emotional deformity, ranging
as it does from passionate love through a strong religious instinct to passionate hate. The warped religious sentiments of the speaker of the
Soliloquy of the Spanish Cloister are obvious enough. *The Laboratory*,
which is also grouped with these poems, is more sinister than grotesque.
It is essentially a picture of aesthetic deformity, of noxious beauty: a
dancer bent on murder, a richly coloured liquid disguising a poison
('And yonder soft phial, the exquisite blue, / Sure to taste sweetly, – is

that poison too?' 15–16). *Sibrandus Schafnaburgensis*, the second section of *Garden Fancies*, is concerned with pedantry or intellectual deformity, and the fate of the offending book is suitably grotesque.

For Browning, the grotesque, though often horrible, is rarely repulsive. The tone of the *Soliloquy of the Spanish Cloister* and *The Laboratory* is melodramatic while *Sibrandus Schafnaburgensis* is treated with no small sense of humour. Browning was, in fact, fascinated with the grotesque, and the descriptions of the beetles, slugs, and toadstools in *Sibrandus Schafnaburgensis* is presented with noticeable relish. Browning confessed his delight with creatures of this sort while speaking to Miss Barrett of Horne's *Ballad Romances*: 'I suppose "Delora" will stand alone still – but I got pleasantly smothered with that odd shower of wood-spoils at the end, the dwarf-story; cup-masses and fern and spotty yellow leaves, – all that, I love heartily ...'[22] The 'dwarf-story' Browning is referring to is *The Elf of the Woodlands: A Child's Story*, which contains a long catalogue of all the creatures, plants, and other accessories of the elf's world. In the same letter Browning goes on to speak of another feature of Horne's poems that seems to have some relation to *The Laboratory*: 'Oh, while it strikes me, good, too, *is* that Swineshead-Monk-ballad! Only I miss the old chronicler's touch on the method of concocting the poison: "Then stole this Monk into the Garden and under a certain herb found out a Toad, which, squeezing into a cup," &c. something to that effect.'[23] One can imagine the delight with which Browning described the making of the poison in *The Laboratory*. Finally Browning confesses to Miss Barrett:

> I suspect, *par parenthèse*, you have found out by this time my odd liking for 'vermin' – you once wrote '*your* snails' – and certainly snails are old clients of mine – but efts! – Horne traced a line to me – in the rhymes of a 'prentice-hand' I used to look over and correct occasionally – taxed me (last week) with having altered the wise line 'Cold as a *lizard* in a *sunny* stream' to 'Cold as a newt hid in a shady brook' ...[24]

It is evident, then, in Browning's attitude towards the grotesque, that the observation of the external world is just as imaginatively exciting as looking within the self. Outsight is, in fact, another mode of revelation. If we only have eyes to see, Browning says, small creatures can teach us a great deal about creation:

> I always loved all those wild creatures God '*sets up for themselves*' so independently of us, so successfully, with their strange happy

minute inch of a candle, as it were, to light them; while we run about and against each other with our great cressets and fire-pots. I once saw a solitary bee nipping a leaf round till it exactly fitted the front of a hole ... Well, it seemed awful to watch that bee – he seemed so *instantly* from the teaching of God![25]

Even at the bottom of the cycle, then, the poet's insight is still intense. As the cycle turns upward again, the poems show a greater sense of gain. The gain is represented, initially, by the discovery of a standard by which the anomalies and complexities of the world are judged. The application of such a standard is, of course, the method of the satirist. In *Popularity*, for instance, the posthumous fame of John Keats is set over against Keats' true significance (Browning recognizes him as a 'star'). Browning compares Keats to a fisherman and his poetry (every rift loaded with ore) to a blue dye. The dye becomes very popular, but it is appreciated for the wrong reasons and is badly imitated. Browning mocks the critics, and through them the ways of the world. A similar approach is used in the first few stanzas of *Old Pictures in Florence*. Here there is a certain nostalgia for the Florence of the great artists, and an impatience with the imperfections of man and his inability to appreciate art: 'For oh, this world and the wrong it does!' (49). As the poem proceeds, however, the satire softens and the poet's attitude to the imperfections of the world changes. Through the medium of art he sees that imperfection is necessary, for man 'receives life in parts to live in a whole, / And grow here according to God's own plan' (111–12). And he realizes that man's potential is worth more than the static beauty of a work of art. With stanza xxiv he returns to his 'special grievance,' the neglect that the Old Masters suffer. Instead of looking back, now, he looks forward to the Florence of the future, with its political freedom and its completed Campanile.

It is evident that, in the poems of this part of the cycle, Browning treats the confusion of ordinary experience as having some purpose and meaning. The question that Browning asks of *Master Hugues of Saxe-Gotha* ('What do you mean by your mountainous fugues?' 4) is the question that every individual must ask of his own complex experience. Browning's answer (that 'comments and glozes' [120], do not lead us to 'God's gold' [114], but that mastering the difficult fugue makes us aware of the infinite) is the answer of all those who realize they must work out the significance of life for themselves. Life is, to use Browning's image in *Master Hugues*, a web full of 'zigzags and dodges, / Ins and outs' (112–13), a web which both hides and reveals the infinite. And so Browning, looking at men 'With such various intentions' (123) down through history, exhorts: 'Leave the web all its dimensions!' (125).

If one accepts life as it is, and is aware at the same time of a purpose in its imperfection, one's conduct becomes of paramount importance. Since the criteria for choosing and the consequences of acting are never fully known, conduct is a matter for argument, and the debate and the colloquy (which is what Browning calls *Master Hugues*) come to the fore. The companion poems *Before* and *After* are essentially a debate on duelling, *Before* representing the positive, and *After* the negative side. The speaker of *Before*, one of the seconds, argues for duelling, insisting that, for the culprit, 'Better sin the whole sin, sure that God observes ...' (13), and for the innocent party, 'While God's champion lives, / Wrong shall be resisted: dead, why, he forgives' (33–4). *After* is spoken by the victor in the duel, who discovers that his victory has solved nothing: 'Ha, what avails death to erase / His offence, my disgrace?' (11–12).

As soon as one begins to look beyond ordinary experience, the conduct of life becomes a quest for moments of special happiness. Such is the theme of *Love in a Life* and *Life in a Love*. In both poems the quest is unsuccessful, and life is consequently an endless and fruitless pursuit. Although the poet views the pursuit with some spirit, there is an underlying tone of boredom and frustration that comes through in the repetition in the opening lines of *Love in a Life* ('Room after room, / I hunt the house through') and in the admission in *Life in a Love* that 'the chace takes up one's life, that's all' (15). The anticipation of the speaker in *In Three Days* seems much more likely to be satisfied, and the passing of time is almost speeded up by the looked-for reunion with his lady.

The moment of pleasure usually centres in a person, a loved one, or an object that has some connection with love. The presence of such a person is often a promise that the experience is possible, and an assurance that it can be renewed. Sometimes, of course, the promise is not fulfilled, as in the case of *A Pretty Woman*, whose beauty is only skin-deep. More often the pleasure is real if transitory. The speaker of *Meeting at Night* and *Parting at Morning* confesses, in Browning's words, 'how fleeting is the belief (implied in the first part) that such raptures are self-sufficient and enduring – as for the time they appear.'[26] The transitory nature of love is deeply felt in *A Lovers' Quarrel*, where the intimacy occasioned by the chill of winter gives way to dissension at the return of spring. Similarly, the concern of the wife in *A Woman's Last Word* is to prolong and maintain the happiness of love, in spite of occasional 'wild words.' In *Love Among the Ruins* the moment of pleasure, represented by the 'girl with eager eyes and yellow hair' (51) who waits in the turret, is juxtaposed with 'whole centuries of folly, noise and sin!' (75). The quiet pastoral landscape (the Harvard manuscript of the poem is entitled *Sicilian Pastoral*)[27] gives the added dimension of an idealized world that contrasts with the former 'city great and gay' (6) much as in romance. The moment of pleasure may be evoked by such a landscape, as it is in *'De Gustibus –,'* where the poet's attraction to Italy is treated as a love affair ('Open my heart and you will see / Graved inside of it, "Italy" ' 43–4). If the poet is attracted, not to the country but to the city, then we have an inverted pastoral, such as *Up at a Villa – Down in the City.* Here rural life (serene and virtuous in the traditional pastoral) is associated with all sorts of physical discomfort, while urban events (frantic and vicious in the traditional pastoral) afford endless pleasure and amusement: 'Bang, *whang, whang*, goes the drum, *tootle-de-tootle* the fife. / Oh, a day in the city-square, there is no such pleasure in life!' (53–4).

As we continue to move upwards in the cycle of themes, the pleasures of life begin to point to something beyond life itself. The basic imagery for this expanded vision is provided by *A Woman's Last Word*. This poem represents the experience of love as an Eden and the 'wild words' that destroy happiness as the serpent or the apple. The lovers are represented as birds in debate; the traditional image of the soul as a bird in the Tree of Life is relevant here, as are such medieval love debates as Chaucer's *Parliament of Fowls*. The point is that the moment of happiness is associated with paradise, and that the pleasure provided by ordinary experience brings an awareness of an imaginative or spiritual world not unlike that sought in romance.

The kind of love that can lead to such an awareness is represented by the poem *Respectability*, where the unconventional nature of true love is contrasted with the conventions of society (represented by Guizot's hypocritical welcome to Montalembert upon his election to the Academie française). Such social conventions are felt to be 'a vegetable existence,' while love represents 'a real life,' though one still within the grasp of ordinary experience. The intense experience of such 'a real life' leads to an awareness of the infinite. In *The Flower's Name*, the first of the *Garden Fancies*, the garden with which the lady is associated has overtones of Eden, and in particular the 'soft meandering Spanish name' (20) of the flower she touched points to the infinite within the finite. For Browning refers to the name in the same way that he refers to the old gipsy's tale in *The Flight of the Duchess*, as 'Speech half-asleep, or song half-awake' (22). An object as well as a sound can symbolize the infinite. In *Memorabilia* the eagle feather that the poet picks up on the moor represents the transcendent vision provided by Shelley's poetry. The painting of *The Guardian-Angel* has a somewhat similar function. Browning's contemplation of the picture (in which he recognizes the angel as 'Thou bird of God!' 18) brings him peace ('All lay quiet, happy and supprest' 28) which in turn enables him to view the world as a kind of Eden. In spite of the fact that the experience is shared ('My angel with me too ...' 46) it develops into a highly individual vision which Browning expresses in a poem: 'I took one thought his picture struck from me, / And spread it out, translating it to song' (52–3).

In Browning's poetry, the moment of insight, the moment when the relation of the infinite and the finite is seen in an ecstatic vision, typically occurs when lovers experience complete unity of their beings. In *Cristina* Browning describes this experience as a mingling of souls, moments 'When the spirit's true endowments / Stand out plainly from its false ones ...' (20–1). Such 'flashes' (25) seem 'the sole work of a life-time' (31). The best-known expression of such an experience is in the poem *By the Fire-Side*, where the 'moment, one and infinite' (181) comes when the poet and his wife are admiring an Italian scene that has for them a highly personal meaning. However, the poetic conventions that are involved in Browning's careful description of this setting give it a universal poetic significance. When the poem opens, it is autumn, and the poet is seated by the fire-side; the atmosphere suggests the intimacy of the winter months in *A Lovers' Quarrel*. There follows his memories of a day's excursion in Italy. The ascent up the mountain is, like that of *The Englishman in Italy*, a quest for a moment of vision. There is even the suggestion, in the twenty-first stanza, that the poet is a type of Orpheus, and that in their ascent they are leaving the underworld behind:

> My perfect wife, my Leonor,
>   Oh, heart my own, oh, eyes, mine too,
> Whom else could I dare look backward for,
>   With whom beside should I dare pursue
> The path grey heads abhor?   (101–5)

During the ascent they consider the coming of a new Heaven and a new Earth (stanza xxvii). Their discussion is mingled with comments on the trees, the little stream, and the lonely chapel, and consequently, when the moment of vision comes, it is closely associated with the natural setting: 'The forests had done it ...' (236). The moment makes both their lives complete, and heightens and perfects their ordinary experiences.

This heightening is conveyed by the fireside setting and its mood of quiet happiness.

As the poet concentrates more and more on the vision, it not only heightens ordinary experience, but causes it to appear as an illusion, while the vision itself is recognized as reality. When translated into poetic conventions, this theme causes the usual associations of dream and waking to be reversed, the latter being the illusion and the former the reality. Such a poem is *Women and Roses*, the record of a dream which seems derived from medieval love visions. Certainly the central symbol (the rose) has affinities with the symbolism of *The Romance of the Rose*, and the poem is built on a medieval *question d'amour*: 'Which of its roses three / Is the dearest rose to me?' (2–3). The three roses represent women of the past, present, and future, who also appear as figures dancing round the tree. The poet is unable to answer his question, since his efforts to fix any one of the three roses in either his life or his art are frustrated. Yet the women continue to circle the tree, a reminder that the desirable vision they represent is unchanging and eternal, even though the particular manifestations of it (the three roses) are subject to change and decay. Because the poet is involved in time, eternity appears to him as an endless circle, and hence the tone of the vision is not one of ecstasy, but of frustration.

Women and Roses points up the limitations of human understanding; no human being can have complete knowledge of the infinite, for such knowledge is God's alone. The most he can hope for is an understanding of the significance that life has for him personally. Such is the import of the very short poem *My Star*, where the different colours (red and blue) and images (bird, flower) represent the kind of insight that cannot be explained to anyone else.[28]

The *Dramatic Lyrics* thus include a wide variety of poems, poems that differ greatly in metrical and stanzaic patterns, in speakers, and in particular lyric forms. The purpose of Browning's wide-ranging experiments is made clear in a letter of 24 February 1853, when Browning wrote to Milsand: 'I am writing — a first step towards popularity with me – lyrics with more music and painting than before, so as to get people to hear and see ...' The statement is a characteristic expression of Browning's not quite compatible intentions: his desire to be popular, and his firm resolution to create his own audience. Here he calls attention to his task as a Maker-see, just as, over a year later, he called attention to the experiments by which he hoped to better his performance. In a letter dated 5 June 1854, he told Forster that in the 'number of poems of all sorts and sizes and styles and subjects' which he had written, 'the manner will be newer than the matter.'[29] Browning's comment reminds us that his treatment of form remained as unconventional in the 1850s as it had in any of his earlier work.

Men and Women

The two volumes called *Men and Women* were published in 1855, and contained a total of fifty poems plus an epilogue. In the distribution of 1863 only thirteen poems were retained under the title. *Artemis Prologizes* seems to have been included among these dramatic pieces because it is a fragment of a drama; *One Word More* retains its original place as the epilogue, and *Rudel to the Lady of Tripoli* serves to introduce it, since the poem is concerned with the sources of inspiration and with the nature of dedications. The rest of the poems usually have a central place in any discussion of Browning's treatment of the 'dramatic monologue': a term which Browning himself did not use, but which has become so generally accepted that it would be confusing to discard it. In this section I will concern myself with this genre which is a combination of the drama and the lyric, the two poems Browning placed at the beginning of the section – 'Transcendentalism: A Poem in Twelve Books' and *How It Strikes a Contemporary* – suggesting the nature of the combination. Browning found the combination a flexible one, and his treatment of it varies widely.

In structure and mode of presentation, the poems in this group are primarily dramatic. Since Browning was not writing for the stage, he was free of the limitations of ordinary dramatic structure (that is, action forwarded by dialogue), for he was not concerned with plot, and was concerned only incidentally with action. In other technical aspects, however, the poems resemble works written for the theatre. With the exception of *Johannes Agricola in Meditation* and *Pictor Ignotus*, both of which have a rhyme scheme, the monologues are written in blank verse, and the iambic metre approximates the rhythms of ordinary speech. In mode of presentation, too, the poems are dramatic, and are spoken by a well-defined character who is not the poet himself. Park Honan's definition of the dramatic monologue sums up this aspect of the genre; it is, he says, 'a single discourse by one whose presence is indicated by the poet but who is not the poet himself.'[30] Similarly, Robert Langbaum treats the dramatic element in the monologues as 'perspective' or 'angle of vision.' The monologue 'imitates not life but a particular perspective toward life, somebody's experience of it.'[31]

To complete our understanding of the dramatic monologue, we must, as Langbaum has said, 'abandon the exclusive concern with objective criteria,'[32] and take into account the characteristics which the Victorian critics were most interested in: that is, mode of composition, and the spirit or attitude which is both revealed by the poet and aroused in the reader. Of these characteristics, the former is the more problematical, since it is impossible to recover and describe the poetic process itself. But conjecture is greatly aided by Browning's comments on his problems of composition, and particularly by his comments on *Luria*. The chief problem Browning faced was to enable the audience to, in Miss Barrett's phrase, 'discern between the vivid & the earnest.'[33] Browning realized that, to create vivid, well-rounded characters the dramatist must enter sympathetically into many feelings and points of view that are not his own. But at the same time Browning was dealing with the development of the soul, and had a clear idea about the rightness or wrongness of his characters' thoughts and actions. Such moral insight demanded expression too. Whatever Browning's solution to this problem, it is clear that the process of composition includes what Mrs Orr would have called two distinct 'forms of mental activity':[34] the sympathy that enables the poet to imitate all the diverse aspects of human life, and the insight (particularly moral insight) that enables him to judge his characters and to assess the development of their souls. Sympathy is the chief characteristic of the dramatist; to such feeling should be attributed the concreteness, the attentiveness to detail that defines the speaker and locates him in a particular time and place. The characteristics that I.B. Sessions assigns to the dramatic monologue – 'speaker, audience, occasion, revelation of character, interplay between speaker and audience, dramatic action, and action which takes place in the present'[35] – sum up the particulars which the dramatist must realize. Insight, on the other hand, is the chief characteristic of the lyricist. He composes, in Browning's words, 'not so much with reference to the many below as to the One above him';[36] hence the lyric impulse tends to subsume the particularity of the dramatist's portrayal by revealing the pattern of a character's whole life; it tends too to subsume the individuality of such a pattern by suggesting that it is a common aspect of human behaviour, that it has universal significance, and that it is to be judged by a scheme of values that God reveals to the poet. It is this lyric impulse in the dramatic monologue that bothers most critics, from the harried freshman who is concerned with what Browning 'really means,' to Hoxie N. Fairchild, who argues that the poet always includes a 'giveaway' that indicates what he himself

thinks or what he wants us to think.[37] Yet it is precisely the tension between the two 'forms of mental activity' that is the characteristic spirit
of the dramatic monologue.

For this reason, Robert Langbaum is surely right when he defines the
effect of the dramatic monologue as 'the tension between sympathy and
moral judgment.'[38] For the feelings the poet has in approaching his material are precisely the feelings he wishes to arouse in his readers. Like
him, they must enter into, and try to understand, points of view not
their own; and like him, they must go beyond such immediate experience, and judge its moral qualities. Because of such mental activity, the
poem becomes as much a part of the development of the reader's soul
as the composition of it was of the poet's.

The two impulses were defined as early as 1856 by Browning's friend
Milsand, when he reviewed *Men and Women* for the *Revue contemporaine*. Milsand set himself the problem of explaining how the English
poets, whose avowed purpose was dramatic and realistic ('toujours de
peindre d'après nature'), managed at the same time 'à écrire en vue d'ex-
primer l'état de leur esprit,' so that 'l'individualité du poète se mêle dans
ses vers à la peinture des choses.' Milsand argued that the mixture was
possible only because the poet combined the lyric and dramatic impulses
in the process of composition. Using terms from Browning's essay on
Shelley, he argued that Browning was both subjective and objective,
lyrical and dramatic ('simultanément, lyrique et dramatique, subjectif
et pittoresque'). In another part of the essay, Milsand called the two
impulses 'réalisme' and 'idéalisme.' 'Réalisme' is 'la tendance à repre-
senter les choses que l'on peut voir, et rien que cela'; 'idéalisme' is 'ce que
l'esprit seul peut percevoir.'[39] Milsand's definition of the term 'idéalisme'
is particularly interesting, for Browning himself seems to have thought
of the lyric impulse as idealization. Julia Wedgwood, commenting on
The Ring and the Book, objected to Browning's voice in the characterization of Pompilia ('It seems to me one of the many instances where
your thoughts overflow the dramatic channel'), in Guido ('It is your
lending so much of yourself to your contemptible characters makes me
so hate them'), and in the lawyers ('I cannot endure to hear your voice
in these Advocates' pleadings'). In reply, Browning characteristically de-
nied the revelation of himself, but admitted the heightening of character,
especially in order to show moral differences:

I don't admit even your objections to my artistry – the undramatic
bits of myself you see peep thro' the disguised people. In that sense,
Shakespeare is always undramatic, for he makes his foolish people

all clever. I don't think I do more than better their thoughts and instructions, and [word illegible], up to the general bettering, and intended tone of the whole composition – what one calls, idealization of the characters. What is in the *thought* about the 'charter' impossible to Pompilia, if you accept the general elevation of her character?[40]

Clearly Browning is characterizing Pompilia, not only through the particulars that the eye perceives, but through the patterns that the poet's imagination conceives.

This combination of dramatic and lyric genres is suggested by the poems which Browning placed at the beginning of *Men and Women* when he regrouped them: '*Transcendentalism: A Poem in Twelve Books*' and *How It Strikes a Contemporary*. In the latter poem Browning describes what is primarily the acute and sympathetic observation of the dramatist, a 'recording chief-inquisitor' (39):

He took such cognisance of men and things,
If any beat a horse, you felt he saw;
If any cursed a woman, he took note;
Yet stared at nobody, – they stared at him,
And found, less to their pleasure than surprise,
He seemed to know them and expect as much.   (30–5)

Although the poet's knowledge of human nature enables him to accept equally all he sees, his letters to 'our Lord the King' (44) suggest that 'all thought, said, and acted' (43) has a significance that goes far beyond the daily life of the city. If one takes 'our Lord the King' to represent God, the poet of Valladolid is not unlike Browning himself, who wrote to Ruskin on 10 December 1855: 'A poet's affair is with God, to whom he is accountable, and of whom is his reward.'[41] The poet is then concerned mainly with what is revealed to him about the relation of the finite and the infinite, and about the development of the soul. In '*Transcendentalism: A Poem in Twelve Books*' Browning speaks about conveying such insights to others, about evoking in them the lyric impulse that produced the poem. As always, Browning insists that the poet's insights cannot be conveyed by 'naked thoughts' (3); rather, he says, thoughts must be draped 'in sights and sounds' (4). When they are embodied in something concrete, the reader is able to perceive their wholeness or unity, and so arrive at insights of his own. The method of the magician John of Halberstadt seems best:

He with a 'look you!' vents a brace of rhymes,
And in there breaks the sudden rose herself,
Over us, under, round us every side,
Nay, in and out the tables and the chairs
And musty volumes, Boehme's book and all, –
Buries us with a glory, young once more,
Pouring heaven into this shut house of life. (39–45)

These two poems make it clear that the dramatic and lyric impulses rarely function alone, for the dramatist is always moving toward recurring patterns of action and thought, and the lyricist is always moving toward concrete particulars that embody such patterns. On the one hand, the characters of *Men and Women* are dramatic creations whose outlook we must experience through identification, and judge with whatever insights we have; on the other hand, these characters embody the poet's lyric insight, his understanding of human nature and its relation to the infinite. There are, then, two voices in the dramatic monologue, the speaker's and the poet's.[42] Each constantly merges in the other, so that the reader is forced to rely on his own powers of sympathy and judgment when considering the meaning of the poem.

The combination of characteristics of both the lyric and the drama made a very flexible genre, and, in this group of poems, as in the others we have been examining, Browning made the most of such flexibility. In particular he exploited the various kinds of irony inherent in the genre, and especially the kind of irony that appears when dramatic particulars are considered in a wider lyric context. But irony arises from other situations as well: from the discrepancy between motives and actions; from the discrepancy between what is said and what is meant by the speaker, between what is said by the speaker and understood by his listener, between what is said by the speaker and understood by the reader, and so on. Browning's treatment varies as much as do the speakers of each poem.

An Epistle Containing the Strange Medical Experience of Karshish, The Arab Physician portrays an individual's discovery of the Christian concept of the Incarnation. Browning treats this discovery in a dramatic manner, as one specific stage in the development of Karshish's soul, for he is as yet only attracted by the idea of the Incarnation, and is just starting to move along the path toward faith. As always in Browning's dramatic pieces, this 'Action in Character' is full of irony. For Karshish is an empiricist, a medical man in search of knowledge, and hence is ill prepared to cope with a spiritual experience. That he has never worked out the implications of his world view is evident in the inconsistencies in his thought: even though he is an empiricist, he sets down the conventional view of the soul (3–6); he accepts without question the efficacy of charms, yet assumes, on the basis of empirical evidence, that a miracle (such as Lazarus' return to life) cannot happen. He makes the most of the empirical facts he has gathered, certain that they are correct, and sure that they are valuable. Yet these things, which he hesitates to entrust to the Syrian messenger, have, we know, no value at all, and are medically unsound; all the things that Karshish doubts (the resurrection of Lazarus, the Incarnation) are, on the other hand, extremely significant in his life, yet he dismisses them as harmless and without value. Such irony is relatively simple, yet it becomes more complicated as the poem proceeds. The reader, I think, tends to feel patronizing toward Karshish because he is so obviously wrong and Lazarus is so obviously right. There is a tendency to compare Lazarus and Karshish to the disadvantage of the latter, to take Lazarus as a model for human life, and Karshish as a bad example of ignorance. But, as he continues the letter the reader begins to realize that Lazarus need no longer cope with human life, while Karshish merits a good deal of sympathy. His curiosity, his search for truth, his falling into error, his weighing of evidence, his choices and decisions – all these things make him the type of the questing man. Lazarus is the symbol of how not to live; Karshish is Everyman whose spiritual instincts urge him towards truth and salvation.

What makes Lazarus unfit for life is his knowledge of ultimate things – the immortality of the soul, and the true scale of moral values. For Lazarus these things are not a matter of faith; he has experienced them, and hence can be absolutely certain about them. Because he knows the absolute scale of values, he places the physical and the spiritual in their proper proportion; he sees tremendous issues, but they are not the issues that Karshish sees or that the ordinary human being sees. Karshish, for instance, tries to arouse Lazarus from what he thinks is apathy by reminding him of purely physical things, such as the huge army approaching the city. To Lazarus this event is insignificant. But in 'some trifling fact' (150), 'a word, gesture, glance' (162) he sees tremendous moral import. It is clear, then, that Lazarus has a detailed knowledge of moral consequences; it is equally clear that such absolute knowledge makes him totally unfitted for human life. One of the most constant themes in Browning's poetry is the idea that the limitations of earthly life are designed to give man the opportunity for moral development; man acts only when he has made a choice, and choice can be made only when man has incomplete knowledge. Absolute knowledge, of the kind that Lazarus has, precludes moral choice. Faith, on the other hand, is, as Tennyson said, 'Believing where we cannot prove'; as such, faith is the basis of moral action. Each individual faces a unique set of moral problems and decisions, and the choice that he makes determines the whole pattern of his life.

Although Lazarus cannot make such a choice, Karshish is moving toward one. He is alternately attracted and repelled by the idea of the miracle, and by what Lazarus says about Christ. The idea that attracts him most is the one he leaves until the end of the letter: the idea of the Incarnation. He accounts for his reluctance in speaking of the Incarnation by labelling the idea as insane or trivial; yet his very reticence indicates that this idea is the most staggering one of all. The fact that he is moved to express it shows that it has already become a part of his life, even though he has not yet accepted it intellectually.[43]

Johannes Agricola in Meditation was classified as a romance in 1863, and did not become one of the *Men and Women* until 1868. As a romance it can be considered along with *The Heretic's Tragedy* and *Holy-Cross Day* as a portrayal of perverted religious feeling. In grouping it in *Men and Women*, Browning placed it directly after *An Epistle*, thus emphasizing the contrast between the two poems. Karshish's search for truth, his growing faith, his errors, his curiosity, his decisions – all these qualities make him a representative and (for Browning) admirable human being. Johannes Agricola is just the opposite. He does not seek truth because he thinks he is certain of it, and he confuses faith with knowledge. He is convinced that he has no decisions to make and no errors to fall into. Karshish's curiosity is replaced by Agricola's complacent acquiescence ('God, whom I praise; how could I praise, / If such as I might understand ...' 56–7). Coming to this poem immediately after *An Epistle*, a reader with any knowledge of Browning's views on the development of the soul cannot but judge the pattern of Johannes Agricola's life as inadequate.

The next three poems, *Pictor Ignotus*, *Fra Lippo Lippi*, and *Andrea del Sarto*, form a distinct group, since the central character in each is a Renaissance painter. In each, dramatic and lyric elements are combined, but Browning's treatment of the combination varies considerably.

In *Pictor Ignotus* Browning portrays an artist incapable of making full use of his talents, and at the same time keenly aware of the discrepancy between what he might have been and what he actually is. Implicit throughout the monologue is a sense of the painter's failure both as an artist and as a human being. What he might have been is suggested by the youth's pictures, at the sight of which his soul springs up. He remembers the 'gift / Of fires from God' (5–6), the power to paint human passion in the portrayal of externals. In the midst of his dream of public acclaim, love, and praise, there is a sudden change, marked by the shift from the present to the past tense. 'The thought grew frightful, 'twas so wildly dear! / But a voice changed it!' (39–40). Whether the voice is fear of criticism, or timidity, or conscience, it is clear that it represents the deep psychological aberration in the painter's personality. A nightmarish stream of consciousness follows; attraction and repulsion, love and vitality along with mistrust and hate, mingle confusedly. The painter aspires to do great work for the 'loving trusting ones' (45), but also realizes that the world will judge his work, and him too. The reader is left wondering about the nature of the choice that the unknown painter made. Was it an act of cowardice, a psychologically dangerous withdrawal from the give-and-take of life? Or was it a defiant act, in which the painter showed his displeasure with a society incapable of appreciating art, except in terms of buying and selling, or on the arbitrary basis of taste? Whatever the reasons (and we may sympathize with both), we usually judge the choice adversely. When the painter says, 'What did ye give me that I have not saved?' the reader cannot help recalling the parable of the talents, and the failure of the man who simply possessed God's gifts and did not use them. Similarly, the rhetorical question at the end ('Tastes sweet the water with such specks of earth?' 71), which the painter means to be answered negatively, must of course be answered affirmatively, for the specks give the water whatever taste it has. Through such devices as these, Browning directs our moral judgment of the speaker, and emphasizes his inability to see any purpose in the imperfections of the world. We are left with a sense not of the tragedy of failure, but rather of the pathos of promise unfulfilled, and of the grotesqueness of human feelings gone awry.

Pictor Ignotus presents us with a man who does not understand himself, and hence the gap between what he says of himself, and what the reader understands of him, is full of irony. The irony in *Fra Lippo Lippi* is rather different. For Fra Lippo Lippi does understand himself, and knows how to manipulate his listener, the watchman. He is, moreover, himself aware of the discrepancy between his view of life and art, on the one hand, and the view of the prior and the other monks, on the other. The poem, then, is quite different in treatment from *Pictor Ignotus*. It is a portrayal not of a psychologically abnormal personality, but of the confident new outlook that marked the shift from the Middle Ages to the Renaissance. And where the irony in *Pictor Ignotus* suggested a tragic waste of talent, the irony in *Fra Lippo Lippi* suggests the comic realization of a particular outlook on life and art.

The poem begins with the incongruous and the laughable (the monk who pursues worldly things with gusto), moves on to divine comedy (the revelation of God's purposes in life), and ends with a seemingly inappropriate but wholly characteristic linking of the two. The broader irony of the poem lies in the fact that in the crude and rather farcical discrepancies that evoke laughter the pattern of divine purpose is evident.

The setting and the situation realize vividly the kind of irony which is laughable. A monk is caught, after midnight, lurking in a dark alley in a disreputable part of Florence, 'Where sportive ladies leave their doors ajar' (6). As Roma King points out, the situation is symbolic: 'The street and monastery represent apparently contradictory forces, both religious and artistic, which Lippo is challenged to reconcile.'[44] The reconciliation takes the form of a proper understanding of the finite, the infinite, and the relation between them. And that understanding is the substance of Fra Lippo Lippi's apology.

The broad comedy of the first part of the monk's apology – the account of his escape from the Medici palace to join the pre-Lenten revelry in the city – is obvious enough. By shutting the painter up in the palace, Cosimo de Medici made painting an ascetic discipline not very different from monastic life; and the assumption that spirit can be exalted only at the expense of flesh is represented by Fra Lippo Lippi's subject, 'Jerome knocking at his poor old breast / With his great round stone to subdue the flesh ...' (73–4). The discrepancy between this assumption and Fra Lippo Lippi's activities (as suggested in the snatches of song) is laughable, and the reaction of the officer ('Though your eye twinkles still, you shake your head ...' 76) is an ironic mingling of approval and disapproval. But the monk gives an ironic twist to the officer's charge that he is a 'beast.' He tells the officer how he came to be a monk, and how he promised to renounce the world and lead an ascetic life. The irony in his account is all too evident. What he renounces ('the world, its pride and greed, / Palace, farm, villa, shop and banking-house ...' 98–9) are things he never had anyway; and what he escapes from is a life of poverty so extreme that he did indeed live as a beast

'On fig-skins, melon-parings, rinds and shucks, / Refuse and rubbish' (84–5). Fra Lippo Lippi's comments might have been a bitter satire on the worldliness of the church. Instead, the tone suggests a realistic acceptance of things as they are, an acceptance which is based on certain assumptions about the nature of earthly life. These assumptions become clear when the monk goes on to talk about his art, and so we move from the broad comedy of a man hot in pursuit of earthly pleasures to the divine comedy of a man who is aware of God's purposes working through earthly life.

When Fra Lippo Lippi sets out his views of art, he presents in effect a sacramental view of life. The medieval preference for art that was formal, cold, and stylized was based on the assumption that a too realistic rendering of earthly things hampered spiritual insight. Fra Lippo Lippi, on the other hand, assumes that flesh is a symbol which does not hide but rather reveals spiritual things. Hence it is the painter's task to reproduce carefully the look of things, and in doing so to lead the viewer on to a consideration of the spiritual significance of them: 'Can't I take breath and try to add life's flash / And then add soul and heighten them threefold?' (213–14). Here 'breath' seems to represent physical existence, 'life's flash' whatever the painter does with his material to make it lifelike, and 'soul' whatever the painter does with his material to make it represent, not just the particular thing he is painting, but the essence of life itself, something universal and unchanging. The implications of this three-fold process are evoked by Fra Lippo Lippi's reference to the creation (266–9), which implies in turn his belief that man is made in the image of God, and that it is the painter's task to portray him as such. In short, his purposes as a painter imply a Trinitarian analogy, and that analogy helps us understand his argument that the three aspects of painting are not separate and distinct, but inseparably fused, a paradoxical three-in-one unit. The unity would be destroyed should any one part be neglected. Hence, if a painter is to portray man in the image of God, the body, and whatever it is that makes it lifelike, are just as important as the soul.

When the watchman lets it be known that he still thinks Fra Lippo Lippi a beast, the painter goes on to set out the moral value of art, and in doing so provides one answer to the age-old question about the value of earthly life. The artist, he argues, is more than just (in modern terms) a photographer; that is, he gives more than an exact, accurate representation of nature. Instead, he lifts what Coleridge called the 'veil of familiarity' from the world, so that we are seeing it as if for the first time. Art, then, cannot be accepted passively. Instead, it evokes a response from the viewer, a response that involves a keen sense of God's purposes working through creation. The value of art implies the value of life:

> This world's no blot for us,
> Nor blank – it means intensely, and means good:
> To find its meaning is my meat and drink.   (313–15)

The high seriousness of the central part of the monologue is varied by the comedy of Fra Lippo Lippi's retraction. At first glance, the all-too-obvious irony of a retraction designed to pacify a suspicious and rather stupid officer of the law suggests that Browning is returning to the broadly comic treatment of the first part of the poem. A more careful examination makes clear that the irony is more complex than it would at first seem, and that the tone strikes a balance between the low comedy at the beginning and the divine comedy of the central section.

There is much about the retraction that is conventional. As one might expect, the artist in effect confesses his sin in being so involved with worldly things (all of which are vanity) and promises to return to spiritual things. The subject – the Coronation of the Virgin – seems proper for such a mood, and the composition ('God in the midst, Madonna and her babe, / Ringed by a bowery, flowery angel-brood, / Lilies and vestments and white faces ...' 348–50) is to be as conventional as the retraction itself. We, of course, are aware of the irony in the retraction. The subject, which seems so conventional, is in fact a subject of special significance for the painter: an earthly woman crowned Queen of Heaven. Mary's spiritual exaltation came about through her physical being, and hence Mary's life is the type of each individual's existence. And the composition, which seemed so conventional too, is in fact to be varied with an unconventional portrayal of the painter himself making eyes at Saint Lucy. The picture, on the surface a representation of a heavenly affair, is also Fra Lippo Lippi's representation of what is apparently his own very earthly affair with the Prior's niece. The irony in the painter's multiple purposes should, one might think, be accompanied by a sense of incongruity. The fact that Fra Lippo Lippi gives no indication that he feels the combination of elements inappropriate clinches his argument for us, and forces us to re-examine our assumption that worldly pleasures are somehow not a part of divine purpose.

The irony in *Andrea del Sarto* works in a way quite different from

Fra Lippo Lippi. The poem has some of the pathetic elements of *Pictor Ignotus*, for one has a sense of a not inconsiderable talent going to waste. But whereas the unknown painter seemed largely unconscious of the psychological state that determined his choice of a particular kind of art, Andrea is fully conscious of the choice he has made, and indeed reiterates it in the monologue itself. Andrea's sense of what he might have been and what he is, though confused, is far keener than that of the 'pictor ignotus,' as is his sense of his deficiencies and limitations. The irony in the poem emphasizes the discrepancy between promise and achievement, and hence the treatment shifts from the pathos of promise unfulfilled to the satiric sense of not measuring up to a standard.

Andrea is a failure both as a painter and as a man. As Roma King points out, 'He comes to see that his failure is at least twofold – both as artist and as lover – and that somehow these two are inseparably related.'[45] The relationship of the two is suggested by the ironic subtitle of the poem, 'Called "The Faultless Painter." ' Andrea's painting is technically perfect, but it shows no insight, and lacks depth of feeling and understanding. Similarly, when Andrea describes Lucrezia, he speaks readily of the perfection of her appearance, and seems in those passages to overlook her moral and emotional deficiencies. The imagery associated both with Lucrezia and with Andrea's work emphasizes this limited perfection: both are gray rather than golden. Andrea compares Lucrezia to pearls and the moon; so, too, his art: 'A common grayness silvers everything ...' (35); 'All is silver-gray, / Placid and perfect with my art ...' (98–9). The perfection which Andrea sees in Lucrezia's appearance and in technical aspects of his art is, ironically, a measure of his limitations. 'A man's reach should exceed his grasp, / Or what's a heaven for?' (97–8). Heaven, in other words, is perfect and complete, and the imperfection of earth implies the perfection of heaven. An artist who understands this strives to realize that understanding in his painting. On the other hand, art which is perfect and complete in itself, like Andrea's, suggests nothing beyond itself, and in fact hinders man's perception of heaven. Art which is perfect paradoxically fails; art which is imperfect paradoxically succeeds, because it goads the viewer to complete it, and hence to see what the painter has seen.

Andrea's limitations are summed up by the shifting meaning of the gold imagery. At the French court, the ostentatious display of gold is linked with energy, vitality, creativity, and the insight suggested by the phrase, 'fire of souls' (160). The Renaissance view of gold as the king of metals and the sum of all metallic virtues seems relevant here, since it suggests by analogy the complexion of man, and the most desirable combination of the elements and humours. When Andrea leaves the French court to return to Lucrezia, gold becomes associated with Lucrezia's hair (175), with the perfection of outward appearance. Finally, gold becomes synonymous with money, and with the financial troubles with which Andrea is plagued. Andrea speaks of gold in business terms, and such words as 'gain' and 'profitless' 'depict the degeneration of Andrea's standards of values, his genuine confusion, and ultimately his compromise with the tawdry and commonplace.'[46]

Both Roma King and David Shaw have pointed out that the poem lacks a formal structure, and that its form is 'random and non-progressive, as sporadic and meandering as its speaker.'[47] Such a manner of proceeding suggests the failure of Andrea just as much as the progress of Fra Lippo Lippi's monologue suggests the realization of his view of art. It also indicates the moral confusion of his repeated choice to stay with Lucrezia and to do as she wishes. This constant evidence of Andrea's limitations, and the constant sense we have of how far he has fallen short of the golden days at the French court, suggest that Browning's treatment is satiric.

In each of these three monologues Browning combines the dramatic and the lyric. Each is carefully located in time and place; in each the occasion is vividly realized, and in two of the three the listener is characterized with some care. At the same time we sense that in these dramatic particulars the patterns of three lives are summed up. These patterns are common rather than unique: the pathos of promise unfulfilled in *Pictor Ignotus*; the comedy of views realized in *Fra Lippo Lippi*; and the satire of a foolish choice repeated by a man with limited insight in *Andrea del Sarto*.

The last three monologues show a similar combination of dramatic and lyric elements, a tendency toward the particular and the local, on the one hand, and toward the comprehensive and the universal, on the other. *The Bishop Orders his Tomb at Saint Praxed's Church* presents us with a death-bed scene, but at the same time reveals to us what Ruskin defined as 'the Renaissance spirit, – its worldliness, inconsistency, pride, hypocrisy, ignorance of itself, love of art, of luxury, and of good Latin.'[48] In *Bishop Blougram's Apology* the argument is a dramatic one, since Blougram argues from premises that Gigadibs will accept and understand.[49] The apology, though framed for a particular speaker and a particular time, nevertheless discloses the nature of Blougram's own faith, and the heightened expression of certain passages (182–97, 560–3, 621–5, 647–61, 693–7, 845–51) reveals to us Blougram's whole approach to life; biographical evidence makes it clear that Browning's own approach to life was not very different. *Cleon* begins his letter by describing the arrival of Protus' letter, thus setting his words in a particular time and place. But he too reveals the pattern of his life, a pattern not unlike that of *Andrea del Sarto*.

Like 'pictor ignotus,' the Bishop who 'Orders his Tomb at Saint Praxed's Church' is incapable of understanding himself. Consequently, his monologue is shot through with inconsistencies (as Ruskin pointed out) and these evoke in the reader a sense of irony. For, while the Bishop mouths the platitudes of the church ('Vanity, saith the preacher, vanity!' 1), he is in fact engaged in an intense search for sensation, sensation which is physical (his memories of his mistress and her beauty), intellectual (his love for good Ciceronian Latin, his promise that his sons will have 'brown Greek manuscripts' 74), and aesthetic (his description of the design of the tomb, the basalt, 'peach-blossom marble' 29, and the lapis lazuli). It is the design of the 'bas-relief in bronze' (56) which best sums up the Bishop's indiscriminate sensation-seeking:

> Those Pans and Nymphs ye wot of, and perchance
> Some tripod, thyrsus, with a vase or so,
> The Saviour at his sermon on the mount,
> Saint Praxed in a glory, and one Pan
> Ready to twitch the Nymph's last garment off,
> And Moses with the tables ... (57–62)

Here, as in *Pictor Ignotus*, one is left with a sense, not of the tragedy of such limited understanding, but of the pathos of a man for whom there is nothing but sensation, and of the grotesqueness of such limited humanity.

It is possible to see a similar parallel between *Fra Lippo Lippi* and *Bishop Blougram's Apology*. Like the painter, the Bishop is fully conscious of the discrepancy between his view of life, on the one hand, and the view of those around him, on the other. And he, like Fra Lippo Lippi, realizes his particular outlook on life, and is capable of the ironic manipulation of a listener who does not understand him. Browning's treatment of the monologue is, then comic. As in *Fra Lippo Lippi*, the comic ranges from the apparent incongruity of a bishop who enjoys worldly things to the divine comedy which is the revelation of God's purposes in earthly life.

The comedy which lies in incongruity is developed through Blougram's ironic acceptance of Gigadibs' premises (never thought out, of course) that a bishop ought to lead an ascetic life – if he doesn't, he's a knave – and that an intelligent man ought to enjoy the good things in life – if he doesn't, he's a fool. Blougram is, of course, fully aware of the inconsistencies in such a point of view. Hence he takes the premises, whittles away at one inconsistency after another, and brings Gigadibs round to an understanding of God's purposes working through ordinary life. He argues that any view of life must be based on life as it actually is, and not on an 'abstract intellectual plan of life / Quite irrespective of life's plainest laws ...' (92–3). And he goes on to argue that the purpose of such life, admittedly full of discrepancies, is moral growth (693–7). Hence the divine purpose of life:

> You own your instincts – why what else do I,
> Who want, am made for, and must have a God
> Ere I can be aught, do aught? – no mere name
> Want, but the true thing with what proves its truth,
> To wit, a relation from that thing to me,
> Touching from head to foot – which touch I feel,
> And with it take the rest, this life of ours!   (845–51)

Thus Blougram makes Gigadibs realize that a life of faith does not involve the rejection of material things, and realize at the same time that the full value of temporal and material things is evident only in a spiritual context. Like Fra Lippo Lippi, Blougram does not expect to be fully understood. But in fact his argument is realized in an unexpected way, when Gigadibs gives up his life as a journalist and emigrates to Australia.

The final poem in this group – *Cleon* – is given the same kind of satiric treatment as *Andrea del Sarto*. Like Andrea, Cleon knows what he is, and knows too what he would like to be. And, also like Andrea, he reiterates the choice that makes his life a failure. The reader constantly judges Cleon in terms of what he might have been. The satire lies in this sense of the discrepancy between the man and the standard he has failed to achieve.

Like *An Epistle*, the monologue is in the form of a letter from Cleon to Protus, his king, a letter in which Cleon answers three questions put to him by the king. Protus had apparently asked Cleon if he were the perfect man, and Cleon answers that he is. In this context, 'perfect' means 'complete' or 'fully developed,' for Cleon has mastered all arts, and has encyclopaedic knowledge. He denies, however, that the development of the complete man is the working out of divine purpose, and in doing so reveals himself as an empiricist, like Karshish. He distinguishes carefully between facts, which are true because they are empirically demonstrable, and fiction, which is not true because it is made up. Hence the story which he has written about the incarnation is fiction. The limitations of such a position become clear in Cleon's negative answer to Protus' second question: Is the development of the complete man 'The very crown and proper end of life?' (164). The complete man is still a finite creature, who can conceive of infinity. Hence, to finite eyes 'imperfection means perfection hid ...' (185). Cleon asks if such divine excellence is empirically verifiable, and finds that it is not. He treats the desire of the soul for immortal life in exactly the same way. For Cleon, such a desire is valid only if confirmed by empirical evidence, such as a sign from God. But such evidence is, of course, never available. It is ironic that Cleon should use the same arguments and follow the same line of reasoning that David does in *Saul*, and yet be unable to take the final step and affirm truth which is revealed. To Protus' third question (Does the artist enjoy immortality through his works?) Cleon gives a qualified, 'Yes.' Such immortality is unsatisfactory, because the artist himself perishes. Throughout the monologue, it is clear that Cleon is capable of conceiving of immortality for the soul, but incapable of believing in it, since belief is for him a matter of empirical demonstration. And when the teachings of Paul and the Christians reach him, Cleon confirms his position and rejects them: 'Their doctrines could be held by no sane man' (353).

4 The Ring and the Book

When Henry James delivered his lecture on 'The Novel in *The Ring and the Book*,' he, like many other critics, remarked on the seeming formlessness, the 'clustered hugeness or inordinate muchness' of the poem. 'All the while,' he continued, 'we are in presence not at all of an achieved form, but of a mere preparation for one, though on the hugest scale ...'[1] James and other critics are responsible for the assumption that too often passes for an axiom, that Browning's poetry is difficult because it lacks form, order, and an easily recognized structure. *The Ring and the Book* often does seem shapeless, partly because we do not know how to approach a poem that demands as much activity on the part of the reader as it did on the poet's, and partly because we are not familiar with the structural signposts that Browning places strategically throughout the poem. In dealing with book 1, for instance, most critics are so concerned with the gold-and-alloy image that they fail to ask themselves why Browning not only describes the contents of the Old Yellow Book, but three times presents the materials he derives from it. Each presentation is generically distinct, and provides the key to the structure of the books that follow. Yet this careful piece of patterning, which is typical of the tight construction of the whole poem, has been almost totally ignored.*

* Except by Mary Rose Sullivan, *Browning's Voices in the Ring and the Book* 13–

The principal image of book I, the ring which is produced from the processing of gold and alloy, points directly to the structure of the poem, and ironically to the truth the poem contains. The structure, as we shall see, is circular, and the titles of the first and last books indicate the way in which Browning rounds off the poem. As for the second aspect of the ring: the circle, we already know, is one of Browning's favourite images for truth. When the image appears in *Abt Vogler* ('On the earth the broken arcs; in the heaven, a perfect round' 72) the circle represents ultimate truth, the arc of the circle finite truth. Browning often speaks of the artist as gifted with insight into ultimate truth, and so the circle (which is limited to a single plane) may be a symbol for truth as the artist sees it, while the sphere (with its infinite number of planes) may represent truth as God sees it.

The making of the ring raises other problems, though the primary meaning is simple enough. The gold represents the facts, the alloy the poet's fancy (that is, imagination), and the ring the truth which is the poem. But when we come to consider why fact needs fancy to become truth, and why, moreover, Browning seems to contradict himself and have the alloy washed away by 'a spirt / O' the proper fiery acid' (I 23–4), it quickly becomes apparent that the image is not as simple as it first appeared. And so we begin to suspect that here, as so often before, Browning is making use of irony.

The irony arises from Browning's consciousness of his audience, the British public, 'ye who like me not ...' (I 410). He is fully aware, when he discusses such concepts as truth, value, and the imagination, that his audience has a completely different idea of the terms. The poet exploits these differences by seeming to share these assumptions about truth and value, and yet at the same time enlightens his audience by presenting inconsistencies that force them to consider the real meaning of the terms. When we examine these concepts, then, we must watch for both the ironic sense and the true or authentic sense. In every case the

18. Sullivan argues that the account of the contents of the Old Yellow Book is a presentation of the facts, that the second telling is 'an imaginative re-creation' of the facts, and that the third is 'factual narration ... without interpretation or editorial comment,' which 'represents a kind of prologue to the next, most important stage of the poetic process, which is the introduction of the individual voices of the monologues.' Sullivan relates this process to the fashioning of the ring: 'first, the preparation of the crude material (finding and studying the written record); second, the moulding of it by mixing in a firmer, more malleable material (his emotional and imaginative re-creating of the scenes leading up to the trial); and third, the purifying of the shaped ring by the withdrawal of the alloy (suppression of his own personality in the dramatization of the events surrounding the trial).'

ironic sense corresponds with the popular understanding of the term. In dealing with truth, for instance, Browning plays with the popular assumption that what is true is what is factual, an assumption based on the empiricist philosophy dominant in his time. Browning knew that the British public would approach his work with the conviction that what was in his source, the Old Yellow Book, was true, because it was factual, and what was in *The Ring and the Book* was not true, because it was poetry, ' "make-believe" ' (ı 455). Browning appears to support this view by washing away the alloy (his fancy), and by saying that the Old Yellow Book contains 'pure crude fact' (ı 35), 'fanciless fact' (ı 144), 'absolutely truth' (ı 143). Other comments give these statements an ironic twist. The 'truth' the Old Yellow Book contains is 'all i' the heads and hearts of Rome' (ı 415); it contains, not facts, but interpretations of facts, lawyers' opinions, 'Pages of proof this way, and that way proof ...' (ı 239). From these opinions the facts, the bare outline of the case, can be deduced. There is seldom any doubt about these facts; the real problem is to get at their meaning. Knowing that his audience would equate the facts with truth, Browning asks,

> Was this truth of force?
> Able to take its own part as truth should,
> Sufficient, self-sustaining? (ı 372–4)

The answer is, of course, no, for, while the reader is satisfied as to the who and what, the how and why escape him. Facts alone, then, are not truth, until a pattern of relationships reveals their significance.

Browning treats the concept of value in a similar way. Knowing full well that gold is looked upon as a 'precious' metal, he sets up an ironic analogy between it and the material in the Old Yellow Book (note the usefulness of the colour for Browning's ironic purposes):

> This is the bookful; thus far take the truth,
> The untempered gold, the fact untampered with,
> The mere ring-metal ere the ring be made! (ı 364–6)

Browning thus makes the most of the popular equation of gold with value, and strengthens his ironic equation of fact with truth. The authentic sense of the term, on the other hand, is close to Ruskin's definition of wealth in *Unto This Last*; that is, wealth must be defined not only as possessions but also as the individual's ability to use his possessions to preserve and enhance his life. Gold is not wealth unless it is useful; similarly, facts alone have no use and therefore no value. To be

in possession of a fact is not to have truth; truth is the individual's outlook on life, the point of view that fits the facts into the pattern by which
he lives. Hence the facts must be shaped by the poet's fancy, and so
made serviceable.

If we drop the metaphor here, we are left with the relativist position
that one truth is as good as another, so long as they are both equally
useful. But Browning is no relativist. There is such a thing as absolute
truth, and it is intuited by the imagination, which Browning ironically
calls the fancy. He well knew that in the popular sense fancy is the organ
of fiction; it makes things up, and is therefore fundamentally opposed
to truth. In the true sense, fancy is what the Romantics called the imagination. It is the faculty by which the poet intuits ultimate reality, and
is therefore fundamentally concerned with truth. Fancy establishes
relationships among facts; it creates patterns, and chooses those that
seem to approximate most closely the ultimate truth revealed to it.
Fancy, therefore, both sees into the infinite, and judges the finite.

In its true sense, then, the ring metaphor emphasizes the shaping
power of the poet, and directs our attention to the problem he faces
in organizing and constructing his work. It also emphasizes the response
of the reader, and the process he will use to arrive at truth. For Browning is clearly not interested in simply telling a story, and hence disposes
quickly of his primary source. Once he has described the documents in
the Old Yellow Book and outlined their contents, he says, 'You know the
tale already ...' (I 377); that is, the reader knows the facts of the tale,
' "the story, now, in off-hand style, / Straight from the book" ' (I 451–2).
But when Browning asks about the moral significance of the course each
character took – 'was it right or wrong or both?' (I 388) – the reader
is unable to answer. Moral insight is, therefore, a major aspect of the
poet's fancy, this 'Something of mine which, mixed up with the mass, /
Made it bear hammer and be firm to file' (I 462–3). From the letters to
Julia Wedgwood we know that it was just such insight that first
attracted the poet to the story: 'I was struck with the enormous wickedness and weakness of the main composition of the piece, and with the
incidental evolution of good thereby – good to the priest, to the poor
girl, to the old Pope, who judges anon – and, I would fain hope, to who
reads and applies my reasoning to his own experience, which is not
likely to fail him.'[2] The reader, then, must repeat with the poem what
Browning has done with the Old Yellow Book. From the reader's point
of view, as Browning says, 'Fancy with fact is just one fact the more
...' (I 464). Traditionally, however, the poet has greater insight than

other men, and the working of his fancy is a particularly significant fact. Browning describes his insight as giving the facts shape, like rings on the djereed. This shape is, on the one hand, moral truth, and, on the other, the literary form or genre which contains this truth. The structure of the poem depends, then, not on the facts as they are borrowed from the Old Yellow Book, but on the insight with which Browning offers these facts for the consideration of the reader.

Having explained, indirectly, the purpose and effect of his poem, Browning proceeds with the construction of it. Three times he ranges over his material, and each time he distinguishes a different generic pattern. He presents the information from the Old Yellow Book, first as a lyric (1 523–652), then as a narrative (1 780–823), and finally as a drama (1 838–1329). In the principal part of the poem these genres will be combined, but here Browning is anxious to show differences, and to set forth his concept of each mode.

Lyric

The lyric is marked by the moral insight that is realized in the various literary kinds Browning uses, and in the treatment of characters and events. The mode of composition becomes clear when Browning compares himself as poet to Elisha as prophet (1 760–72). Elisha is portrayed, not only as divinely inspired, but as inspiring (literally) the dead. Similarly, Browning 'creates, no, but resuscitates, perhaps' (1 719). His is a 'mimic creation' (1 740), as opposed to God's creative power, but it is nevertheless 'a glory portioned in the scale' (1 741). This divinely inspired insight Browning conveys, not by assertion and explanation, but through the concreteness of characters and images:

> The life in me abolished the death of things,
> Deep calling unto deep: as then and there
> Acted itself over again once more
> The tragic piece.   (1 520–3)

In spite of the dramatic metaphor, Browning is speaking of the resuscitation by which he may express his own insight, his own approach to life. This oblique lyric expression is clear from such lines as: 'I fused my live soul and that inert stuff ...' (1 469). And Browning causes his 'mage' (1 742) (who usually represents for him a lyric poet) to say: ' "I can detach from me, commission forth / Half of my soul ..." ' (1 749–50).

121

What is expressed is a remarkably full view of life. The mage speaks of '"a special gift, an art of arts, / More insight and more outsight"' (I 746–7) and thereby suggests, as I noted in the previous chapter, the whole range of human experience. Consequently, the lyric impulse is realized in a wide range of literary kinds.

The way in which moral insight gives generic shape to crude facts ('my fancy with those facts ...' I 679) becomes clear when we apply the dialectic between right and wrong to characterization. Translated into poetic terms, this dialectic can be represented by man's affinity to the angels, on one hand, and his affinity to beasts, on the other. If beastlike men overcome good characters, the action is tragic; if the good characters triumph, the action is comic. Between these two extremes is a wide range of characters who are neither wholly good nor wholly bad, but innocent, on the one hand, and worldly wise, on the other. The former belong to the world of romance, the latter to the world of satire. These four moral distinctions, then, provide us with four pregeneric categories. These categories function in somewhat the same way as key signatures in music. They are the tonal elements which the poet combines according to his own particular purposes. Browning uses these categories to shape each phase of the story according to his own insight.

The events of the story represent a ring, 'this round from Rome to Rome ...' (I 526), and it is a 'tragic piece' (I 523) insofar as two of the principal characters die, and evil seems more prominent than good. The story falls into five more or less equal phases, but any similarity to a five-act tragedy is largely coincidental. The phases are based on moral distinctions, which influence characterization and give shape to the action.

The first phase (I 523–43) presents Pompilia's upbringing and her marriage. The action is comic, from the point of view of the Comparini, and ironic, from our point of view. It has two moral aspects (the Comparini act 'Part God's way, part the other way than God's ...' I 530), and takes place on two levels: the 'world's mud' (I 532) in which the Comparini make 'a shift and scramble' (I 531), and a 'sphere of purer life' (I 536), supposedly represented by Guido, the nobleman. Pompilia's parents move upwards from one level to the other, and the move has a double significance. On the one hand the marriage is a step up the social scale; it represents the traditional comic achievement of the new society which they have struggled to bring about through their plots and intrigues. On the other it represents the promise of personal salvation. Here Guido as a 'star' (I 538) represents metaphorically the One Man who is the Son of God. Through her marriage Pompilia becomes a star too, and hence this phase of the action fittingly concludes with a Nunc Dimittis: ' "Now let us depart in peace, / Having beheld thy glory, Guido's wife!" ' (1 542–3). It is significant that throughout this comic action Pompilia remains a conventional heroine; like Shakespeare's Hero, she is beautiful, innocent, passive, and generally colourless.

In the second phase of the story (1 544–77) the Comparini visit Pompilia at Arezzo and are sadly disillusioned. The action is generally satiric, since it takes place on the level of the 'world's mud' and involves characters who are worldly wise. Guido, it turns out, is more worldly wise than the Comparini, and, in retrospect, the action of phase one is seen as ironic. As the 'sweetness of Pompilia' (1 556) is contrasted with the animality of the Franceschini the extremes of the moral dialectic begin to appear. Abate Paul ('fox-faced' 1 549), Canon Girolamo ('cat-clawed' 1 550) and their mother ('with a monkey-mein ...' 1 571) are little better than beasts, while Guido is the devil himself ('the Prince o' the power of the Air' 1 567). The palace at Arezzo is as close to hell in metaphor as it is in Pompilia's experience:

> a fissure in the honest earth
> Whence long ago had curled the vapour first,
> Blown big by nether fires to appal day ... (1 559–61)

The palace contains a nightmare world ruled by a 'satyr-family' (1 570). Here Pompilia is kept a prisoner, and from here the Comparini escape.

In the third phase (1 577–602) Pompilia's escape and capture are presented as a romance with an ironic ending. At this point, the romance depends entirely upon action. Into the demonic world of imprisonment and torture ('Fire laid and cauldron set ...' 1 581) springs 'the young good beauteous priest' (1 586) 'in a glory of armour like Saint George ...' (1 585). His quest is only partially completed for although he rescues the lady in distress, he fails to destroy the demons. The incompleteness of the quest immediately changes the action from the world of romance, where moral distinctions are clear, to the everyday world of ordinary experience, where such distinctions are often ambiguous and obscure. An ironic figure, 'the angel of this life' (1 594), appears, causes Pompilia to be recaptured, and allows the priest to escape. The ambiguous moral significance of the things of this world is suggested by the metaphors applied to the sky: 'earth's roof' and 'heaven's floor' (1 599), 'grate o' the trap' and 'outlet of the cage' (1 600).

The ambiguities are cleared away in the fourth phase (1 603–27), which describes the murder. Here there is the greatest possible contrast between the victim, an innocent and much-harried mother, and the murderers, 'a pack of were-wolves' (i 611). Consequently, this phase is a tragedy, and the tragic action takes place in the middle of winter, the lowest point in the cycle of the seasons ('it was eve, / The second of the year, and oh so cold!' i 605–6). The murder is the turning point; after it, writes Browning, 'I knew a necessary change in things ...' (i 630).

Although Browning's statement about 'a necessary change' may suggest a happy ending of some sort, the fifth phase (i 627–52) is not comic (as one might expect), but ironic, since it treats events and characters, whether good or bad, in terms of the inconsistencies and shifting ambiguities of ordinary life. The arrest is the 'first ray' (i 635) of a more enlightened standard by which Guido and his companions are to be judged. This standard is obscured, however, by a satiric interlude, the arguments of the lawyers, which confuse the issues until 'you scarce distinguished fell from fleece ...' (i 647). Although the lawyers and their clients represent a world of beasts (sheep and wolves) there is an implicit moral distinction in the metaphor, and it is this distinction that is made clear by the Pope, the 'great guardian of the fold ...' (i 648). Although the Pope's judgment is made with reference only to the limited understanding of man, it is arrived at with a consciousness of the infinite and of the way in which it impinges on the finite. The action thus swings upward to a comic ending. The dénouement is qualified, however, by the continued wrangling ('Vex truth a little longer ...' i 658) which leaves the reader with the sense that the world goes on much as it always has.

Shaped thus by the moral distinctions, the story reflects accurately Browning's own reaction to it: 'the enormous wickedness and weakness of the main composition of the piece,' and 'the incidental evolution of good thereby ... ' In effect it is Browning's reading of life, a vision of grays and blacks relieved sporadically, and thrown into relief, by white. The five phases of the story (comic, satiric, romantic, tragic, ironic) are the expression of Browning's moral insight, and it is this insight, divinely inspired, that makes this particular account a lyric.

Narrative

Having fully examined the lyrical aspects of his material, Browning turns from himself ('Enough of me!' i 773) and presents the facts of the

Old Yellow Book in a new manner. The 'spirit' by which he resuscitates the dead is quite different from his initial inspiration; it has all the energy and moral disinterestedness of nature herself: 'A spirit laughs and leaps through every limb, / And lights my eye, and lifts me by the hair ...' (1 776–7). Though this 'spirit' embodies the mode of composition Browning usually identifies with dramatic poetry, he here links it with narrative. As we might expect, we are given a vivid and lively description of externals. Count Guido, for instance, is

> A beak-nosed bushy-bearded blackhaired lord,
> Lean, pallid, low of stature yet robust,
> Fifty years old ... (1 782–4)

The account is factual:

> [Guido] killed the three,
> Aged, they, seventy each, and she, seventeen,
> And, two weeks since, the mother of his babe ... (1 797–9)

The court case and the issue ('Injury to his honour' 1 806) are presented with as much moral neutrality as possible, and the principal interest for the reader lies in how the story will turn out. The brevity with which Browning deals with the narrative genre indicates the relative importance he assigned to it.

Drama

At line 824 Browning turns to the drama which is to be his principal mode in the poem: 'Let this old woe step on the stage again!' (1 824). In spite of this direction, Browning is not writing for the stage, 'the very sense and sight' (1 826). As usual, he notes that stage presentation restricts the poet, and that it provides the audience with 'at best imperfect cognizance' of 'how heart moves brain, and how both move hand ...' (1 827–8). Instead, Browning gives us 'voices' (1 833) which provide as much evidence of this interior action as mere words can show. 'For how else know we,' asks Browning, 'save by worth of word?' (1 837).

Browning then proceeds to give an account of the voices which 'presently shall sound / In due succession' (1 839–9). These accounts serve as useful introductions to the succeeding books, and therefore a detailed discussion of each will be deferred until we come to examine the monologues themselves. It should be noted, however, that Browning combines the two modes of composition he has just distinguished, since he delineates vividly each character's perspective, his approach to truth, and at the same time directs the reader's attention to the moral qualities that such an approach reveals. The poet's judgment of the first three speakers is relatively clear. Both Half-Rome and Other Half-Rome have a 'source of swerving ...' (i 859) while Tertium Quid courts the approbation of high society. The judgment of the actors themselves seems much more tentative. Guido's evil nature manifests itself only as a shifty avoidance of truth; Caponsacchi is still the 'young frank personable priest ...' (i 1022), though he speaks, one should note, not to the court but to God (i 1072–4). Pompilia's devotion to truth is suggested by the fact that she gives details significance: 'Nothings that were, grown something very much ...' (i 1094). The trial, and the 'frothy talk' (i 1106) of the lawyers, serve as an interlude before the Pope's careful judgment. And finally Guido speaks again, 'the same man, another voice' (i 1285), and 'the true words come last' (i 1281).

The patterns of the poem

When we consider the way in which these three basic genres may be combined in the central portion of The Ring and the Book, we find a broad range of possible patterns. The sequence of events remains unchanged, but now this, now that, part of it can be emphasized according to the speaker's point of view. Just as Browning's insight into the moral qualities of each of his characters gives a certain shape to each of the five phases of the story, so each character's account of the affair will cause the events to take on generic characteristics which may or may not correspond to those Browning has already assigned to them. This dramatic interpretation is, of course, Browning's way of indicating the moral qualities of the speaker, and so our attention is divided between the poet and the characters he is creating. Moreover, the thread of the story is never lost, and hence we must keep in mind three generic points of view: the narrative, in which the facts of the story are presented simply as facts susceptible of varying interpretations (only one of which is right); the dramatic, in which each character interprets the story according to his own approach to life; and the lyric, in which the poet applies his moral and artistic insight to both the story he tells and the characters he creates, and so in effect makes the entire poem his reading of life.

There are other patterns as well. The monologues fall into three groups of three each, and each group includes a speaker *pro* and *con*, and a *tertium quid*. The first three speakers represent 'the world's outcry' (I 839). Half-Rome speaks against Pompilia, the Other Half-Rome speaks for her, while Tertium Quid refuses to be involved or to make a choice. The next group of three, Guido, Caponsacchi, and Pompilia, have all been desperately involved in the action. Guido speaks against Pompilia, Caponsacchi defends her, while Pompilia herself is detached from the situation by her purity of spirit and her devotion to truth. The last group, the two lawyers and the Pope, represents a reversal of the pattern of the first group. For the lawyers the case is a professional exercise; they are not involved even to the extent that Half-Rome and the Other Half-Rome are. And, while Tertium Quid is farthest from the truth, the Pope is perhaps closest to it; he feels the urgency and difficulty of making a choice.

The sequence of literary modes in each group of books is similar – not precisely the same, but similar insofar as the pattern is varied in repetition. The first book in each group belongs to the satiric mode; the second uses elements of comedy and romance, while the final book in each group is a 'third something' not so easily categorized as the other two.

Half-Rome

Half-Rome begins by emphasizing the plots and intrigues of Violante, and speaks of 'the wife's trade,' 'the sex's trick' (II 75). The foibles of women are a traditional subject of satire, and when the speaker applies the same characteristics to Pompilia (and, by implication, to his own wife) the entire story takes on a satiric cast. In effect, Half-Rome takes the satiric aspects that Browning distinguished in the first two phases of his narrative, and expands them to include the entire story. As far as moral distinctions are concerned, he deals principally with worldly wise people. As he proceeds, the object of his satiric wrath and the standard by which the characters are judged become evident. For he constantly lashes out at the world's wickedness (represented by women, in the main) and constantly praises the virtues of civilized society (represented by Guido).

The world's wickedness is summed up visually by the bodies in the church. Half-Rome describes the sight, and tells of the reaction of old Luca Cini:

'Here the world's wickedness seals up the sum:
'What with Molinos' doctrine and this deed,
'Antichrist's surely come and doomsday near.
'May I depart in peace, I have seen my see.'   (II 125–8)

This Nunc Dimittis, like the Nunc Dimittis of the Comparini in book I, is ultimately ironic. The Comparini believed theirs was a vision of social prominence, on the one hand, and personal salvation, on the other. For the reader, however, the vision becomes ironic as he moves on to the second phase of the story. When Luca Cini views the bodies of the Comparini, he recognizes in the deed the sum of the world's wickedness. Half-Rome, however, takes, not the deed, but the Comparini themselves, as wicked, and so reveals, ironically, an understanding just as limited as that of Pompilia's parents. He has no concept of the metaphysical import of evil, and sees it only as worldly wisdom turned to selfish ends. Nevertheless he speaks of it in the traditional terms, as a 'crime' (II 164) and as a sin which must be confessed (II 1447–50). When he uses the Garden of Eden story, he casts the characters as follows:

The gallant, Caponsacchi, Lucifer
I' the garden where Pompilia, Eve-like, lured
Her Adam Guido to his fault and fall.   (II 167–9)

In spite of such passages as these, Half-Rome's concept of sin is not Christian or even Hebraic. Instead, he presents the Comparini and Pompilia much as type characters in a comedy. He emphasizes the plots of Violante and the intrigues of Pompilia, finding in them evidence that all women are culpable. The words 'trick,' 'lie,' 'contrive' and 'gull' keep recurring in his account, and consequently the action is for him something of a farce (II 622, 1461).

Just as feminine failings are treated in a non-theological context, so Guido's virtue, against which Half-Rome measures all other actions, is not so much Christian as it is pagan. Guido is just as worldly wise as the Comparini, especially if one considers his early life in Rome. Family difficulties – poverty, the need for an heir – compel him to marry Pompilia, and subsequently his home life at Arezzo is a comedy in which the Count struggles to maintain appearances against overwhelming odds:

You had the Countship holding head aloft
Bravely although bespattered, shifts and straits
In keeping out o' the way o' the wheels o' the world,
The comic of those home-contrivances

When the old lady-mother's wit was taxed
To find six clamorous mouths in food more real
Than fruit plucked off the cobwebbed family tree ...   (II 668–74)

What permits Guido to hold his head aloft is his virtue, which Half-Rome equates with 'honour in Rome, civility i' the world' (II 1473). Half-Rome approves of Guido's plea of *honoris causâ* (II 29) as an entirely adequate defence. He does not worry, as Bottini does, about proving honour a Christian virtue, nor does he understand, as the Pope does, that a sense of honour often runs counter to God's laws. For him it is a natural virtue that corresponds to the customs of civilized society ('Revenged his own wrong like a gentleman' II 1529) and of a pagan golden age ('Take the old way trod when men were men!' II 1524). This sense of honour, of civility, belongs to the order of nature,[3] and certainly Half-Rome equates it with 'the natural law' (II 1477) as opposed, first, to the written law of the courts, and secondly, to the Christian law of the church. The former law Half-Rome dismisses as inadequate, since it discovers ' "scandal on both sides, / Plenty of fault to find, no absolute crime ..." ' (II 1170–1). The latter, which in seventeenth-century Rome was never distinct from the former, is just as inadequate, and in discrediting them Half-Rome frequently lumps them together as 'Rome's law and gospel' (II 1396). Guido's conduct, as Half-Rome describes it, fully exemplifies the virtue of civility. His simplicity and his candour, for instance, are emphasized (II 862, 1308, 1504), and his conduct in the most aggravating circumstances is marked by thoughtful restraint and a consideration of the usages of society. These qualities the speaker attributes to 'birth and breeding, and compassion too' (II 639).

It is evident, then, that in his telling of the story Half-Rome develops the elements necessary for satire: an object to be ridiculed, and a standard by which it is made to appear ridiculous. Although one might expect that the literary background of this satire would be found in the complaints and homilies of the Christian Middle Ages (in which the foibles of women were a favourite subject), one must in fact look farther for literary analogies, to the Latin literature of pagan Rome, and particularly to the satires of Horace. Horace had set up a contrast between the city and the country, observing in one all the vices he deplored, and in the other all the virtues he admired. As if conscious of this literary tradition, Half-Rome describes Guido's life in terms of such a contrast. Guido's stay in Rome, his seeking for preferment, and his pursuit of unearned wealth, are viewed with Horatian disapprobation. In fact, Half-

Rome mentions the 'ancient,' and uses a phrase from one of the satires (I vii 3):

> The Count had lounged somewhat too long in Rome,
> Made himself cheap; with him were hand and glove
> Barbers and blear-eyed, as the ancient sings. (II 113–75)

While Guido's parasitic existence at Rome is thus presented as a subject for satire, his return to Arezzo is interpreted as an attempt to regain his honour and his self-respect. For Guido gave up the game,

> Determined on returning to his town,
> Making the best of bad incurable,
> Patching the old palace up and lingering there
> The customary life out with his kin,
> Where honour helps to spice the scanty bread. (II 313–17)

Guido's retreat to Arezzo, and to his villa, has much the same significance as Horace's retreat to his Sabine farm. Life there is frugal, and the work is hard; nevertheless, because of its very frugality and simplicity, it represents the simple virtues of the natural man. Although Guido's hardships are the discipline which produces virtue, a sense of outraged honour makes them quickly intolerable. The news of the birth of Gaetano (whom Guido takes to be Caponsacchi's son) reaches Guido while he is at work and he immediately reacts with the righteous indignation of the natural man whom circumstances have given too much to bear:

> Why, the overburdened mind
> Broke down, what was a brain became a blaze.
> In the fury of the moment – (that first news
> Fell on the Count among his vines, it seems,
> Doing his farm-work,) – why, he summoned steward,
> Called in the first four hard hands and stout hearts
> From field and furrow, poured forth his appeal ... (II 1389–95)

Guido's patience and forbearance, though they have their limits, are great enough for Half-Rome to suggest that he is ' "the male-Grissel or the modern Job!" ' (II 1487).

Half-Rome's use of pagan myth is as revealing as his references to Horace. He barely mentions Caponsacchi as a Christian knight, but instead depicts him as a pagan saint and then as Apollo:

> The courtly Christian, not so much Saint Paul
> As a saint of Caesar's household: there posed he

Sending his god-glance after his shot shaft,
Apollos turned Apollo, while the snake
Pompilia writhed transfixed through all her spires. (II 791–5)

Pompilia is the python, the female dragon of classical myth, perhaps the
archetype of feminine wiles. Half-Rome also depicts Caponsacchi and
Pompilia as Paris and Helen (thus implying the righteous wrath of the
wronged husband); significantly, they are shown, not as heroic Homeric
figures, but as a decadent gallant and his paramour:

And just as she, I presently shall show,
Pompilia, soon looked Helen to the life,
Recumbent upstairs in her pink and white,
So, in the inn-yard, bold as 't were Troy-town,
There strutted Paris in correct costume,
Cloak, cap and feather, no appointment missed,
Even to a wicked-looking sword at side,
He seemed to find and feel familiar at. (II 1002–9)

The way in which the Homeric tale serves the speaker's satiric purpose
is obvious.

Nearly all the episodes of the story are presented in this book.[4] Although the narrative is the primary interest, the reader is always aware
that he is listening to a particular interpretation of events. Half-Rome's
approach to the truth of the case is crude and, in the poet's judgment,
completely wrong. Although he gives the impression that he is presenting facts without bias (II 1048, 1213–15), his account is in fact 'the instinctive theorizing whence a fact / Looks to the eye as the eye likes the
look' (I 863–4). In making Half-Rome speak as he does, Browning reveals not only what he calls his 'source of swerving' (I 859) – his fear that
his wife is about to take a lover – but his moral status, his entire approach
to life. For in telling the story Half-Rome reveals obliquely his own situation. The simplicity and candour with which he purports to present the
case are the same qualities he attributes to Guido, and the threats of a
whipping for the cousin arise from the same sense of outraged honour
that he discovers in Guido's action. The cousin that worries him so much
is a decadent gallant like Caponsacchi, an anti-Guidoite who has given
the case quite a different interpretation (II 190), a 'wag' like Caponsacchi's friend Guillichini (II 937), and a courtly lover:

a certain what's-his-name and jackanapes
Somewhat too civil of eves with lute and song
About a house here, where I keep a wife. (II 1544–6)

In effect, the entire story is told, not as a piece of idle gossip, but as a warning: 'You, being his cousin, may go tell him so' (II 1547). Half-Rome, then, is fiercely involved in just the kind of world he portrays, a society where the crafty, the selfish, the worldly wise pursue their own vicious ways, where a measure of self-respect is gained only by preserving one's honour. It is significant that Half-Rome conceives of nothing beyond the pagan virtue he derives from his experience of society. He has no other standard by which to satirise and correct the vices he observes. His insight into the story itself is, therefore, completely inadequate. On the other hand, Browning's insight into the character he is creating is more than adequate. This insight is the lyrical element which helps us to judge the dramatic portrayal, and at the same time the element in the dramatic portrayal which gives the narrative its satiric shape.

The Other Half-Rome

In book III, as in book II, most of the story up to the point just before Pompilia's death is told. The book is designed to contrast as much as possible with book II, yet the speaker is never allowed to raise the basic issues that the Pope does. The Other Half-Rome remains on the same level as his counterpart; that is, there is a strong sense of the community, of the story in its social significance. This is accomplished by using the comic aspects of the first two phases of the story as set forth by Browning, and by extending the moral implications of this part of the narrative throughout the tale. The comic aspects have two separate but related narrative elements. One involves the machinations of the Comparini as they attempt to arrive at a better situation in society, and the subsequent purging of their illusion. The other involves Pompilia's reaction, or rather lack of action; for she remains pure and essentially colourless, a passive Griselda figure who patiently endures the trials imposed by her husband. This second narrative element is susceptible of far-reaching moral interpretation, especially if one takes into account its literary origins. Chaucer used the Griselda story (in the *Clerk's Tale*) and so did Boccaccio; Chaucer gave the tale strong religious implications, and its source – the Patience Group of the Cupid and Psyche genre – raises questions of right and wrong on a cosmic, if not a Christian scale. Browning avoids such broad implications by balancing the Griselda aspects of his tale with the comic intrigues of the Comparini. As a result, the significance of the Other Half-Rome's interpretation is narrowed to the speaker's society.

Without its deeper moral implications, the Griselda story becomes only
a sentimental tale of a cruel husband and a wronged wife:

> One wears drab, one, pink;
> Who wears pink, ask him 'Which shall win the race,
> 'Of coupled runners like as egg and egg?'
> ' – Why, if I must choose, he with the pink scarf.'   (I 888–91)

Such is the extent of the Other Half-Rome's moral insight.

The comic elements of the Other Half-Rome's narrative are less obvious than the sentimental ones. Just as Half-Rome cast his characters in
the Adam-and-Eve story, so the speaker of book III hands round the
parts, though with important differences. Pietro is Adam, Violante is
Eve, and Guido the serpent; Pompilia is significantly omitted:

> Adam-like, Pietro sighed and said no more:
> Eve saw the apple was fair and good to taste,
> So, plucked it, having asked the snake advice.   (III 169–71)

Once again the use of the Eden myth is not meant to have religious overtones. It simply emphasizes the foolish, good-hearted nature of the Comparini. They appear, not as objects of satire, nor as tragic figures (as is
possible if the Eden analogy were developed), but as comic characters.
In fact, they are treated explicitly according to the Renaissance theory
of humours. Initially their life is presented as a golden mean:

> Nor low i' the social scale nor yet too high,
> Nor poor nor richer than comports with ease,
> Nor bright and envied, nor obscure and scorned,
> Nor so young that their pleasures fell too thick,
> Nor old past catching pleasure when it fell,
> Nothing above, below the just degree,
> All at the mean where joy's components mix.   (III 120–6)

This happy medium has a further aspect, the balance of two different
natures in marriage:

> The acquiescent and recipient side
> Was Pietro's, and the stirring striving one
> Violante's: both in union gave the due
> Quietude, enterprise, craving and content,
> Which go to bodily health and peace of mind.   (III 132–6)

Just as in Renaissance comedy one humour predominated, so here one
desire (to have a child) comes to the fore:

But, as 't is said a body, rightly mixed,
Each element in equipoise, would last
Too long and live for ever, – accordingly
Holds a germ – sand-grain weight too much i' the scale –
Ordained to get predominance one day
And so bring all to ruin and release, –
Not otherwise a fatal germ lurked here ...   (III 137–43)

The action, then, represents the working-out and the purging of this predominant desire.

In the Other Half-Rome's account of the action, certain themes from the earlier books are put to good use. It will be remembered that in Browning's account of the story Pompilia's marriage was viewed by the Comparini both as a step up the social scale and as the promise of personal salvation. The Christian context of Browning's interpretation is replaced here by the pagan context presented by the Abate Paul. He describes Guido in the same way as Half-Rome, as virtuous in the pagan Horatian manner, 'humble but self-sustaining ...' (III 301). Pompilia he views as a prize of classical myth, the golden apples of the Hesperides (III 384–7). Violante echoes the myth when informing Pietro of the proposal, and has 'gold dreams' (III 439) in which Danae, who attracted Zeus, figures prominently. Such a pagan context should warn Violante that all is not well, but of course she does not realize that Guido's pagan virtues may be Christian vices. The purging of the Comparini's humour does not in fact come about until they move to Arezzo. There 'they touched bottom' (III 521). Their eyes are opened by the

craft and greed
Quickened by penury and pretentious hate
Of plain truth ...   (III 522–4)

and they appear as comic characters at last purged of their humour, a 'starved, stripped, beaten brace of stupid dupes' (III 529) who slink back in shame to Rome. The speaker concludes the episode with an essentially comic view of the characters; that is, he keeps his eye on their society rather than on their ultimate destiny. They

carried their wrongs
To Rome, – I nothing doubt, with such remorse
As folly feels, since pain can make it wise,
But crime, past wisdom, which is innocence,
Needs not be plagued with till a later day.   (III 535–9)

Although the speaker notes the finger of God in this retribution (III 551–3), he typically looks to the middle course pursued by men, and especially by the law court in its attempt to compensate everyone (III 670–1).

The Griselda aspects of the narrative extend the comedy of book III to include the moral dialectic and the sentiment of the popular romance tradition. Pompilia and Caponsacchi are constantly associated with a paradisal world of primal innocence, while Guido is depicted as a demonic figure. Pompilia is spoken of as a flower (III 5, 72, 365, etc.) and as a bird or bird's egg (III 63–4, 215, 1122, etc.) and the 'lamb-pure, lion-brave' (III 29) Caponsacchi is described as a ' "warm-day" ' (III 1125) and the ' "south wind" ' (III 1126). Pompilia is also described as a garden (III 229–41), an image derived perhaps from the *hortus conclusus* of the Song of Songs. These metaphors, in spite of their theological significance, are exploited principally for their sentimental value. One has only to glance at the opening lines of the book to recognize the use to which they are put:

Another day that finds her living yet,
Little Pompilia, with the patient brow
And lamentable smile on those poor lips,
And, under the white hospital-array,
A flower-like body, to frighten at a bruise
You'd think, yet now, stabbed through and through again,
Alive i' the ruins. 'T is a miracle. (III 1–7)

When Pompilia, thus described, comes into contact with the world, the particular quality that she exhibits is patient endurance. The Other Half-Rome speaks of her 'undue experience' (III 107) and concludes: 'Thus saintship is effected probably; / No sparing saints the process!' (III 111–12). In spite of the fact that Guido is theologically the devil, he acts more like the comic villain, the Walter (Gualteri) of the Griselda story. For the speaker emphasizes, not his evil and her good, but his cruelty and her weakness. The process begins with what the speaker calls 'the tenebrific passage of the tale ...' (III 789), when Guido plans to spring his 'cruelty / On the weak shoulders of his wife' (III 966–7). Guido is portrayed as cunning and wise in the ways of the world; Pompilia on the other hand is 'helpless, simple-sweet / Or silly-sooth' (III 805–6). She appears to be completely lacking in sophistication, and the adjective 'silly-sooth' in particular suggests that she is easily deceived. At any rate, her virtue is entirely passive; she is 'unskilled to break one blow / At her good fame by putting finger forth ...' (III 806–7). Her moral elevation is not much higher than that of the creatures with which she is usually associated, and hence it is no surprise that the speaker should interpret her flight from Arezzo as instinctive, like the migration of a bird (III 1121–2). The murder itself is never seen as anything more than the logical climax of Guido's cruelty. Guido is upbraided, not for a mortal sin, but for a fault which pressed the powers of endurance beyond their limit: ' "You wronged and they endured wrong; yours the fault " ' (III 1655).

Although the Other Half-Rome recognizes Pompilia's innocence, then, he does not portray it as an active virtue, nor does he allow her the moral elevation she deserves. This incomplete insight is the result of his 'source of swerving': 'I ... have no wife, / Being yet sensitive in my degree ...' (III 1678–9). Such sensitivity, such sentimentality blinds the speaker to the deeper moral implications of the affair. He is indeed the counterpart of Half-Rome and not the equal of the Pope, although he reaches the same conclusions.

Tertium Quid

In contrast to Half-Rome and the Other Half-Rome, Tertium Quid is detached from 'this rabble's-brabble of dolts and fools / Who make up reasonless unreasoning Rome' (IV 10–11). 'We lift the case / Out of the shade into the shine ...' (IV 6–7), he says, and he proceeds with 'a reasoned statement' (I 920) that represents, Browning tells us, 'how quality dissertated on the case' (I 924). As far as Browning is concerned, Tertium Quid's detachment is morally culpable, for at each stage he defers judgment and refuses to make a choice. Here is one of his typical statements:

You see so far i' the story, who was right,
Who wrong, who neither, don't you? What, you don't?
Eh? Well, admit there's somewhat dark i' the case,
Let's on ... (IV 314–17)

Tertium Quid defers his judgment, partly because he is more interested in presenting 'a reasoned statement of the case' than he is in drawing conclusions, partly because he does not want to run the risk of offending any one of his listeners by preferring one side to the other, and partly because his moral insight is, like that of the other two speakers in this group, extremely limited. He is, in fact, farther from the truth than either

Half-Rome or Other Half-Rome. Although he treats the story as both a satire and a comedy, he presents it with such moral neutrality that it becomes inconsequential, a few minutes' amusement in a pleasant social evening.

When the satiric and comic interpretations of the previous two books are emptied of their moral content, there is a general levelling of all human action. Any ultimate significance such action may imply is replaced by the relativist view that all is temporary and transient, and that truth is a matter of individual opinion. When this approach to life is translated into comic terms – as it is by Tertium Quid – we are presented with a picture of society as an aggregate of individuals moved by conflicting but nonetheless similar impulses. These impulses, according to Tertium Quid's view of things, generally correspond to those on which the classical economists based their theories; that is, self-interest and unrestricted competition. Such laws are 'natural,' and are essentially non-moral. As the basis of comic action, they represent, not the promise of a new society, but the guarantee that the old one will last as long as human nature remains unchanged. Consequently Tertium Quid's account of the life of Pietro and Violante is comic only because it reflects the way of the world. He tells of their middle-class existence, their falling into debt, and their efforts to gain money. The basis of their actions is simple enough: 'Themselves love themselves ...' (IV 72). Their life is conceived largely in terms of profit and gain. When Guido offers to marry Pompilia, they have a vision of almost infinite wealth, and consequently when there recurs the Nunc Dimittis – which by now must be recognized as the key to the moral character of the speaker – it is evidence, not of personal salvation nor of a new society, but of more money:

> Themselves would help the choice with heart and soul,
> Throw their late savings in a common heap
> Should go with the dowry, to be followed in time
> By the heritage legitimately hers:
> And when such paragon was found and fixed,
> Why, they might chant their 'Nunc Dimittas' straight.   (IV 333–8)

Guido, of course, is moved by exactly the same impulses. Consequently both he and the Comparini are knaves, and, insofar as each is duped by the other, fools. 'Who / was fool, who knave?' Tertium Quid asks, only to conclude, 'Neither and both, perchance' (IV 507). His statement of what he considers the essence of the case – a statement sometimes praised by critics for its clarity, its simplicity, its avoidance of fine phrases and its reliance on the 'facts' – is no more than his own limited view of the relation of man to man:

> There was a bargain mentally proposed
> On each side, straight and plain and fair enough;
> Mind knew its own mind ... (iv 508–10)

> Guido gives
> Money for money, – and they, bride for groom,
> Having, he, not a doit, they, not a child
> Honestly theirs, but this poor waif and stray. (iv 523–6)

> In the inexpressive barter of thoughts,
> Each did give and did take the thing designed,
> The rank on this side and the cash on that –
> Attained the object of the traffic, so.
> The way of the world, the daily bargain struck
> In the first market! (iv 528–33)

Profits are gained, however, only at the expense of others, and consequently each party discovers that he has been cheated. Neither side can be blamed, for such is the way of the world. Of the Comparini Tertium Quid says:

> The pair had nobody but themselves to blame,
> Being selfish beasts throughout, no less, no more:
> – Cared for themselves, their supposed good, nought else,
> And brought about the marriage; good proved bad ... (iv 701–4)

If the speaker is inclined to prefer any side in this comedy, it is Guido's, partly because he is noble, partly because he has a way of doing things that Tertium Quid finds attractive. And this brings us to the satiric aspects of the monologue.

It is at first difficult to understand how satire can arise from a view of life in which human beings of all ranks are moved by the same basic impulses, for in effect the satirist then has no vantage point from which he can ridicule his fellow man. And certainly Tertium Quid sees all of society as moved by self-interest and the desire for profit, as gaining here and falling into debt there. He speaks of Pietro, for instance, as 'in debt at last, / As he were any lordling of us all ...' (iv 97–8). But Pietro is not a nobleman, and this, for Tertium Quid, makes all the difference between him and Guido. For while Guido acts on the same motives as Pietro, he 'shrinks from clownish coarseness in disgust ...' (iv 759). He has about him, says Tertium Quid, a 'touch / O' the subtle air that breeds the subtle wit ...' (IV 756–7), and such wit gives his actions what the speaker calls elsewhere a 'decent wrappage' (IV 523). While all men, then, are subject to natural laws and impulses, some classes of men can make them more acceptable than others. The crime of the Comparini is not that they pursued their self-interest, but that they did so openly, coarsely, and without taste. And while Tertium Quid condemns the crime before God and man (IV 216), it is clear that the real offence is to 'nature and civility and the mode ...' (IV 217). Guido's murder of the Comparini, and his plot against Pompilia, are far less culpable, because they represent 'the finer vengeance' (IV 769). Hence the actions of Guido are gently approved, and those of the Comparini mildly ridiculed – mildly, because the satire has no moral basis, and hence gives no occasion for righteous indignation.

This concept of an acceptable and an unacceptable way of doing things is the basis, not only of the satiric aspects of the story, but of the detachment which the speaker professes. His monologue is a 'sample-speech' (I 941), partly because he presents the story in a way he knows will be acceptable to the social rank of his listeners (Browning says he 'harangues in silvery and selectest phrase' I 933), partly because he cuts through the false wrappage of words with which the case is usually presented. His is the 'clarity of candour, history's soul, / The critical mind, in short ...' (I 925–6). Tertium Quid's detachment, then, is both a style and a method of argument. As far as style is concerned, his 'silvery' phrases are carefully balanced, whether parallel or antithetical in sense. The distance achieved by such artificiality strengthens his claims to candour (IV 853, 1444) and clarity of presentation. He ridicules ingenious theories about Pompilia's reasons for accepting Caponsacchi's help:

What an elaborate theory have we here,
Ingeniously nursed up, pretentiously
Brought forth, pushed forward amid trumpet-blast,
To account for the thawing of an icicle ...   (IV 860–3)

We must not want all this elaborate work
To solve the problem why young fancy-and-flesh
Slips from the dull side of a spouse in years,
Betakes it to the breast of brisk-and-bold
Whose love-scrapes furnish talk for all the town!   (IV 898–902)

Not only does he pride himself on his ability to lay bare the facts, he also makes a show of carefully considering all sides of the question. His transitional phrases often are 'So they say. / On the other hand, so much is easily said ...' (IV 698–9), or 'But then on the other side again ...' (IV

1043). The detachment that this method of argument achieves is obvious; 'I simply take the facts, ask what they show' (IV 1353), he says, and refuses to draw conclusions, even though he is reasoning by the 'steady lights / Of after-knowledge' (IV 1185–6).

Detachment, of course, is not solely a matter of style and technique. It is also the attitude of the person who feels that all is temporary and transient, and that commitment to any single point of view is a wilful disregard of the social process. For the flux of life causes all things – especially moral differences – to change and fade. 'Healthy minds,' Tertium Quid says,

> let bygones be,
> Leave old crimes to grow young and virtuous-like
> I' the sun and air; so time treats ugly deeds:
> They take the natural blessing of all change.   (IV 238–41)

Such a 'natural blessing' eventually levels out all moral distinctions. The levelling process is nowhere better illustrated than in the account of Guido's flight and the law's pursuit. The 'journey of twenty miles' (IV 1403) wearies Guido and brings about his capture, while it overheats the officer Patrizj and causes his death. And so it brings 'just and unjust to a level, you see' (IV 1404).

If one views life as flux and change as meaningless, human beings are little better than puppets, and life itself is a farce. Hence it is no accident that the last part of the story is likened to a puppet play (IV 1280–99). Here Guido and Pompilia and the Comparini are involved in a farcical struggle where 'threats pass, blows are dealt, / And a crisis comes ...' (IV 1283–4) again and again, the difference between each struggle, each adventure, being represented only by a change of costume. And so the murder is no more than the climax of a number of costume changes:

> What you thought tragedy was farce.
> Note, that the climax and the crown of things
> Invariably is, the devil appears himself,
> Armed and accoutred, horns and hoofs and tail!
> Just so, nor otherwise it proved – you'll see:
> Move to the murder, never mind the rest!   (IV 1294–9)

For underneath it all Guido is ' a mere man – / Born, bred and brought up in the usual way' (IV 1603–4) while Pompilia is ' "a little weak" ' (IV 1587). There is no more difference between them than between Punch and Judy.

While Tertium Quid tells the story, then, as comedy and satire that eventually disintegrate into farce, the whole monologue may be seen as a carefully controlled but nonetheless farcical interlude in a social evening. One might draw an analogy with the tradition of having the masque relieved by an antimasque. For at the beginning 'civility and the mode' are very much in evidence; the speaker is surrounded by

> Eminence This and All-Illustrious That
> Who take snuff softly, range in well-bred ring,
> Card-table-quitters for observance' sake ...   (I 937–9)

At the end of the speech there is a general exodus of the people of quality. These two actions – approach and retreat – frame a tale of knaves and fools. For although 'the world wags still ...' (IV 869), the nobility manage to contain all the disagreeable aspects of life, to set them off as a controlled interlude in sophisticated but essentially empty lives.

The speakers of the second ring of books are all characters closely involved in the story, and consequently their speeches further the sequence of events with which we are now so familiar. While the first ring of books sets the stage and gives us the necessary background, the second ring draws us into the drama itself. Primarily, then, these central books are dramatic speeches which, like all of Browning's dramatic speeches, point not to outer but to inner action, to the workings, conscious and unconscious, of each character's mind. This inner action often seems to have a significance that goes beyond the revelation of individual character. Pompilia, for instance, is not just a particular woman in a particular situation, she is the type of innocent and wronged womanhood, and she, like Guido and Caponsacchi, reveals what Browning calls in the essay on Shelley 'the primal elements of humanity.' Browning assigns these elements to the lyric poet, because his recognition of them depends upon his understanding of the human condition, and because his judgment of them depends upon his moral insight. And so the characteristic combination of the drama and the lyric continues in the central books of the poem.

Count Guido Franceschini

Guido's monologue is carefully set as to time and place. He has just been tortured, and is 'ripe for declaring truth' (I 953). Seated in 'a small chamber that adjoins the court ...' (I 950), he addresses his judges, and

141

defends his actions. His defence, however, is not only a justification of the murder, as it would be if the monologue were purely dramatic, it is an apology for the whole course of his life.

Guido's speech is sometimes praised by the critics as a masterly and convincing defence, and it is indeed difficult to see through the cleverness and shrewdness to the falseness that underlies his argument. But the falseness is there, and Browning warned Julia Wedgwood, who found the monologue too able a statement for a wicked man, that 'the whole of his speech, as I premise, is untrue – cant and cleverness – as you see when the second speech comes ...'[5] Browning hints at the substance of the falseness in his description of the monologue in book I:

> He proffers his defence, in tones subdued
> Near to mock-mildness now, so mournful seems
> The obtuser sense truth fails to satisfy;
> Now, moved, from pathos at the wrong endured,
> To passion; for the natural man is roused
> At fools who first do wrong, then pour the blame
> Of their wrong-doing, Satan-like, on Job.   (I 957–63)

Guido's emotions imply two points of view: acquiescence in the course of one's life and submission to an ordained order, on the one hand, and remonstrance against such a course and the attempt to remedy it, on the other. Hence the pathos (submission) and the passion (remonstrance). As Guido proceeds with his argument, these two reactions develop into two intellectual frames of reference. By shifting from one to the other Guido appears to both explain and excuse what he has done. His explanation is of course shot through with inconsistency because of the shifting point of view, but the falseness is sometimes hard to detect because each frame of reference is in itself a plausible view of life. The argument is a clever piece of work, and is of necessity so; for Guido cannot deny the facts of the case (having admitted them under torture) and is forced therefore to defend all that he has done in the best manner possible.

The two frames of reference are distinct in their structure and moral implications, though not in the human institutions they embrace. The first looks primarily to human society, and views the church as an extension of it. In Renaissance terms, this view is that of the order of nature,[6] in spite of the fact that sometimes, for Guido, it includes the institution proper to the order of grace (the church). Here self-interest, the pursuit of wealth, unrestricted competition, and militant individualism are given a certain approbation not unlike that of Max Weber's Protestant Ethic. From this point of view, life is described as 'cramped and grasping, high and dry' (v 180). The second frame of reference looks to the church as God's institution on earth, and views society as an extension of it. In a limited sense this point of view corresponds to the order of grace, since it deals with man's place and ultimate destiny in the scheme of things. Guido emphasizes the scheme of things as an orderly hierarchy, a Great Chain of Being extending upwards from human society to God Himself: 'The public weal, which hangs to the law, which holds / By the Church, which happens to be through God himself' (v 245–6). In this scheme man is expected to keep his place, as in Weber's 'traditionalism'; hence the necessity for humility, obedience, a sense of responsibility, and an observance of the duties by which one maintains one's position. The way in which Guido can defend himself by shifting between these two frames of reference is obvious enough. On the one hand he can picture himself as a martyr, the victim of unrestricted competition in his society; on the other he can picture himself as a servant of God holding the place ordained for him. Hence his grasping for money and his discipline of his wife claim pity from one point of view and moral approbation from the other. The fact that the two points of view are not morally compatible, to say nothing of their logical consistency, is obscured by the ease with which Guido slips from one to the other.

Once Guido's frames of reference have been distinguished, it is easier to recognize the literary form of his monologue. He attacks those aspects of human life that are not to his liking, and he does so by measuring them against a scheme of values of which he approves. His method is that of the satirist, but, unlike the traditional satirist, he judges the objects of his attack by a standard which is constantly shifting. Sometimes he attacks unrestricted competition and militant individualism by emphasizing the moral value of order and degree in human society; at other times he attacks such a static scheme of things as unrealistic in a world dominated by self-interest and torn by the struggle for existence. Whatever the matter of his argument, however, the form remains constant, and the fact that the second ring of books begins with satire confirms the pattern established in the first ring.

Like Pope at the beginning of the *Epistle to Dr. Arbuthnot*, Guido begins by appealing for sympathy, and by attempting to establish his own character as a satirist, a superior individual afflicted by physical and mental agonies. He hints that he is a Christ figure when he expresses surprise at being given wine, 'and not vinegar and gall...' (v 5), and insists that torture of his noble flesh was less difficult to bear than the torment of spirit he has suffered at the hands of Pompilia and the Comparini. He directs his listeners' attention to his place in society and the wrong done to 'my self-respect, my care for a good name, / Pride in an old one, love of kindred ...' (v 31–2). Pompilia, 'the mongrel of a drab' (v 88), has of course violated this order by her conduct. As for his own conduct, Guido emphasizes

> my persistent treading in the paths
> Where I was trained to go, — wearing that yoke
> My shoulder was predestined to receive,
> Born to the hereditary stoop and crease ...   (I 124–7)

Guido goes on to discuss the duties, responsibilities, and rights of his position. As the 'representative of a great line ...' (v 140), he reminds the judges of the public service of his family:

> None o' the line
> Having a single gift beyond brave blood,
> Or able to do aught but give, give, give
> In blood and brain, in house and land and cash,
> Not get and garner as the vulgar may ...   (v 159–63)

When the means for such service was used up, Guido was forced to turn from his place, ' "by the hearth and altar" ' (v 214), and to look to either the army or the church for help. He describes both as extensions of a grasping, fiercely competitive society, a society from which he is removed by his virtue, his humility as a servant of the church: 'Humbly I helped the Church till here I stand ...' (v 247). He emphasized his obedience, his patient wait for recognition, his disinterested attempt to maintain his place in life, and his belief in a cosmic order descending from God. From this point of view, he condemns the cruel competition of which he was the victim:

> I waited thirty years, may it please the Court:
> Saw meanwhile many a denizen o' the dung
> Hop, skip, jump o'er my shoulder, make him wings
> And fly aloft, – succeed, in the usual phrase.   (v 292–5)

He describes his own patient merit in turning from such vulgar struggles:

> While I – kept fasts and feasts innumerable,
> Matins and vespers, functions to no end

I' the train of monsignor and Eminence,
As gentleman-squire ... (v 336–9)

Disappointed in his expectations, Guido looked to marriage and a dowry. At this juncture his point of view shifts. The transition is a clever appeal from one who would not be condemned for following the ways of the world – clever because it uses words and phrases equally appropriate to his first point of view:

Will the Court of its charity teach poor me
Anxious to learn, of any way i' the world,
Allowed by custom and convenience, save
This same which, taught from my youth up, I trod? (v 431–4)

Once the transition is successfully made, he treats the marriage contract in terms of a bargain, 'mere rank against mere wealth ...' (v 475):

Admit that honour is a privilege,
The question follows, privilege worth what?
Why, worth the market-price, – now up, now down,
Just so with this as with all other ware:
Therefore essay the market, sell your name,
Style and condition to who buys them best! (v 460–5)

Such a bargain is not without some vestige of moral principles: 'I thought / To deal o' the square ...' (v 477–8). His own false pretenses in the matter he dismisses as a 'mere grace' (v 497), 'a flourish ... / For fashion's sake ...' (v 498–9). Anyone who has any knowledge of the ways of the world, he says, should recognize the contract for what it is:

The veritable back-bone, understood
Essence of this same bargain, blank and bare,
Being the exchange of quality for wealth ... (v 500–2)

Having thus defended his own actions from the world's point of view, Guido immediately proceeds to condemn those of the Comparini from the church's point of view. The transition is again cleverly handled. He ridicules Pietro and Violante for wanting to move out of their place in the hierarchy ordained by God and he echoes the reactions of the author of Ecclesiastes to the things of this world: 'They found that all was vanity ...' (v 523). Each social class, he insists, should stay in its place and fulfil its proper duties, even if it means the endurance of hardship and poverty. The attempt of one rank to assume the duties and responsibilities of another is inevitably disastrous.

145

Throughout his monologue, Guido constantly transfers the terms of one frame of reference to the other. When he considers his marriage, for instance, he talks of his 'profit or loss i' the matter ...' (v 568), but what he is really speaking of is not the dowry that he bargained to get, but the wifely 'loyalty and odedience' (v 578) ordained by God (see v 716–29). Similarly, the idea that the wife should keep her proper position, and fulfil the duties ordained by the law of God and man Guido treats in terms of a bargain:

Such was the pact: Pompilia from the first
Broke it, refused from the beginning day
Either in body or soul to cleave to mine ...   (v 607–9)

Consequently, Guido argues, she 'proves a plague-prodigy to God and man' (v 664). Throughout the account of the marriage and the separation, Guido switches freely from one frame of reference to the other. On the one hand he is the victim of the ways of the world (' "I am irremediably beaten here ..." ' v 1393) and on the other a martyr to the course of life set out for him by God: ' "God's decree, / In which I, bowing bruised head, acquiesce" ' (v 1417–18).

When Guido comes to deal with the murder, the shifts in his argument become more complex. Obedience to ' "God's decree" ' he treats as a motive for action rather than a virtue of passive endurance: 'A voice beyond the law / Enters my heart, *Quis est pro Domino?*' (v 1548–9). In spite of the fact that this law is revealed, it points to a system of natural ethics, and consequently to a concept of natural law as an extension of divine law, and in opposition to the codified law, both civil and ecclesiastical, of Rome. The man who follows his natural impulses is, then, closer to God than the man who keeps his place in, and is regulated by, society. It is on such a basis that Guido defends his murder of Pompilia: 'I did / God's bidding and man's duty, so, breathe free ...' (v 1702–3).

This abrogation of the codified law is a dangerous move for a man speaking to judges, but as always Guido forestalls the wider implications of his argument. Once he has made his point, he voices his conviction that the law he is being tried by is but the natural law codified, and that both take their validity from God himself (v 1761–77). Having thus linked the natural law to the revealed and the codified law, Guido in effect challenges the court to execute justice and to 'Protect your own defender ...' (v 2004). He ends his argument with a Utopian vision of Rome, where the divinely sanctioned social order to which he had first appealed is at last realized:

Rome rife with honest women and strong men,
Manners reformed, old habits back once more,
Customs that recognize the standard worth –
The wholesome household rule in force again,
Husbands once more God's representative,
Wives like the typical Spouse once more, and Priests
No longer men of Belial, with no aim
At leading silly women captive, but
Of rising to such duties as yours now ... (v 2039–47)

With this last remark Guido reaffirms the superior position he had established at the beginning of his monologue, and lays upon his judges the burden of bringing into existence this Utopia for which he himself has already struck a blow.

Guido's argument is indeed a clever defence, but the cleverness is as much Browning's as it is Guido's. For Browning in effect idealizes Guido's shrewdness, presenting it in a far more sustained and concentrated fashion than ever appears in the actual depositions. Insofar as this concentration, this heightening of character, reveals to us Guido the man, the monologue is dramatic, but insofar as it gives us Browning's insight into the workings of an evil mind, the monologue is lyric.

Giuseppe Caponsacchi

In contrast to the subtle and involved nature of Guido's argument, Caponsacchi's monologue is frank, open, and straightforward. Although it is an impassioned utterance, its purpose is not so much to persuade as to inform: 'My part was just to tell you how things stand, / State facts and not be flustered at their fume' (vi 1967–8).

Just as Guido's monologue is an adaptation of the satiric mode, so Caponsacchi's is a modification of the romance mode. As one might expect, the romance elements do not lie in the action and much less in the flight, which from another point of view might be considered the most romantic incident of all. Rather, Browning is concerned with the growing understanding of the priest, and this inner action he treats in much the same way as in the earlier *Dramatic Romances*, in three stages: an uncomfortable awareness of the complexity of ordinary life, a vision of ultimate reality, and an attempt to embody that vision in an ideally human world. Similarly, Caponsacchi starts off totally involved in his society; the sight of Pompilia brings him an ecstatic vision (she is 'the glory of life, the beauty of the world, / The splendour of heaven ...' VI 118–19), a vision which enables him to recognize clearly good and evil; thereafter he tries to pursue the good, but is not entirely successful. And so, as in the third phase of the lyric part of book I, we are dealing with a romance with an ironic ending.

Caponsacchi's account of his early life may be taken as the first of the three stages of romance. He was born a younger son of a noble family, and, like many younger sons of his time, looked to the church for a livelihood. His assumption of the priesthood had all the complexity and ambiguity typical of the first stage of romance. He took seriously the vows to renounce the world, but was at the same time aware of his own weaknesses and shortcomings. The terms proposed by the church ('"Renounce the world? Nay, keep and give it us!"' VI 309) were a suitable compromise: 'I was good enough for that, nor cheated so ...' (VI 337). And so he became something of a priest and something of a lover:

> According to prescription did I live,
> – Conformed myself, both read the breviary
> And wrote the rhymes, was punctual to my place
> I' the Pieve, and as diligent at my post
> Where beauty and fashion rule.   (VI 343–7)

The theatre episode, where the priest sees Pompilia with 'the beautiful sad strange smile' (VI 412), is the vision which enables him to recognize his life for what it is:

> my life
> Had shaken under me, – broke short indeed
> And showed the gap 'twixt what is, what should be...   (VI 485–7)

Thus the first stage of romance is illuminated by the second. The rest of the monologue is an account which corresponds essentially to the third stage of romance, the stage where the quest for good and against evil is carried out, in the hope of bringing about an idealized world.

For Caponsacchi the quest takes the form of an expansion of vision that leads to a significant choice. The sight of Pompilia is the turning point of his life, but it by no means provides a total guide for his conduct, nor does it preclude the choice which he recognizes as necessary for action. And consequently we are given a fairly detailed account of the facts and issues which confronted him. These facts and issues are of course obscured by the machinations of Guido, but, throughout, Capon-

148

sacchi has the vision of Pompilia against which to measure everything. Thus, though he is for some time confused and upset by the forged letters, he begins to understand that the letters could no more come from Pompilia than a scorpion from a Madonna's mouth (vi 667–76). Significantly, the understanding is arrived at, not by a logical process, but by a subtle combination of reason and intuition. His references to Pompilia as the Madonna enrich this subtle process. For when he represents Pompilia's speech, he remembers her emphasis on the strangeness, the wonder, the mystery of her life (vi 755–68). Her statement is, of course, an oblique reference to her pregnancy, and, by implication, to the mystery of the Annunciation. Caponsacchi immediately discovers that what he has been seeking cannot be found by reason alone:

> God and man, and what duty I owe both, –
> I dare to say I have confronted these
> In thought: but no such faculty helped here. (v 942–4)

He realizes too that his refusal to help Pompilia is a 'veil / Hiding all gain my wisdom strove to grasp ...' (vi 955–6). Confronted with the mystery of Pompilia's existence, a new means of insight opens up to him: 'Into another state, under new rule / I knew myself was passing swift and sure ...' (vi 964–5). But even this new insight is not enough, and for days he ponders his decision.

His decision turns on the attempt to arrive at a clear conception of good and evil. The basis for his decision is provided by Pompilia herself, and is described by Caponsacchi in terms of classical myth. He speaks of the 'fabled garden' (vi 1002) of the Hesperides and of his own quest as a 'great adventure' (vi 1003). At first he plucks only 'hedge-fruit' (vi 1004), but at the sight of 'the prize o' the place, the thing of perfect gold, / The apple's self' (vi 1007–8) he begins to recognize true value. At the same time he becomes aware of the dragon guarding the apples. In moral terms the 'hedge-fruit' is a thing indifferent, like Milton's apple; but the golden apple (Pompilia) is clearly good, and the dragon (Guido) is clearly evil. Once Caponsacchi has distinguished the characters confronting him the choice is equally clear: ' "Duty to God is duty to her ..." ' (vi 1030).

Although the characters for a romantic narrative are all present – a knight, a maiden in distress, and a dragon – Caponsacchi continues to emphasize, not the events themselves, but his expanding vision, his growing understanding. Even the flight itself is treated as a quest for greater insight rather than an escape from a dragon.

Throughout the journey from Arezzo to Castelnuovo Caponsacchi
seeks what can only be described as spiritual communion with Pompilia.
He calls her a 'perfect soul' (ɪ 1162) and links her with music (which for
Browning always points to the infinite): 'music seemed / Always to
hover just above her lips ...' (vɪ 1196–7). Twice they approach a communion and fail. On the first occasion Pompilia speaks of his kindness
and the priest comments, 'I did not like that word' (vɪ 1234). On the
second occasion she has him read and pray for her. 'I did not like that,
neither, but I read' (vɪ 1274). They achieve a communion when Pompilia
praises his constancy:

> 'I want
> 'No fact nor voice that change and grow unkind.'
> That I liked, that was the best thing she said.   (vɪ 1317–19)

Caponsacchi's insight enables him to see things as they are, and consequently, as his monologue moves toward its conclusion, romance is replaced by irony. The priest knows that he is not the pure and spotless
knight of romance:

> If I pretended simply to be pure
> Honest and Christian in the case, – absurd!
> As well go boast myself above the needs
> O' the human nature ...   (vɪ 1717–20)

Romance, he says, is impossible in actual life, nor would 'the officious
priest ... personate Saint George / For a mock Princess in undragoned
days ...' (vɪ 1771–2). Nevertheless (and here the irony becomes more
complex), 'the revelation of Pompilia' (vɪ 1866), initially so fantastic, is
now part of the reality of his life, and permits him to see his existence as
a significant part of God's plan for the world. Like Guido, he ends with
a Utopian vision, but it is a Utopia that depends, not on a change in
human nature, as Guido's did, but on the expansion of human perception:

> To live, and see her learn, and learn by her,
> Out of the low obscure and petty world –
> Or only see one purpose and one will
> Evolve themselves i' the world, change wrong to right:
> To have to do with nothing but the true,
> The good, the eternal – and these, not alone
> In the main current of the general life,
> But small experiences of every day,

Concerns of the particular hearth and home:
To learn not only by a comet's rush
But a rose's birth, – not by the grandeur, God –
But the comfort, Christ. All this, how far away!
Mere delectation, meet for a minute's dream ...   (vi 2085–97)

With this Utopian vision the total shape of Caponsacchi's monologue becomes apparent. It is a movement from unimaginative involvement in one's situation, through a world of romance with all its heightened awareness, towards a lyric insight. This same kind of movement is yet another pattern in the second ring of monologues. Guido is shrewdly but unimaginatively involved in himself and his situation; Caponsacchi is a romantic figure, aware of what he is seeking but unable to realize his vision; Pompilia completes the pattern with her lyric insight, her devotion to truth, and her consequent detachment from her situation.

Pompilia

While Guido's and Caponsacchi's monologues belong to the satiric and romance modes respectively, Pompilia's makes use of the characteristics of the lyric. Browning attributes to Pompilia lyric insight, which appears as a devotion to truth, and as a purity of heart which enables her to see God. Such treatment creates the sense of detachment that one feels in reading the monologue, and indicates the place that the poem would occupy in the cycle of lyric themes which we examined earlier. It will be remembered that near the top of the cycle there was a point where the imaginative vision became so vivid that it caused the usual associations of dreaming and waking to be reversed. Ordinary life becomes unreal and insubstantial; the dream, on the other hand, points to ultimate reality. This same pattern characterizes Pompilia's monologue. At one point she speaks of the 'history of me' (vii 109) as 'sheer dreaming and impossibility ...' (vii 112). And later she says:

Thus, all my life, –
As well what was, as what, like this, was not, –
Looks old, fantastic and impossible:
I touch a fairy thing that fades and fades.   (vii 198–201)

Even her son, taken from her, becomes a dream (vii 213).
While Pompilia's life is a dream, the moment of her dying is reality. In effect, her deathbed is a vantage point from which she can survey her life

and her situation, but remain detached from both. The strife of her past experience, and the calm of the present moment, are conveyed in what she calls 'a fancy' (vii 360), the hovel metaphor (vii 360–72). Inside the hovel is a bestial existence where animal-like human beings savagely pursue their self-interest. Outside is moonlight and peace, a peace which she associates, by extension, with Christ walking on the waves. The contrast of strife and calm is mentioned again in book vii, 999–1000. The calmness represents, among other things, both the peace of God and the withdrawal of Pompilia from the demoralizing conflict of the ordinary world. From one point of view her detachment is a circle which isolates her from mankind:

> I wish nor want
> One point o' the circle plainer, where I stand
> Traced round about with white to front the world.   (vii 1644–6)

From another point of view it is a step closer to God: 'I withdraw from earth and man / To my own soul, compose myself for God' (vii 1769–70).

Because Pompilia's detachment is analogous to a lyric vision, she typically sees issues, particularly moral issues, very clearly: 'Now I have got to die and see things clear' (vii 733). Her understanding of Guido's plot against her is especially incisive, and she realizes his true intent:

> to bring about a wicked change
> Of sport to earnest, tempt a thoughtless man
> To write indeed, and pass the house, and more,
> Till both of us were taken in a crime.   (vii 696–9)

Her insight, however, goes beyond these particular circumstances to a metaphysical view of good and evil. She associates the latter with a blank nothingness, and the former with eternity. At the same time she links the blankness to the earlier contrast between dreaming and waking. The dream, her ordinary experience, represents the insubstantial nature of evil, while her waking life – significantly pastoral and idyllic – points to eternal good:

> All since is one blank,
> Over and ended; a terrific dream.
> It is the good of dreams – so soon they go!
> Wake in a horror of heart-beats, you may –
> Cry, 'The dread thing will never from my thoughts!'
> Still, a few daylight doses of plain life,

Cock-crow and sparrow-chirp, or bleat and bell
Of goats that trot by, tinkling, to be milked;
And when you rub your eyes awake and wide,
Where is the harm o' the horror? Gone! So here.
I know I wake, – but from what? Blank, I say!
This is the note of evil: for good lasts.   (vii 584–95)

Aside from the moral issues, Pompilia's vantage point enables her to discern in life the things of eternal worth. Initially she sees all as flux. At the birth of her child she thought 'something began for once that would not end ...' (vii 203) but he too fades into insubstantiality. Similarly she sees all human plans as vanity: 'All human plans and projects come to nought, / My life, and what I know of other lives ...' (vii 902–3). At the same time she realizes that 'God shall care!' (vii 904) (note the emphatic future). That God does care is made evident by certain truths in life that have an absolute and eternal value:

I am held up, amid the nothingness,
By one or two truths only – thence I hang,
And there I live, – the rest is death or dream,
All but those points of my support.   (vii 603–6)

These truths are extremely significant; they are the principal topics of her monologue, the content of the insight which she is given through the grace of God, and the inspiration itself, the vitality which sustains her speech. It is evident, of course, that we are dealing with something more than a logical process. She mentions Caponsacchi's name and declares, 'There, / Strength comes already with the utterance!' (vii 942–3). Or she remembers her child and says, 'There, enough! I have my support again ...' (vii 895).

The truths are three: the efficacy of prayer, the presence of a soldier-saint, and the blessing of motherhood. Of prayer to God she says relatively little. She recounts her attempts to gain help from the archbishop and the governor, and when they fail her she turns to God: 'Henceforth I asked God counsel, not mankind' (vii 859). Caponsacchi is treated at much greater length. Pompilia describes him as 'a lustrous and pellucid soul' (vii 935) and associates him with the white light of the infinite. She speaks of his 'purity in quintessence' (vii 925), the 'glory of his nature' (vii 921) which 'blazed the truth / Through every atom of his act with me ...' (vii 922–3). As in book vi, the priest is not seen as the conventional knight of romance. Caponsacchi, of course, was too aware of his own shortcomings to portray himself as a pure knight. Pompilia idealizes him, not as a knight of romance, but rather as a 'soldier-saint' (vii 1786). The distinction may seem a tenuous one, but it is nonetheless real, and it is significant that it is Conti who describes the priest as Saint George: ' "Our Caponsacchi, he's your true Saint George / To slay the monster, set the Princess free ..." ' (vii 1323–4), Saint George having associations with both spiritual, and courtly and sexual, love. It must be remembered that the rescue of the maiden from the dragon usually culminates in a marriage of rescuer and rescued (as in the first book of *The Faerie Queene*). Browning naturally wished to avoid any sexual implications (since the whole case for Pompilia rests upon her purity in body, mind, and spirit) but found the analogy with Saint George too useful a poetic device to discard altogether. And so he presents Caponsacchi as a saintly knight, and usually mentions Saint George by name only where wild adventure culminating in physical love is clearly implied.

When Pompilia apostrophizes Caponsacchi as 'O lover of my life, O soldier-saint' (vii 1786) she is thinking of him in a purely spiritual manner, as but a particular manifestation of the soldier-saint who is present in every age to do God's work in the world. So she can say of him: 'No change / Here, though all else changed in the changing world!' (vii 1414–15). He is present throughout time: 'He was mine, he is mine, he will be mine' (vii 1457). She refers to him six times as a star (vii 1143, 1405, 1448, 1467, 1568, 1785), thus identifying him with truth, with the white brilliance that reveals the infinite.[7] When redness does appear, it stands, not for the flesh and for sexual love (as it does, for instance, in *The Faerie Queene* and in *Idylls of the King*) but for a sapping of the vital purpose revealed by the white star. For instance, when Caponsacchi considers the folly of flight, Pompilia says:

> I felt that, the same loyalty – one star
> Turning now red that was so white before –
> One service apprehended newly: just
> A word of mine and there the white was back!   (vii 1467–70)

The third truth of Pompilia's life is her child. At the beginning of the monologue she insists that she wants to be known as the mother of a son (vii 9–14). And certainly the recognition of her pregnancy is a cardinal point in her narrative:

> Up I sprang alive,
> Light in me, light without me, everywhere

Change! A broad yellow sunbeam was let fall
From heaven to earth ...   (vii 1223–6)

The sunbeam from heaven is yet another image for a vision, but its
primary purpose is not so much revelation as it is renewal of purpose:
' "I too have something I must care about ..." ' (vii 1238); ' "have my
purpose and my motive too ..." ' (vii 1245). And, as if to confirm Caponsacchi's suggestion, Pompilia sees herself as the Madonna: 'I felt like
Mary, had my babe / Lying a little on my breast like hers' (vii 1692–3).

Like Guido and Caponsacchi before her, Pompilia ends her monologue with a vision. But, unlike theirs, her vision looks, not to a Utopia
on earth, but to perfection in heaven. Significantly, she looks to the
perfection of spiritual love:

Marriage on earth seems such a counterfeit,
Mere imitation of the inimitable:
In heaven we have the real and true and sure.
'Tis there they neither marry nor are given
In marriage but are as the angels ...
                                        ... who, apart,
Know themselves into one, are found at length
Married, but marry never, no, nor give
In marriage; they are man and wife at once
When the true time is: here we have to wait
Not so long neither!   (vii 1824–8; 1833–8)

Just as the Nunc Dimittis was the key to the moral elevation and insight
of each character in the first ring of monologues, so the Utopian vision
is the key to moral elevation in the second ring. Pompilia's general elevation is of course greater than that of either Guido or Caponsacchi,
and, since she is at the same time less learned than they, idealization of
character is more in evidence here than elsewhere. Browning spoke of
her 'Italian ignorance, quite compatible with extraordinary insight and
power of expression too ... '[8] but it is of course obvious that the artistic
and moral insight into Pompilia herself is Browning's alone. Consequently the lyric elements that are the result of Pompilia's moral elevation are complemented by the lyric insight of the poet himself.

The lawyers (who, with the Pope, are the speakers of the third ring of
books) are mentioned by Browning several times in his letters to Julia
Wedgwood. From these letters it would appear that their function is

two-fold. On the one hand they provide comic relief: 'The buffoon lawyers (not a bit, intellectually and morally, beneath lawyers I have known) serve an artistic purpose and let you breathe a little before the last vial is poured out ...'[9] On the other hand their buffoonery has a serious purpose in relation to the moral insight which plays so important a part in the poem. The comic is never presented for its own sake, and Browning makes it clear that the comic qualities of the lawyers are marks of his own moral disapprobation: 'I hate the lawyers: and confess to tasting something of ... satisfaction, as I emphasize their buffoonery ...'[10] Their buffoonery lies partly in their personal qualities, but more especially in their methods of argument, and hence Browning emphasizes, as he does with Guido, their cleverness. Here is how he defends their portrayal against the strictures of Julia Wedgwood: 'As for the lawyers, why, *Who* is going to find fault with me, in the other world, for writing about what *I*, at least, wish had never been made? But made they are, and just so, – apart, as in the other case, from more shrewdness and learning than they are likely to have, – just so, I have known them ...'[11]

Dominus Hyacinthus de Archangelis

The comic elements in book vIII are largely personal and domestic in nature. Archangeli's size is the primary comic device, and the phrase in which Browning describes it fairly overflows with vowels and monosyllables: 'The jolly learned man of middle age, / Cheek and jowl all in laps with fat and law ...' (I 1131–2). With his size goes his love of good food, and his monologue is constantly interrupted with thoughts about the preparation of his son's birthday feast (vIII 15–17, 116–25, 541–7, 1096–1105, 1378–85). Most of his digressions, however, are concerned with his 'dear domestic ties' (I 1136): his 'old mother' (vIII 1751), his 'good fat little wife' (vIII 1780), and, most important of all, his son and heir. His use of a wide range of diminutives, his pride in his son's ability at Latin, his concern with the birthday feast – these make up the humour Browning describes as 'Paternity at smiling strife with law ...' (I 1146). The gentle nature of this humour seems quite different from the buffoonery Browning intended, and consequently we must look farther to discover its relation to the disregard of moral responsibility for which Browning hated lawyers.

In Browning's scheme of things, shrewdness and intelligence are, one might assume, gifts of considerable value for a moral life, since they make possible clearer judgment and more dispassionate choices. But in Browning's lawyers a shrewd and calculating mind goes hand in hand with moral laxity. Archangeli's wit might have been treated in a comic fashion, and indeed, when we consider it in relation to his awkward and ungainly body, the comic possibilities are obvious. 'Thick at throat, with waterish under-eye' (I 1148), he 'wheezes out law and whiffles Latin forth ...' (I 1151), and he has

> Ovidian quip or Ciceronian crank,
> A-bubble in the larynx while he laughs,
> As he had fritters deep down frying there. (I 1157–9)

Just as an agile mind in an ungainly body is comic, so an agile mind without a sense of moral responsibility is villainous. He 'makes logic levigate the big crime small ...' (I 1153). The sense in which Archangeli is a buffoon now becomes evident. The case is, for him, an exercise in mental agility, and is made out with an eye, not to the persons involved in it, but to his legal rival, the judges, etc. He is not involved in the case morally or emotionally. It is simply an intellectual problem that is to be shaped into a virtuoso legal performance.

This moral laxity helps us define the literary mode to which Archangeli's monologue belongs. He welcomes the opportunity to defend Guido, not because he is convinced of Guido's innocence, or because the affair moves him personally, but because he can set an excellent example for his boy: 'illustration from his sire, / Stimulus to himself!' (VIII 79–80). The moral gaps in his argument are but a reflection of the larger gap between his private and his professional life. Early in his monologue he praises 'home-joy, the family board, / Altar and hearth!' (VIII 51–2) as 'a source of honest profit and good fame ...' (VIII 53), and contrasts such joy with 'revel and rout and pleasures that make mad!' (VIII 50). The theme comes from Horace, as Archangeli points out (VIII 58), and was used by both Half-Rome and Guido. Yet the lawyer does not use domestic virtues as standards by which to judge the case. Archangeli, like Wemmick in *Great Expectations*, shuts his home life off from his career: 'ambition's range / Is nowise tethered by domestic tie ...' (VIII 1767–8). As the Horatian theme is expanded, the more the gap becomes obvious. 'The fact is,' Archangeli says, 'there's a blessing on the hearth, / A special providence for fatherhood!' (VIII 82–3). Yet, after one swift parallel between his boy and Gaetano (VIII 87) he sees no further connection. His constant references to his own son only emphasize his constant refusal to judge Guido as a father. It gradually becomes evident, then, that Archangeli is a satirist *manqué*, and that his monologue, though deficient in moral judgment, belongs to the same mode with which Browning began the first two rings of books. But Archangeli differs from Half-Rome and Guido in that he is even farther from the truth than they.

He is, as Browning points out, concerned with 'the manner of the making out a case ...' (I 1125). Two things are to be considered: the shape of the argument itself, and the style in which it is couched. For centuries forensic rhetoric followed a well-established pattern laid down by Cicero in his *De Inventione* and by Quintilian in his *Institutio Oratoria.* Oratory was divided into three kinds (epideictic or occasional, deliberative, and forensic) and the oration itself into seven parts (*exordium, narratio, partitio, confirmatio, refutatio, digressio,* and *peroratio*). In addition, forensic oratory had four basic kinds of arguments (*constitutio coniecturalis, definitiva, translativa,* and *generalis*). Although these divisions and the rules connected with them did not vary greatly in the expositions of a long succession of theorists, in actual practice there were two traditions: the Aristotelian tradition of rhetoric as a system of general culture based on the art of speaking and writing well on all subjects, and the scholastic tradition, derived from Gorgias and the Sophists, where the conduct of the argument itself was considered more important than its truthfulness.[12] This latter tradition is best exemplified by Bottini when he says, 'Anything, anything to let the wheels / Of argument run glibly to their goal!' (IX 471–2). In the matter of style, the classical tradition of clarity, perspicuity, and decorum (as in Cicero) contrasted with the sophist tradition of ornament, glitter, and striking utterance. Archangeli avoids the glittering style, as is evident by his pride in good Ciceronian Latin, but his argument itself shows some of the vicious ingenuity that is usually associated with sophistry. Consequently there is a gap between his style and his method of argument, a gap that corresponds to the disjunction between his mental agility and his sense of moral responsibility. The clarity and elegance of the style he is striving for undoubtedly give a sense of competence and integrity which disguises the baseness of his argument. Such ingenuity would, of course, have been approved by most lawyers, for he follows the traditional rules fairly closely, and very competently applies them to the case before him.

Archangeli begins his defence by asking, 'Where are we weak?' (VIII 307). He is faced with the fact that Guido has confessed to the murder ('Our murder, – we call, killing, – is a fact / Confessed, defended, made a boast of ...' vii 309–10), and hence he must decide on the type of argument best suited to these circumstances. *Constitutio coniecturalis* involves a question of fact; that is, whether or not the man has actually done the deed. According to Quintilian (*Institutio Oratoria* iii vi 10) a denial of the facts is always a strong line of defence, and hence Archangeli considers the possibility of suggesting that Caponsacchi did the murder, and that Guido was accused only because he happened to arrive at that particular time to forgive his wife (viii 358–82). Guido's confession, however, rules out this line of defence. Archangeli considers also *constitutio translativa*, a question as to the proper legal procedure. He doubts the legality of the use of torture on a nobleman, wonders why noblemen cannot better withstand pain (viii 403–20) and finally decides, 'We'll take it as spontaneously / Confessed ... ' (viii 356–7). Archangeli does not directly consider *constitutio definitiva*, where there is a dispute about the name by which an act is described, although he does speak of the murder as a 'killing' (viii 309). The question of definition forms but a part of the principal means of defence, the kind of argument called *constitutio generalis*, where the question is about the import, the nature, and the essence of the act. Here, in vindication of Guido's honour, Archangeli finds his strongest defence: '*Honoris causa*; so we make our stand: / Honour in us had injury, we shall prove' (vii 424–5).

Once he has decided on his general line of defence, he quickly outlines his argument:

> We shall demonstrate first of all
> That Honour is a gift of God to man
> Precious beyond compare, – which natural sense
> Of human rectitude and purity, –
> Which white, man's soul is born with, brooks no touch ... (viii 457–61)

While he thus attributes honour to God, he treats it in fact as a 'natural sense.' In doing so he seems to follow the example of Cicero, who taught that nature provided man with all the instincts necessary for the preservation not only of his life but of his proper place in the created order. These instincts are the basis of natural law, from which not only statute law but all social ties and obligations are derived. Archangeli proves that honour is natural by illustrating the sense of honour in animals, then in man, and then in the Christian, though he must, to take this last step, twist a Biblical text. Unlike Guido, Archangeli argues that Christ did not abrogate the Mosaic law – if he did the law would no longer have a natural origin and development – and consequently 'Law, Gospel and the Church subjoin' (vɪɪɪ 718). Such an argument in effect makes the Mosaic law, Christ's gospel, and the church itself progressive refinements of natural law. And consequently in the final stage he looks beyond these particulars to the general manifestation of the natural law in civilized society as a whole. Although he speaks of this stage as a 'revealment' (vɪɪɪ 730), it is clearly a natural development that has reached the high degree of sophistication evident in 'the acknowledged use and wont' (vɪɪɪ 741) of Roman society.

Archangeli refers to his argument as 'my miracle, my monster of defence – / Leviathan' (vɪɪɪ 1730–1), and seems to be pointing out its size and complexity. The moral implication of the metaphor is ignored, but the reader of course remembers the Biblical significance of the monster (as the incarnation of evil). This double awareness of the reader accounts for the irony that underlies all of Archangeli's monologue. For if his argument is indeed a monster, and morally reprehensible, it is at the same time a perfect specimen of its kind, well constructed and presented with good style. One must admire his preference for Ciceronian Latin (vɪɪɪ 129–35, 157–215, 1741–5), although his use of it to appeal to one of the judges ('It's Venturini that decides for style' vɪɪɪ 218) is less admirable although shrewd and practical. Similarly, his use of scriptural references and quotations gives sound support to his argument, especially in the eyes of ecclesiastical judges (vɪɪɪ 1736–40) but involves at the same time a sophistic twisting of the texts to make them yield the interpretation he desires. Although Archangeli argues that 'a good thing done unhandsomely turns ill ... ' (vɪɪɪ 809), the reverse is not true: a bad thing done handsomely does not turn good – and that, of course, is the point Browning is making, ironically, about the lawyer.

Archangeli's moral laxity is ultimately culpable, and, had it appeared in the second ring of books, its relation to the ultimate scheme of things would have been emphasized. But here Browning is less concerned with the standards of heaven than he is with the ways of the world. In the essay on Shelley Browning tells us that the poet who deals with 'the doings of men,' with 'the manifested action of the human heart and brain,' is a dramatic poet. Consequently this book is more purely dramatic than its predecessors, for attention is directed less to the various narrative patterns, and to the relation of the character to the infinite, and more to the perspective of one man and his view of society. The relief of which Browning spoke to Julia Wedgwood is hence not solely comic; it is to some degree a lessening of the intensity of the moral light

Browning attributes to his characters. After the badness of Guido, and the goodness of Pompilia, the indifference of the lawyer does indeed allow us to 'breathe a little.'

Juris Doctor Johannes-Baptista Bottinius

The moral laxity is continued in book IX, although the devices through which it is developed are carefully varied so as to present as great a contrast as possible to book VIII. The contrasting comic elements are obvious. Where Archangeli is fat, Bottini is thin; Archangeli is a family man, Bottini is a bachelor; and while Archangeli is portrayed in the initial stages of the preparation of his argument, Bottini presents his finished argument in an imaginary court. It is his delivery, in fact, that accounts for much of the humour, and Browning describes it twice (I 1200–19; VIII 237–42).

Like that of Archangeli, Bottini's argument follows the usual form from *exordium* to *peroratio*. Both lawyers observe what Bottini calls 'the sacredness of argument' (IX 469), but, where Archangeli cultivates refinement of style, Bottini makes use of a highly ornamented rhetoric that is often as involved as his argument itself. Consequently the moral indifference of his monologue lies in the manner as much as the matter.

The lengthy *exordium* (IX 17–118) draws a comparison between a lawyer's preparation of his case and a painter's work on a picture. The meaning of the comparison is a favourite doctrine of Browning's: that truth is something more than 'those mere fragmentary studied facts / Which answer to the outward frame and flesh ... ' (IX 102–3), that it is in fact 'a spirit-birth' (IX 106). The length of the comparison, however, throws the reader's attention, not on the meaning, but on the device itself. The reader is left, in fact, with a picture, the function of which is ultimately decorative. It is no accident that the word 'paint' turns up frequently (IX 122, 130, 192, etc.) nor is it purely by chance that Bottini ends the *exordium* with what might well be a painting: a tableau of Pompilia and Gaetano and the Comparini as the Holy Family, and of Guido as Herod. What is emphasized is not the moral and religious significance of the 'parallel' (IX 122), but its pictorial values. Hence the confusion of Pompilia's physical and moral perfection. She is placed incongruously between the beautiful Greek courtesan Phryne and the sternly moral Roman matron Lucretia, but the moral incongruity scarcely disturbs the decorative effect. It is clear of course that Bottini, like Archangeli, has his eye on his art and not on his client.

Had he taken a good look at Pompilia, he might have seen what Caponsacchi saw:

> Her brow had not the right line, leaned too much,
> Painters would say; they like the straight-up Greek:
> This seemed bent somewhat with an invisible crown
> Of martyr and saint, not such as art approves. (VI 1989–92)

But Bottini is more interested in the symmetry of his argument, and
hence he sets out to paint 'a faultless nature in a flawless form' (IX 195).
Moving in an orderly fashion to the *propositio*, Bottini presents his
'great theme' (IX 191): 'that the innocency shown is safe ...' (IX 184).
The way in which he 'shows' Pompilia's innocence is that of the painter
in words, and is well illustrated by the extended jewel image with which
he describes Pompilia's life (IX 196–212). Here the literary antecedents
of this kind of poetry become evident. The delicate colour, the sensu-
ous atmosphere, the pristine richness, all suggest Ovidian poetry, and
the typical Ovidian combination of innocence and sensuousness, shy-
ness and forwardness, comes to the fore:

> Womanliness and wifehood opaline,
> Its milk-white pallor, – chastity, – suffused
> With here and there a tint and hint of flame, –
> Desire ... (IX 204–7)

It would appear, then, that we are indeed to be given a picture of
innocence, but it is not Pompilia's innocence. Pompilia is merely a
figure on whom is focused an entire literary tradition. She is Ovid's
Daphne and Salmacis, Marlowe's Hero, Chapman's Corinna, and
many others of the same tradition, a beautiful, innocent – and passionate – maid. The way in which the style contributes to the effect
is also Ovidian. The imagery is rich and profuse; Browning describes
it as 'some finished butterfly, / Some breathing diamond-flake with
leaf-gold fans ...' (I 1168–9). Bottini does not allow the reader to
dwell too long on each facet of the rich decoration; instead he rushes
on to the next embellishment. He indicates the tempo by such phrases
as 'Which is to say, – lose no time but begin!' (IX 213), 'I dare the epic
plunge – / Begin at once with marriage ...' (IX 217–18) and 'But time
fleets: / Let us not linger: hurry to the end ...' (IX 837–8). The swift
movement thus prevents the rich texture from cloying.

The Ovidian tradition helps us to define not only the style of Bottini's
argument, but also the literary mode Browning is using in this book.
I have argued that Archangeli's monologue, like the first monologue in

each of the other two groups of books, belongs to the satiric mode. If Browning is to maintain the pattern he has established, Bottini's monologue should be either a comedy, like the Other Half-Rome's, or a romance, like Caponsacchi's. In fact, it combines elements of both. The basis of such treatment is the legal argument which Bottini uses. Throughout the monologue he insists that Pompilia is innocent, because she has always been true to the promptings of her own nature: 'What is greatest sin of womanhood? / That which unwomans it ... ' (IX 791-2). In effect, if not in so many words, Bottini concedes his opponent's points and admits the charges against Pompilia, then argues that, as a maturing woman, she could not have done otherwise. When this argument is translated into literary patterns, we have elements of both romance and comedy. The romance elements lie in Pompilia's repeated attempts to satisfy her natural desires, attempts that might be described as a quest for self-fulfilment. The satisfaction of her desires (with Caponsacchi) involves the overcoming of all obstacles (including her husband) and the creation of the kind of social situation where 'doing what comes naturally' is possible. Hence the monologue has comic elements as well.

Pompilia's quest begins when she matures to the point where it is a part of her nature to attract men. Bottini develops an analogy between her and a flower, and argues that it is the purpose of both to attract indiscriminately:

The lady, foes allege, put forth each charm
And proper floweret of feminity,
To whosoever had a nose to smell
Or breast to deck: what if the charge be true?
The fault were graver had she looked with choice,
Fastidiously appointed who should grasp,
Who, in the whole town, go without the prize!   (IX 298-304)

The time comes, however, when Pompilia must act and make decisions of her own and here Bottini's defence becomes particularly sophistic. He argues that Pompilia must act in order to obey the promptings of her own maturing womanhood, and that, far from sinning, she is only fulfilling her own nature. Growing dissatisfied with her husband, Pompilia chooses, not indiscriminately, 'a man of mark' (IX 348). Caponsacchi is introduced with an Ovidian quip (IX 340) and is presented as a typical Ovidian youth: 'Well-born, of culture, young and vigorous, / Comely too ...' (IX 351-2). He is compared to David as he appeared to Abigail, and the comparison emphasizes the sexual attraction which underlies the whole situation. Pompilia proceeds to use all her wiles to seduce Caponsacchi, and Bottini continues to excuse her actions as natural and therefore innocent. In dealing with the love letters, for instance (IX 443–506), he argues that Pompilia must do everything in her power to prevent a crime (Guido's murder of her): 'Who dares blame the use / Of the armoury thus allowed for natural ... ' (IX 430–1). The 'armoury' is 'the magic nod and wink, / The witchery of gesture, spell of word ... ' (IX 436–7). By another standard these 'arts that allure' (IX 436) would be morally culpable, but in Bottini's terms they are natural and therefore innocent. Given this kind of argument, it does not really matter whether Pompilia wrote the love letters or not. Bottini says of course that she did not, but goes on to give the impression that she did:

> Concede she wrote (which were preposterous)
> This and the other epistle, – what of it?
> Where does the figment touch her candid fame? (IX 473–5)

The letters are in effect only an extension of her womanly nature, and must therefore be excused.

As Bottini continues, the story moves to a typical Ovidian situation: 'He is Myrtillus, Amaryllis she, / She burns, he freezes ... ' (IX 539–40). The flight, consequently, is little more than another version of the Venus and Adonis story, in which the ardent Pompilia uses kisses and embraces to overcome the priest's irresoluteness ('Means to the end are lawful' IX 676). The comic resolution of the story is the stay at the inn. Having thoroughly aroused the priest, Pompilia swoons, and is carried to bed, where she remains conveniently unconscious (and therefore innocent) while the priest, Bottini suggests (IX 750–6), has his way with her. There is no sweaty insistence in the proceedings; the delicate sensuousness leaves Pompilia innocent, and leaves Bottini free to attribute Gaetano's birth to 'spontaneous generation' (IX 1350). The moral irresponsibility with which Bottini treats the case is summed up in the problem he extracts – 'How so much beauty is compatible / With so much innocence!' (IX 756–6) – and that is no more than an Ovidian *question d'amour*.

In spite of his failure to make a responsible moral judgment, Bottini insists that

> By painting saintship I depicture sin,
> Beside the pearl, I prove how black the jet,
> And through Pompilia's virtue, Guido's crime. (IX 1409–11)

It is evident that Bottini has done nothing of the sort, that, far from showing sin by the light of virtue, he has done little more than demonstrate that whiteness in one part of a picture must be balanced by blackness in another. In effect, then, Bottini is just as morally indifferent as Archangeli. For both, the case is simply a professional exercise, a virtuoso display of legal techniques. Far from presenting their respective sides of the case with fairness and understanding, as Judge Gest has argued,[13] they ignore the truth for the sake of a well-shaped argument.

The Pope

Book x, the monologue of the Pope, concludes the third ring of books. Unlike the lawyers, the Pope keeps his attention focused, not on the mechanics of his official decision, but on the case itself, and on his his decision as it affects both his own life and the lives of those whom he judges. He thus has a broad view that gives him a detachment similar to that of Pompilia. His moral insight, too, is just as keen as Pompilia's, but it is by no means as simple in its operation. For while Pompilia is a pure soul about to be taken up into heaven, the Pope is very much a man among men, who must arrive at truth painfully, step by step, 'As a mere man may, with no special touch / O' the lynx-gift in each ordinary orb ... ' (x 1243–4). On the one hand, because of his position, he is subject to pressure from the state, from the church, and from the Italian aristocracy; on the other, there is 'what ... / From the other world he feels impress at times ...' (i 1223–4). His insight, then, never has the simplicity, the inspired quality of Pompilia's, and consequently his monologue is less lyrical than Pompilia's, and more dramatic, in Browning's sense of the term.

The lyric elements of the monologue must not, however, be ignored. Argument takes on a lyrical cast when it proceeds on something more subtle than the logic of discursive thought, and certainly the Pope's monologue, in comparison with those of the lawyers, does not have the logical consistency, the careful working-out of an argument, in which they took so much pride. The Pope, in fact, expresses his entire approach to life, and treats the specific task before him, not apart from the general course of his life, as both Archangeli and Bottini did, but as a summary of all the tasks that have ever faced him, and of all the choices that he has ever made. For he imagines his judgment before God, and God's demand:

'Show me thy fruit, the latest act of thine!
'For in the last is summed the first and all, –
'What thy life last put heart and soul into,
'There shall I taste thy product.' (IX 341–4)

It is this sense of the ultimate significance of his decision that gives the Pope's monologue its peculiar character. Centred on a specific judgment, it nevertheless raises eternal questions so that, for the moment, the whole course of a man's life, and his ultimate destiny, rest in one particular act.

In order to act, man must make a choice, and a choice is possible only because man's knowledge is incomplete. The limitations of man's understanding sometimes sap the will and prevent a choice from being made. The Pope is conscious of this danger, and emphasizes, with the story of Formosus at the beginning of his monologue, the inescapable duty of making a decision.

The Pope begins wisely by saying that he must judge motives, so far as is possible, and not acts alone:

For I am ware it is the seed of act,
God holds appraising in His hollow palm,
Not act grown great thence on the world below,
Leafage and branchage, vulgar eyes admire. (x 271–4)

This approach enables him to see through Guido's clever argument, a difficult thing to do, since he has Guido's testimony alone to examine. But he sees clearly that Guido applies to his own actions a double standard. On the one hand he is a nobleman, having 'Great birth, good breeding, with the Church for guide' (x 479); on the other he is a monster, 'body and soul / Prostrate among the filthy feeders ...' (x 501–2). Having recognized these two points of view, the Pope goes straight to the core of Guido's argument:

When Law takes him by surprise at last,
Catches the foul thing on its carrion-prey,
Behold, he points to shell left high and dry,
Pleads, 'But the case out yonder is myself!' (x 503–6)

The Pope mocks the shell, the 'new tribunal now / Higher than God's, – the educated man's!' (x 1975–6) and throws out the argument of *honoris causâ*. For he recognizes the motives underlying Guido's acts: 'He believes in just the vile of life' (x 511). Where Guido had deliberately confused two points of view to make his acts acceptable, the Pope sees the real unity of the deeds in Guido's 'low instinct' and 'base pretension' (x 512). And rather than examining each deed in isolation, as Guido had done, the Pope sees Guido's whole life epitomised in the murder,

> the last deliberate act; as last,
> So, very sum and substance of the soul
> Of him that planned and leaves one perfect piece ...   (x 521–3)

As Guido's principal motive the Pope singles out 'the lust for money' (x 542). With this firm foundation for his judgment the Pope proceeds to examine the course of the story. He concludes that Guido deliberately plotted against Pompilia in order to trap her in sin, and that she stood firm because of her purity and goodness.

Having judged Guido, the Pope proceeds to judge Paolo and Girolamo (x 868–909), their mother (x 909–24), the four confederates (x 924–63), Guido's supporters at Arezzo (x 964–84), and the archbishop of Arezzo (x 985–1002). Each is guilty of contributing to a hell on earth ('Such denizens o' the cave now cluster round / And heat the furnace sevenfold ...' x 993–4) and each, the Pope decides, should be swept away.

The Pope's vindication of Pompilia is brief but perceptive. He pronounces her 'perfect in whiteness' (x 1005) and realizes that her soul has greater knowledge that can be obtained by 'the intellect of man' (x 1013). Like Bottini, he compares her to a flower, but the image points to the purity of her soul, not the beauty of her body. However, he does not exclude her body from her general purity, and he condemns by implication, as Fra Celestino later does specifically (xii 580–4), the argument of Bottini:

> But, brave,
> Thou at first prompting of what I call God,
> And fools call Nature, didst hear, comprehend,
> Accept the obligation laid on thee,
> Mother elect, to save the unborn child ...   (x 1071–5)

And he continues to describe the growth and development of all creatures of nature as 'Life from the Ever Living' (x 1080).

Caponsacchi the Pope describes as an 'irregular noble 'scapegrace' (x 1100), but he praises him for his purity and his resistance to temptation:

> Why comes temptation but for man to meet
> And master and make crouch beneath his foot,
> And so be pedestalled in triumph?   (x 1184–6)

The Comparini he finds culpable because of their 'sadly mixed natures' (x 1217), their refusal to make a clear choice between good and evil:

Never again elude the choice of tints!
White shall not neutralise the black, nor good
Compensate bad in man, absolve him so:
Life's business being just the terrible choice.   (x 1234–7)

With the principal characters thus judged, the first section of the monologue ends.

The rest of the Pope's monologue has sometimes been condemned as a digression, but, as has already been pointed out, it sets these specific decisions in the context of a man's whole approach to life and at the same time gives the case a place in the broad flow of life itself, and indeed in God's plan for the world. For the case raises all the issues which must be faced constantly throughout life: the source and extent of our knowledge, the nature of God, the mystery of good and evil, the purpose of individual life and of human history. To each of these topics the Pope brings wisdom and understanding. He recognizes, first of all, that his knowledge is limited, yet he affirms that it comes from God: 'my poor spark had for its source, the sun ... ' (x 1284); 'Mind is not matter nor from matter, but / Above ... ' (x 1352–3). Perfect knowledge can be God's alone, while man's knowledge, complete in its way, is accommodated to his understanding, 'a whole proportioned to our sense ... ' (x 1316). In dealing with such accommodation Browning uses a favourite image, that of the convex glass that gathers scattered points of revelation (x 1310–22). The Pope, then, has limited knowledge, like all men, but is assured that such knowledge is divine in origin:

All that I do and am
Comes from the truth, or seen or else surmised,
Remembered or divined, as mere man may:
I know just so, nor otherwise.   (x 1826–9)

The Pope proceeds to reason about the nature of God, and, like David, does so in an orderly and logical sequence, concluding, like him, that God's strength and intelligence imply 'goodness in a like degree' (x 1363). But the implication cannot be proved by 'the human eye in the present state ... ' (x 1364), and consequently it is the revelation of Christ that gives us a knowledge of God's love. Logic and revelation thus combine, the one active in definition and clarification, the other supplying intuitive knowledge where the discursive processes fail. The two work hand in hand, and the process is orderly, if not totally explicable. For once God's love has been revealed the Pope can make a further affirmation:

I can believe this dread machinery
Of sin and sorrow, would confound me else,
Devised, – all pain, at most expenditure
Of pain by Who devised pain, – to evolve,
By new machinery in counterpart,
The moral qualities of man – how else? –
To make him love in turn and be beloved,
Creative and self-sacrificing too,
And thus eventually God-like ...   (x 1374–82)

And he goes on to enunciate a favourite Browning doctrine: 'Life is training and a passage ... ' (x 1410); 'the moral sense grows but by exercise' (x 1414); 'life is probation and this earth no goal / But starting-point of man ...' (x 1435–6).

Just as the life of each individual has its dangers and vicissitudes as it moves towards its goal, so the course of human history does not always run smoothly. For faith must constantly be reaffirmed, and hence the Pope sees the necessity for an age of unbelief: 'The impatient anti-masque treads close on kibe / O' the very masque's self it will mock ... ' (x 1903–4). Through the eyes of the Pope Browning may be looking at his own age with all its various manifestations of doubt and unbelief.

It may seem to some critics that the Pope has wandered very far from his specific task, but he has in fact placed the case in the broad perspective not only of human history but of God's plan for the world. For, unlike Pompilia, the Pope does have his eye on the world (though with reference to the other world), and, as he stated in the essay on Shelley, Browning considered a stooping to the finite as primarily dramatic.

Guido

Guido is the only character to be given two monologues, and this fact has an important effect on the pattern of the whole poem. The placing of his second speech – immediately after the Pope's monologue – is important; moreover, the relation between this speech and those in the second ring of books is a complex one, and must be defined carefully.

To begin with, Guido's exposure of himself in book xi reinforces the Pope's judgment, and gives a strong conclusion to the moral pattern that the reader must follow throughout the poem. For Guido is at last telling the truth. 'The true words come last' (I 1281), Browning says of Guido's second monologue, and certainly the reader has the sense that he is at last seeing Guido as he really is. Book v was an argument designed to persuade the judges by confusing the moral issues. Book xi is the exposure of a point of view not unlike that of the speaker in *Time's Revenges*: 'There may be heaven; there must be hell; / Meantime, there is our earth here – well!' In thus allowing Guido to expose himself, Browning is in effect playing God, and giving the reader a degree of certainty about the Pope's decision that the Pope himself may not have.

Though 'the true words come last,' they are the words of an evil nature, and consequently they are shot through with 'the contradictions and self-betrayals that reveal the full extent of [Guido's] duplicity.' Moreover, 'it is impossible to distinguish fully between the true Guido and the actor playing a desperate role.'[14] In addition, Guido's attempt to deceive others is complicated by self-deception. The truth that we get in book xi is, then, a very curious kind of truth, shifting, evasive, and difficult to fix, as the first five hundred lines of the monologue show. Guido begins with some of his old shrewdness, which is almost as effective here as it was in book v. Having just been told by Cardinal Acciaiuoli and Abate Panciatichi that he must die at sunset, he reacts as cleverly as usual. First he appeals for pity ('Help me, Sirs!' xi 15). Then he seems to delude himself wilfully, to consider the information he has just received as a 'vile experiment' (xi 20), a 'well-intentioned trick' (xi 22) to make him speak the truth. Swiftly he recalls the argument he had used, the argument based on natural law and civility: 'All honest Rome approved my part ... ' (xi 39). And, as he did before, he applies one standard to his own actions, and another standard (the Christian one) to the actions of the Pope. Can the Pope be good, he asks, and still order the execution? 'Will my death do credit to his reign / Show he both lived and let live, so was good?' (xi 65–6). Mercy, he insists, should abrogate the law. He again appeals for pity with his long description of Mannaia, the engine of execution (xv 180–258). But the appeal for pity turns to righteous indignation when he uses as an example the execution of Felice, who struck a Duke for kidnapping his sister:

I do the Duke's deed, take Felice's place,
And, being no Felice, lout and clout,
Stomach but ill the phrase 'I lose my head!'   (xi 277–9)

Again he accuses the Pope, and indeed, all men, for not intervening to save him: 'They are not good, / Nowise like Peter ... ' (xi 324–5). These reactions – a combination of shrewdness, confusion, and desperation – presently give way to a single outburst of hatred ('The angry heart explodes, bears off in blaze / The indignant soul, and I'm combustion-ripe' xi 466–7) and the truth pours forth (xi 515 ff).

The truth that Guido reveals is a viciously simple creed:

'Get pleasure, 'scape pain, – give your preference
'To the immediate good, for time is brief,
'And death ends good and ill and everything:
'What's got is gained, what's gained soon is gained twice,
'And, – inasmuch as faith gains most, – feign faith!' (xi 768–72)

Guido, it is clear, is completely involved in material things and in the turning of time. Recognizing no law but that of self-interest, he sees life as a vicious struggle where only the fittest survive.

It is from this point of view that Guido retells the story of the marriage, the flight, and the murder. And it is this point of view which helps us to define the literary mode Browning is using in book xi. In undermining all human aspirations and ideals, and in insisting that all motives may ultimately be reduced to self-interest, Guido is clearly setting himself up as an ironist, aware of the multiple and shifting incongruities of human existence, and capable of penetrating to what (in his view) is 'real.' When such an ironic point of view is applied to the events of the story, the concerns of all the characters, and of Pompilia and Caponsacchi in particular, are reduced to self-interest. The flight which, as I have already pointed out, is, so far as the action of the story alone is concerned, the most romantic incident of all, becomes a parody of romance. And indeed, Guido's point of view inverts the whole story, and makes it an anti-romance.

It was not Browning's practice to treat romance solely in terms of external action; he was concerned rather with the three stages of inner growth: an uncomfortable awareness of the complexity of ordinary life, a vision that brings the individual close to ultimate reality, and an attempt to realize that vision in an ideally human world. Browning's characteristic treatment of romance may be seen in Caponsacchi's monologue in book vi. And it may be seen, turned upside down, in Guido's second monologue. Book vi dealt with inner growth; book xi deals with inner deterioration, and does so in stages that are a distorted reflection of the stages of Caponsacchi's experience. Like Caponsacchi, Guido starts off totally involved in a society where moral issues are confused, and where a thousand distractions sap the will to pursue any one course in life. The sight of Pompilia brings a change to both men, but while she was an ecstatic vision for Caponsacchi, for Guido she is an offence against his manhood and his age, and a threat to his personal well-being. Caponsacchi reacted to Pompilia creatively, and, in trying to realize the good she revealed to him, became a better man. Guido, on the other hand, showed contempt for Pompilia; incapable of using his marriage creatively, he reduced their relationship to a struggle of wills (each pursuing its own selfish ends). Thus the lives of both Guido and Caponsacchi depend upon some kind of relationship with Pompilia. And this relationship in turn defines the moral qualities of both characters.

Guido begins – and this is the first stage of his anti-romance – by describing a society where moral issues are by no means clear. But where Caponsacchi's view of society and his role in it resulted from the lack of a firm purpose and direction in his life, Guido's view is the result of the tendency to reduce human nature to its simplest selfish level, and to find logic only in extremes. What he sets forth is essentially a Hobbesian view of society in which each individual pursues his selfish interests, and where law is a contract (and not a natural right, as Guido argued earlier) which holds selfish interests in check:

> For pleasure is the sole good in the world,
> Anyone's pleasure turns to someone's pain,
> So, let law watch for everyone ... (XI 529–31)

This kind of law is completely non-moral, and does not even imply a system of natural ethics, let alone divine guidance. Hence Guido says, 'I fail to see, above man's law, / God's precept you, the Christians recognize' (XI 551–2). Similarly, when he examines religious practices (such as the veneration of sacred relics), he sees, not the faith thus expressed, but the self-interest involved, the payment of a fee. Faith for him is no more than a 'fancy' (XI 591), though a pretense of faith may be very useful. Unable to understand that faith and doubt are both part of man's relation with God, that man must view death, for instance, both with sorrow, from the worldly point of view, and with joy, from the heavenly point of view, he accuses those who appear to waver in their faith of hypocrisy:

> Entire faith, or else complete unbelief, –
> Aught between has my loathing and contempt,
> Mine and God's also, doubtless ... (XI 730–2)

There may indeed be logic only in extremes, but to insist upon such logic is to deny the richness and variety of human life, the range of man's relations with God, and the potential for growth which such richness implies. But Guido is fundamentally opposed to human development. He finds pleasure only in opposing, reducing, and destroying. The extent to which he denies life is evident in his account of his first meeting with Pompilia.

This first meeting marks the beginning of the second stage of Guido's story. He is offended by Pompilia, and resents her shrinking from him, partly because she is frightened by his unkempt appearance and by his age, and partly because she (apparently) senses his evil nature:

> I resent my wrong,
> Being a man: I only show man's soul
> Through man's flesh: she sees mine, it strikes her thus!
> Is that attractive? (xɪ 985–8)

Guido begins, then, not with a sense of enlightenment, like Caponsacchi, but with a sense of injury:

> Therefore 'tis she begins with wronging me,
> Who cannot but begin with hating her.
> Our marriage follows: there we stand again! (xɪ 1031–3)

Caponsacchi reacted to the vision given him by pursuing it, by trying to make it work in his life. Guido reacts in just the opposite fashion. The offence he has suffered leads to the desire to take revenge, and each new offence strengthens that desire. There is, first of all, the offence of Pompilia's obedience: 'How can I other than remember this, / Resent the very obedience?' (xɪ 1046–7). There is the offence of Pompilia's passivity: Guido expects an animal who will fight back, 'be female to my male,' and 'yield fair sport so ... ' (xɪ 1327, 1331). Instead he finds his wife 'a nullity in female shape ... ' (xɪ 1111). And so the offences mount. '[I] lead [you] by degrees,' Guido says, 'Recounting at each step some fresh offence / Up to the red bed ... ' (xɪ 1294–6). His hatred, it becomes clear, is hatred of Pompilia's very goodness; it has no cause or purpose beyond itself: 'Say that I hated her for no cause / Beyond my pleasure so to do ... ' (xɪ 1432–3). The desire for revenge takes shape in the plot against Pompilia, and when her purity and goodness thwart his subtler scheme, he murders her.

The murder, the ultimate act of destruction, is the logical outcome of Guido's contempt for goodness. His pleasure lies in destroying, just as Caponsacchi's lay in creating. There is one point at which Guido feels he might have found something different in marriage. 'I fare somehow worse / For the way I took ...' (xi 1446–7), and he goes on to speculate on where the fault lies:

– my fault ... as God's my judge
I see not where the fault lies, that's the truth!
I ought ... oh, ought in my own interest
Have let the whole adventure go untried,
This chance by marriage, – or else, trying it,
Ought to have turned it to account some one
O' the hundred otherwise?   (xi 1447–53)

Yet Guido is incapable of 'turning it to account', and can find no gap in the logic of the process that led him to his present situation. The anti-romance culminates, then, not in a joyous affirmation of life and a determination to struggle on, but in a bitter denial of life and the desperation of the damned.

Guido curses his failure to escape after the murder as 'Artistry's haunting curse, the Incomplete!' (xi 1559). The incompleteness, the lack of success, leads him, in spite of his disbelief, to recognize something above himself, 'the luck that lies beyond a man' (xi 1565), 'destiny' (xi 1700). Significantly, this 'luck' is not entirely indiscriminate or blind, but rather a steady and fatalistic turning of the wheel of destiny. As Guido himself says, when considering the fact that his hirelings would have killed him had not the police caught up with him, "Tis fate not fortune! All is of a piece!' (xi 1731). 'So the cards are packed,' he continues, 'Dice loaded, and my life-stake tricked away!' (xi 1753–4). It is evident then that Guido does extend the pattern of his life to the cosmos, where it becomes 'this tenacious hate of fortune, hate / Of all things in, under, and above earth' (xi 1796–7).

Near the end of the monologue the extremes of Guido's situation appear most clearly. On the one hand, there are the statements of heroic defiance not unlike those of Satan in *Paradise Lost*:

Some use
There cannot be but for a mood like mine,
Implacable, persistent in revenge.   (xi 2103–5)

Related to such statements is the wolf image by which Guido characterizes himself throughout the monologue, and the afterlife which he envisions as an eternity of war-like pursuits: 'The strong become a wolf for evermore!' (xi 2051). On the other hand, there is a desperate sense of existence as hollow and empty, and of the self as a prison: 'I have gone inside my soul / And shut its door behind me ...' (XI 2289–90), he says, and what he finds there is the nothingness of evil, the 'something changeless at the heart of me' (XI 2392). There is the sense, then, of failure, and the agony of the situation is evident in Guido's final plea, 'Pompilia, will you let them murder me?' (XI 2425). It is not likely that Guido has at last recognized Pompilia's goodness, or that he recognizes in her a means of salvation. Rather, the cry is a cry of desperation, a recognition that the forces of destruction he turned on other people are now turning on himself. And his lingering sense that he might have turned his marriage to account brings Pompilia's name to his lips.

Although I have emphasized, throughout this analysis, the way in which Browning combines the narrative, dramatic, and lyric modes in each monologue, the variations in treatment fall into a broader pattern that involves the poem as a whole. The primary function of the first three books, as I have already pointed out, is to tell the story. We are allowed to examine the narrative from three different points of view, so that the sequence of events is fixed in our minds, and the problem of moral judgment raised. In the second group of books we are drawn into the action itself. The speakers of these monologues are the central characters of the story, and their words, like those of characters in a play, give the action the immediacy and vividness that can be achieved best through a dramatic presentation. The problem of judgment remains, however, and is dealt with specifically by the speakers in the last group of books. Such is the broad pattern of the poem: the narrative, which presents the facts; the drama, which brings them to life and arouses our sympathy for them; the lyric, which leads us to judge them. However, these three aspects of the poem are not separate and distinct, but are rather inseparable parts of the 'seeing' that Browning referred to as 'the communication of something more subtle than a ratiocinative process ...'[15] For each speaker presents the facts, dramatizes them for us, and gives us his interpretation of them. The visible form of each speaker's approach to truth is the literary mode of the monologue, modified and adapted by the speaker's particular point of view.

Though Browning's approach to genre in each monologue is extremely flexible, the poet seems always to have been conscious of the broader patterns of the poem. The pattern of the monologues in each of the three groups, for instance, is similar, in spite of important variations in treatment. The first speakers in the groups – Half-Rome, Guido, and Archangeli – express themselves in the satiric mode. Each attacks Pompilia, though each does so on different grounds, differences that are reflected in the treatment of the mode. Half-Rome disparages Pompilia from a point of view which is highly personal and highly prejudiced; Guido measures her by shifting standards that are designed to confuse and deceive; and Archangeli, in failing to judge her at all, nevertheless follows the pattern of the satiric mode by speaking against her, and by having at least a potential standard (his domestic life) by which to deal with her. The second speakers in the groups – Other Half-Rome, Caponsacchi, and Bottini – make use of comic and romantic elements. Other Half-Rome tells the story as a sentimental comedy in which innocence, virtue, and love triumph over adversity; Caponsacchi adapts the romance mode in describing his growing insight; and Bottini defends Pompilia in an Ovidian fashion, treating the fulfilment of a young girl's love-longings according to the same comic pattern used by Other Half-Rome. The third speakers in the groups – Tertium Quid, Pompilia, and the Pope – approach the central issues in ways as varied as one would expect of characters whose place in the pattern is defined as 'some third thing.' Tertium Quid combines comic and satiric elements and presents the story with a detachment that often indicates a failure to judge adequately; Pompilia speaking in the lyric mode is detached too, but her detachment is that of an individual so keenly aware of ultimate reality that earthly life becomes insubstantial and dreamlike; the Pope's monologue is a combination of the dramatic (insofar as he is concerned with specific persons and issues) and the lyric (insofar as he is aware of the ultimate significance of his decisions); he makes the judgment that Tertium Quid fails to make, and makes it with the same sense of divine purpose that Pompilia has.

The book and the ring

With such careful patterning in the central part of the poem, it is unlikely that Browning would end his work without affirming the pattern established in book I. At first glance, however, book XII fails to do so. The poem comes to an end in a formal sense only, since the recreating of the truth of the work is a continuous process ('Here were an end, had anything an end ...' XII 1). Moreover, Browning seems to have chosen at random the four 'reports' that make up the material of book XII, and the very fact that there are four of them violates the tripartite pattern of the rest of the poem. If one examines these 'reports' generically, however, it soon becomes apparent that they were carefully chosen for specific purposes. In fact, the three letters (one of which includes two 'reports') parallel the triple presentation of the materials in book I, but with just enough variation in the pattern to bring the poem to a highly satisfactory conclusion.

The first letter is from 'a stranger, man of rank, / Venetian visitor at Rome ...' (XII 27–8). Concerned as it is with a description of externals, with the 'constant shift of entertaining show' (XII 33), it is a good example of narrative poetry as Browning conceived it. For the nobleman describes the carnival, the approaching election of a new pope, and then the most sensational news of the day, the execution of Guido. The writer seems to represent the world of 'civility,' for he says of Guido, 'I reported him as safe, / Re-echoing the conviction of all Rome ...' (XII 77–8). It is obvious, of course, that he sees only the externals of the situation, the actions, and hears only popular opinions. In book I Browning tells us that 'action now shrouds, now shows the informing thought ...' (I 1366). Just how little Guido's actions tell about the real character of the man is evident in the Venetian's description of Guido's execution. For here Guido appears as an admirable representative of his rank, dying an heroic, almost saintly death:

'He begged forgiveness on the part of God,
'And fair construction of his act from men,
'Whose suffrage he entreated for his soul,
'Suggesting that we should forthwith repeat
'A *Pater* and an *Ave*, with the hymn
'*Salve Regina Coeli*, for his sake.
'Which said, he turned to the confessor, crossed
'And reconciled himself, with decency,
'Oft glancing at Saint Mary's opposite
'Where they possess, and showed in shrine to-day,
'The Blessed *Umbilicus* of our Lord,
'(A relic 'tis believed no other church
'In Rome can boast of) – then rose up, as brisk
'Knelt down again, bent head, adapted neck,
'And, with the name of Jesus on his lips,
'Received the fatal blow.' (XII 174–89)

To all external appearances Guido dies a noble death, and his saintly qualities seem proved when the lame beggar suddenly regains the use of his leg through Guido's intercessory prayer. The limitations of narrative are only too evident, and Browning allows the letter to proceed no farther.

177

The second letter, from Archangeli to Cencini, the lawyer who compiled the Old Yellow Book, falls into two parts. The first is the formal statement of a barrister who has fought a case with all the arguments at his disposal, and lost. The second is a familiar letter full of homely details about ' "my boy, your godson, fat-chaps Hyacinth" ' (xii 331). The letter affirms the portrayal of the lawyer in book viii, and serves to remind us that life continues, even though the action of the poem has ended. Of his unsuccessful defence of Guido Archangeli says, ' "Rome will have relished heartily the show ..." ' (xii 309). He is so completely involved in this life that even the execution is no more than an occasion for young Hyacinth to enjoy a spectacle and to amuse Roman society with his wit. The sense of life continuing its ordinary course suggests that the letter might be labelled 'dramatic.'

To complete the pattern, the third letter should be a lyric, but, since it is a letter from Bottini, it too is involved in the world as we know it, and shows little or no concern for the infinite. For Bottini has been engaged by the convent of the Convertites to prove Pompilia guilty of adultery so that they may claim her fortune. And Bottini, being the kind of person he is, relishes the thought of taking up the case 'against the person of dishonest life, / Pompilia, whom last week I sainted so' (xii 705–6). Such material can scarcely be considered as lyric. The letter includes, however, a portion of Fra Celestino's sermon, which shows all the characteristics of the lyric as Browning conceived it. The text of the sermon (from Romans 3: 4, 'Let God be true, but every man a liar') raises the problem of the adequacy of human speech, and questions, by implication, the value of an art whose material is language. Because Fra Celestino does look to the ultimate value of speech, its relation to the infinite, his sermon may be considered a lyric. However, the insight which is usually the mark of the lyric is here somewhat limited. He warns his listeners quite properly that, while good may have triumphed in the present case, it will not always do so, and that it is often further obscured by language, by ' "vapoury films, enwoven circumstance" ' (xii 556):

> 'who trusts
> 'To human testimony for a fact
> Gets this sole fact – himself is proved a fool;
> 'Man's speech being false ...' (xii 601–4)

Nevertheless, he suggests that some human speech, such as poetry, is worth pursuing, and that the arts may well express greatness and goodness. He sees their function, however, as limited, and their only reward earthly fame. While Celestino thus has considerable insight into the ways of the world, and of God's occasional intervention, his view is limited and to some extent pessimistic. The pessimism is deepened by placing the sermon in the context of Bottini's letter. Bottini is the personification of all that Celestino is speaking out against, and it scarcely seems possible that Pompilia can be vindicated a second time. That she is again proved spotless Browning reports with deep satisfaction.

Browning evidently found much of which he approved in Fra Celestino's sermon, but at the same time he makes clear the limitations of the monk's outlook. For the friar has renounced the world – as Browning would never do – and he assigns only a limited usefulness to poetry. Browning concludes, therefore, with his own interpretation of Celestino's text, and thereby completes the lyric insight that the pattern he has set for himself demands.

This conclusion is characteristically ironic. Having in mind the demands of the critics that the poet be a religious and philosophical teacher, Browning provides a moral for the poem, a moral which is in fact a paraphrase of the text from Romans:

> our human speech is naught,
> Our human testimony false, our fame
> And human estimation words and wind.   (XII 834–6)

The statement is both true and not true, as the sermon and its context serve to make clear. It is true insofar as Pompilia's fame is twice vindicated, in spite of the lawyers and all their words. It is not true when we remind ourselves of Browning's earlier comment: 'For how else know we save by worth of word?' (I 837). Though much of what is said in the poem is false or misleading, though many of the judgments are mistaken or biased, nevertheless it is with such 'human speech' and 'human estimation' that truth is discovered. Moreover, an artist whose medium is words surely presents ironically any statement denying the worth of words. The irony becomes particularly evident when Browning goes on to defend poetry as 'the one way possible / Of speaking truth ...' (XII 839–40):

> But Art, – wherein man nowise speaks to men,
> Only to mankind, – Art may tell a truth
> Obliquely, do the thing shall breed the thought,
> Nor wrong the thought, missing the mediate word.
> So may you paint your picture, twice show truth,

179

Beyond mere imagery on the wall, –
So, note by note, being music from your mind,
Deeper than ever the Andante dived, –
So write a book shall mean, beyond the facts,
Suffice the eye and save the soul beside. (xii 854–63)

Now it is evident that Browning gives art a much greater function and significance than Celestino does. First of all, he clearly differentiates it from ordinary speech. It is concerned, not only with particulars, but with universals; it speaks to mankind. And it does not inform in the manner of discursive writing; rather, it 'breeds the thought' and thus tells truth obliquely. For Browning is constantly aware that one does not arrive at the truth passively, that truth cannot be received like facts. Rather, each reader must explore what is given to him, use his imagination on it, and so arrive at its meaning. Even the shape which the poet's fancy has given the facts is yet one more fact for the reader. The poem concludes, then, by pointing back to itself.

Fra Celestino thought the reward of poetry was earthly fame. Browning believed it would save not only his soul, but also the souls of those who read it properly. By thus emphasizing the relation between poetry and the infinite, Browning directs us to the poem itself as one gigantic insight, which is in a wider sense the lyric we have been seeking to complete the pattern of book xii.

Henry James sought 'some centre in our field,' some 'point of control' which would unify the poem, and found it in the 'embracing consciousness of Caponsacchi.'[16] He did not ask whether or not the poet himself played a major role in his own poem. Yet it is evident, I hope, that the only 'consciousness,' the only insight, which embraces the whole poem, is Browning's. The alloy, his fancy, is in fact the generic patterns themselves, that give shape and meaning to the facts. The poem is not spacious and loose, as is often suggested; rather, it is carefully conceived and tightly constructed on a pattern as perfect as that of the 'Etrurian circlet.' The 'book' is not the only significant part of Browning's title; for the 'ring' is his own art as a poet, the shaping power that opened the 'book' and made it his reading of life. In an age when the poet was expected to teach as directly and simply as possible, Browning tried to make his readers aware that the form of his poetry was an integral part of its effect.

Conclusion

An investigation of the literary relations of most of Browning's work up to and including *The Ring and the Book* indicates the extent to which he changed and modified the genres he worked with. His first three published poems – *Pauline, Paracelsus,* and *Sordello* – are experiments with the three primary literary kinds: lyric, drama, and epic or narrative poetry respectively. *Pauline* belongs in a continuing Romantic tradition, and foreshadows in both structure and style the Spasmodic poetry of the 1850s. *Paracelsus* is a 'dramatic poem' which belongs generically with works like *Philip Van Artevelde,* while *Sordello* is related to the metrical romances of Scott and Byron. A knowledge of these relations helps the critic define the changes Browning made in each genre. In *Pauline* he made the confession the speech of an assumed character (though, like the later Spasmodic characters, he was apparently designed to reveal the poet himself), and had that character not only pour out his emotions in a succession of dazzling images, but attempt, rather crudely, an analysis of his mental and spiritual development. Such a description of 'incidents in the development of a soul', Browning soon realized, was unsatisfactory, because he was telling the reader something rather than stimulating his 'co-operating fancy.' In *Paracelsus*, then, he freed himself of all the requirements of the theatre (as Henry Taylor had failed to do) and concentrated on complex patterns of dramatic irony. What he learned in writing *Paracelsus* he consolidated in *Sordello*. Initially, he tells us, he chose the narrative genre because he could, as narrator, explain the significance of the words and actions of his characters. His dissatisfaction with this manner of proceeding led him to reject assertion, and to rely instead on elaborately developed patterns that gradually evoke in the reader's mind insight into motive and character.

The long period in which Browning attempted to write for the theatre eventually brought him back to the conclusions he had reached in writing *Paracelsus*: that the demands of the stage for action, a swiftly moving plot, and relatively simple characterization, placed intolerable restrictions on him, and made it extremely difficult for him to portray the inner action in which he was chiefly interested. Nonetheless, the years of writing for the stage were not wasted. If the poet is not to describe but rather to present 'incidents in the development of a soul,' he must allow characters to speak for themselves. In experimenting with the drama, Browning learned how to realize character, how to show different characters approaching truth in different ways, and how to portray different individuals arriving at decisions affecting the whole course of their lives. In his most successful dramas, such as *Pippa Passes*, he discovered how to make the most of the irony of conflicting motives, desires, and obligations. Finally – and this was perhaps the most important result of his experiments with drama – he learned that the neutrality of the dramatist (who must enter into all his characters and realize them with equal vividness) is not incompatible with the commitment of the moralist (who must try to convey his judgment not by direct statement but by devices – especially irony – that evoke in the reader the poet's insights). And so he moved toward the characteristic combination of the dramatic and the lyric that he had already been experimenting with in some of the shorter poems, the combination that has since been called the dramatic monologue.

Browning experimented just as widely with the other genres as he did with the drama. The 1863 arrangement of his poems, for instance, does not indicate a narrow concept of the genres named in the titles, but suggests rather their flexibility. In the romances Browning was not primarily interested in wild adventures, swift action, and exotic descriptions of far-off lands. While retaining the three-fold pattern of romance, he shifted the emphasis from 'Character in Action' to 'Action in Character,' and made the quest a mental journey from the chaotic complexity of ordinary life, to a vision that illumines the whole pattern of an individual's existence, to an attempt to realize that vision in an ideally human world. In the lyrics Browning experimented with a wide variety of metrical and stanzaic patterns; the poems range in treatment all the way from the vision of *Women and Roses* to the grotesqueness of pieces like *The Laboratory* and *The Confessional*. The treatment of the combination of the drama and the lyric in the dramatic monologues of the *Men and Women* group is similarly wide-ranging. Some are pathetic, others comic, and still others satiric. Such variety of treatment stood Browning in good stead when he came to write his most complex poem, *The Ring and the Book*.

In *The Ring and the Book*, Browning combined the narrative, dramatic, and lyric genres in each monologue. Through the narrative, each speaker presents the facts of the story; his speech itself is dramatic, and so it brings the facts to life and arouses our sympathy; the lyric consists of the 'Something of mine' of the poet, the patterns that help us to arrive at an understanding of what is going on, and hence to judge the characters. Browning's treatment of the combination of these basic genres varies within a set pattern. In each of the three groups of monologues, the first speaker expresses himself in the satiric mode, the second makes use of the conventions of comedy and romance, while the final speaker is 'some third thing' not so easily categorized. Finally, the first and last books of the poem define its structure and suggest the variations in treatment.

A study of Browning's experiments with genre should not, ideally, come to an end with *The Ring and the Book*. Browning experimented relentlessly throughout the 1870s and 1880s, and many of the poems are fascinating puzzles for the critic interested in literary kinds. But a study of those poems would be almost as long as the present study, and some of them – particularly the poems based on the Greek – require an expertise I do not possess.

Without a detailed study of the later poems, it is not, perhaps, wise to generalize about Browning's experiments with genre. But in the period between 1833 and 1870 Browning's poetic purposes seem to have remained remarkably constant. It is possible now, I think, to see how much of a piece his work is, and to suggest that *The Ring and the Book* is in fact the realization of everything Browning set out to do in *Pauline*, though he did it in a way that he himself could not have foreseen in 1833. (The irony of purposes fulfilled in unexpected ways is a kind of irony that

Browning relished.) *Pauline*, he said, 'had for its object the enabling me to assume & realize I know not how many different characters ...,' the poet of the poem being the first of the lot. In *The Ring and the Book* Browning assumes ten characters, one of whom is a dramatic presentation of the poet himself. His complex combination of the lyric and the drama is the full realization of his rather crude linking of the two in *Pauline*. Finally, the structure of *The Ring and the Book* is in effect a more complex version of the structure that Browning attempted in *Pauline*: each part of the poem is part of a wider pattern, each part of the story is narrated by a character who is part of the whole story the poet is telling, each character presents other characters while he himself is presented by the poet; in short, it is a structure which is not unlike the Ptolemaic concept of the universe, a system of sphere within sphere, and a *primum mobile* – the poet – giving life and motion to all. In 1845 Browning told Elizabeth Barrett that he had 'never ... begun, even, what I hope I was born to begin and end, – "R.B. a poem." '[1] But *Pauline* was the beginning, and *The Ring and the Book*, if not the end, was the culmination of his work.

Bibliography

BROWNING'S WORKS

Pauline; A Fragment of a Confession   London: Saunders and Otley 1833
(The copy in the Forster Collection in the Victoria and Albert Museum has MS notes by Browning and John Stuart Mill.)
Pauline: The Text of 1833, compared with that of 1867 and 1888   N.
Hardy Wallis (ed). London: University of London Press 1931
Paracelsus   London: Effingham Wilson 1835
Strafford: An Historical Tragedy   London: Longman, Rees, Orme,
Brown, Green & Longman 1837
Sordello   London: Edward Moxon 1840
Bells and Pomegranates   eight numbers.   London: Edward Moxon
1841-6: no I is *Pippa Passes* (1841); no v is *A Blot in the 'Scutcheon*
(1843); no VIII includes *Luria* (1846)
MS of *A Blot in the 'Scutcheon*   Tinker 408, Beinecke Rare Book and
Manuscript Library, Yale University
'Introductory Essay' to *Letters of Percy Bysshe Shelley*   London: Edward Moxon 1852

The Poetical Works of Robert Browning third Edition. 3 vols. London: Chapman and Hall 1863
Dramatis Personae London: Chapman and Hall 1864
The Ring and the Book 4 vols. London: Smith, Elder 1868–9
The Works of Robert Browning with introductions by F.G. Kenyon. Centenary Edition. 10 vols. London: Smith, Elder 1912

LETTERS

CURLE, RICHARD (ed) *Robert Browning and Julia Wedgwood* London: John Murray and Jonathan Cape 1937

DEVANE, WILLIAM C., and KENNETH L. KNICKERBOCKER (eds) *New Letters of Robert Browning* New Haven: Yale University Press 1950

HOOD, THURMAN L. (ed) *Letters of Robert Browning Collected by Thomas J. Wise* New Haven: Yale University Press 1933

KENYON, F.G. (ed) *Robert Browning and Alfred Domett* London: Smith, Elder 1906

KINTNER, ELVAN (ed) *The Letters of Robert Browning and Elizabeth Barrett Barrett 1845–1846* 2 vols. Cambridge, Mass: Belknap Press 1969

OTHER SOURCES

ABRAMS, M.H. *The Mirror and the Lamp: Romantic Theory and the Critical Tradition* New York: Norton 1958 [first published 1953]

ALFIERI, VITTORIO *The Tragedies of Vittorio Alfieri* trans. Charles Lloyd. 3 vols. London: Longman 1815

ALTICK, RICHARD D., and JAMES F. LOUCKS, II *Browning's Roman Murder Story: A Reading of 'The Ring and the Book'* Chicago and London: University of Chicago Press 1968

ANONYMOUS 'Narrative and Romantic Poems of the Italians' *Quarterly Review* XXI (April 1819) 486–556

– Review of *The Giaour* and *The Bride of Abydos* in *Quarterly Review* X (January 1814) 331–54

– Review of Byron's *Corsair*, and *Lara*, in *Quarterly Review* XI (July 1814) 428–57

– 'Sensation Novels' *London Quarterly Review* (American Edition) CXIII (April 1863) 251–68

ARMSTRONG, ISOBEL (ed) *The Major Victorian Poets: Reconsiderations* London: Routledge & Kegan Paul 1969

ATKINS, J.W.H. *English Literary Criticism: The Medieval Phase* Cambridge: Cambridge University Press 1943

[BAILEY, PHILIP JAMES] *Festus: A Poem* London: William Pickering 1839

BIGG, J. STANYAN *Night and the Soul: A Dramatic Poem* London: Groombridge and Sons 1854

BROCKINGTON, A. ALLEN 'Robert Browning's Answers to Questions concerning some of his Poems' in Kenyon *New Poems*

BUCKLEY, JEROME H. *The Victorian Temper: A Study in Literary Culture* London: Allen & Unwin 1952

BUSK, MRS WILLIAM *Plays and Poems* 2 vols. London: Thomas Hookham 1837

BYRON, GEORGE GORDON, LORD *Poetical Works* London: Oxford University Press 1904

CHARLTON, H.B. 'Browning as Dramatist' *Bulletin of the John Rylands Library* XXIII (1939) 33–67

CICERO, MARCUS TULLIUS *De Inventione; De optimo genere oratum; Topica* H.M. Hubbell (trans) Loeb Classical Library London: W. Heinemann, Ltd. 1949

COLLINGWOOD, WILLIAM G. *The Life and Work of John Ruskin* 2 vols. London: Methuen 1893

COLLINS, THOMAS J. *Robert Browning's Moral-Aesthetic Theory 1833–1855* Lincoln: University of Nebraska Press 1967

COOK, A.K. *A Commentary upon Browning's The Ring and the Book* London: Oxford University Press 1920

COOK, ELEANOR GLEN 'The Meaning and Structure of *Pippa Passes*' *University of Toronto Quarterly* XXIV (July 1955) 410–26

CROWELL, NORTON B. *The Triple Soul: Browning's Theory of Knowledge* Alburquerque: University of New Mexico Press 1963

DALLAS, E.S *Poetics: An Essay on Poetry* London: Smith, Elder 1852

DAVIS, H.I., W.C. DEVANE, and R.C. BALD (eds) *Nineteenth Century Studies* Ithaca, New York: Cornell University Press 1940

DEVANE, WILLIAM C. *A Browning Handbook* second edition. New York: Appleton-Century-Crofts 1955

DOBELL, SYDNEY *Balder:* Part the First London: Smith, Elder 1854

– *Thoughts on Art, Philosophy, and Religion* London: Smith, Elder 1876

DUCKWORTH, F.R.G. *Browning: Background and Conflict* London: Ernest Benn 1931

FAIRCHILD, H.N. 'Browning the Simple-Hearted Casuist' *University of Toronto Quarterly* XVIII (August 1949) 234–40

FITZBALL, EDWARD *Thirty-five Years of a Dramatic Author's Life* 2 vols. London: Newby 1859

FORSTER, JOHN *Life of Charles Dickens* new edition, A.J.Hoppé (ed) 2 vols. London: Dent 1966

– *The Works and Life of Walter Savage Landor* London: Chapman and Hall 1876

FOX, W.J. Review of *Pauline; A Fragment of A Confession*, in *Monthly Repository* ns VII (April 1833) 252–62

FRYE, NORTHROP *Anatomy of Criticism: Four Essays* Princeton: Princeton University Press 1957

GEST, J.N. (ed.) *The Old Yellow Book* Boston: Chipman Law Publishing Company 1925

GRAHAM, JOHN 'The "Caricature Value" of Parody and Fantasy in *Orlando*' *University of Toronto Quarterly* XXX (1960–1) 345–66

GRIFFIN, W. HALL *The Life of Robert Browning: With Notices of his Writings, his Family, & his Friends* H.C. Minchin (ed) London: Methuen 1910

GROTE, GEORGE *A History of Greece* 12 vols. London: Murray 1884

HALLAM, ARTHUR HENRY 'On Some of the Characteristics of Modern Poetry, and on the Lyrical Poems of Alfred Tennyson' *Englishman's Magazine* I (August 1831) 616–28

[HERAUD, J.A.] 'Historical Romance' *Quarterly Review* XXXV (March 1827) 518–66

HONAN, PARK *Browning's Characters: A Study in Poetic Technique* New Haven and London: Yale University Press 1961

HORNE, R.H. *Ballad Romances* London: John Russell Smith, nd

– *A New Spirit of the Age* 2 vols. London: Smith, Elder 1844

JAMES, HENRY 'The Novel in *The Ring and the Book*' in *Notes on Novelists with some Other Notes* London: Dent 1914

[JEFFREY, FRANCIS] Review of Byron's *Corsair*, and *Bride of Abydos*, in *Edinburgh Review* XXIII (April 1814) 198–229

J[OLLY], E. (ed) *The Life and Letters of Sydney Dobell* 2 vols. London: Smith, Elder 1878

KEMPER, CLAUDETTE 'Irony Anew, with Occasional Reference to Byron and Browning' *Studies in English Literature* VII (Autumn 1967) 705–19

KENYON, F.G. (ed) *New Poems by Robert Browning and Elizabeth Barrett Browning* London: Smith, Elder 1914

KING, ROMA A., JR *The Bow and the Lyre: The Art of Robert Browning* Ann Arbor: University of Michigan Press 1957

KINTGEN, EUGENE R. 'Childe Roland and the Perversity of Mind' *Victorian Poetry* IV (Autumn 1966) 253–8

KISSANE, JAMES 'Victorian Mythology' *Victorian Studies* VI (September 1962) 5–28

LANDOR, WALTER SAVAGE *Complete Works* T. Earle Welby (ed) London: Chapman and Hall 1933

LANGBAUM, ROBERT review of Honan's *Browning's Characters*, in *Victorian Studies* V (March 1962) 269–71

– *The Poetry of Experience: The Dramatic Monologue in Modern Literary Tradition* New York: Random House 1957

[LISTER, T.H.] review of *Philip Van Artevelde*, in *Edinburgh Review* (American Edition) LX (October 1834), 1–24

LOUNSBURY, THOMAS R. *The Early Literary Career of Robert Browning* London: T. Fisher Unwin 1912

LUNDGREN, BRUCE R. 'The Function of Romance in *Martin Chuzzlewit, Domby and Son*, and *Hard Times*' unpublished MA thesis, University of Western Ontario, September 1966

LYTTON, EDWARD BULWER *The Dramatic Works* New York: Collier, n.d.

MACREADY, W.C. *The Diaries of William Charles Macready, 1833–1851* William Toynbee (ed) 2 vols. London: Chapman and Hall 1912

MARSTON, JOHN WESTLAND *Gerald; a Dramatic Poem: and Other Poems* London: Mitchell 1842

MCELDERRY, B.R. 'The Narrative Structure of Browning's *The Ring and the Book*' *Research Studies, State College of Washington* XI (1943) 193–233

MCKILLOP, ALAN D. 'A Victorian Faust' *PMLA* XL (September 1925) 743–68

MCLUHAN, MARSHALL (ed) *Alfred Lord Tennyson: Selected Poetry* New York: Holt, Rinehart and Winston 1956

– 'Tennyson and Picturesque Poetry' in *Critical Essays on the Poetry of Tennyson* John Killham (ed) London: Routledge & Kegan Paul 1960 67–85

– 'Tennyson and the Romantic Epic' in *Critical Essays on the Poetry of Tennyson* John Killham (ed) London: Routledge & Kegan Paul 1960 86–95

[MERIVALE, HERMAN] review of Browning's *Strafford: a Tragedy*, in *Edinburgh Review* LXV (July 1837) 132–51

MILL, JOHN STUART 'The Two Kinds of Poetry' *Monthly Repository* ns VII (October 1833) 714–24

MILSAND, J.A. 'La Poésie expressive et dramatique en Angleterre: M. Robert Browning' *Revue contemporaine* XXVII (15 September 1856) 511–46

NEWMAN, JOHN HENRY 'Poetry' *London Review* I (February 1829) 153–71

ORR, MRS SUTHERLAND *Life and Letters of Robert Browning* second edition, London: Smith, Elder 1891

– 'Mrs. Orr's Classification of Browning's Poems' *Browning Society Papers* I (1881–4) 235–8

PETER, JOHN D. *Complaint and Satire in Early English Literature* Oxford: Clarendon Press 1956

PREYER, ROBERT 'Sydney Dobell and the Victorian Epic' *University of Toronto Quarterly* XXX (1960–1) 163–79

PRIESTLEY, F.E.L. 'Blougram's Apologetics' *University of Toronto Quarterly* XV (1945–6) 139–47

– 'Drama and the Social Historian' *Transactions of the Royal Society of Canada* LI (series III, June 1957) 23–9

– 'Some Aspects of Browning's Irony' in Tracy *Browning's Mind and Art* 123–42

– 'The Ironic Pattern of Browning's *Paracelsus*' *University of Toronto Quarterly* XXX (October 1964) 68–81

QUINTILIANUS, MARCUS FABIUS *The Institutio Oratoria of Quintilian* H.E. Butler (trans) 4 vols. Loeb Classical Library. London: W. Heinemann 1921–2

REED, JOSEPH W., JR 'Browning and Macready: The Final Quarrel' *PMLA* LXXV (1960) 597–603

RUSKIN, JOHN *Modern Painters* sixth edition. 5 vols. London: Smith, Elder 1856–60

SCOTT, SIR WALTER *Essays on Chivalry, Romance, and the Drama* The Chandos Classics. London: Frederick Warne & Co., nd

– *Poetical Works* J. Logie Robertson (ed) London: Oxford University Press 1904

SESSIONS, I.B. 'The Dramatic Monologue' *PMLA* LXII (1947) 503–16

SHAW, W. DAVID *The Dialectical Temper: The Rhetorical Art of Robert Browning* Ithaca, New York: Cornell University Press 1968

SMITH, ALEXANDER *Last Leaves: Sketches and Criticism* Patrick Proctor Alexander (ed) Edinburgh: William P. Nimmo 1868

– *Poems* London: David Bogue 1853

SMITH, ALEXANDER (of Banff, Scotland) 'The Philosophy of Poetry' *Blackwood's Edinburgh Magazine* (New American Edition vol I) XXXVIII (December 1835) 827–39

SMITH, C.W. *Browning's Star-Imagery: The Study of a Detail in Poetic Design* Princeton: Princeton University Press 1941

STEMPEL, DANIEL 'Browning's *Sordello:* The Art of the Makers-see' *PMLA* LXXX (December 1965) 554–61

SULLIVAN, MARY ROSE *Browning's Voices in 'The Ring and the Book':* A *Study of Method and Meaning* Toronto: University of Toronto Press 1969

TAYLOR, HENRY *Autobiography* 2 vols. London: Longmans, Green 1885

– *Correspondence of Henry Taylor* Edward Dowden (ed) London: Longmans, Green 1888

– *Philip Van Artevelde: A Dramatic Romance* In two parts. London: Edward Moxon 1834

TRACY, CLARENCE (ed) *Browning's Mind and Art.* Edinburgh and London: Oliver and Boyd 1968

WARREN, ALBA H., JR *English Poetic Theory 1825–1865* Princeton: Princeton University Press 1950

WHITLA, WILLIAM *The Central Truth: The Incarnation in Robert Browning's Poetry* Toronto: University of Toronto Press 1963

WIENER, HAROLD 'Byron and the East: Literary Sources of the "Turkish Tales" ' in Davis, DeVane, and Bald *Nineteenth Century Studies*

WOODHOUSE, A.S.P. 'The Argument of Milton's *Comus*' *University of Toronto Quarterly* XI (1941) 46–71

– 'Nature and Grace in *The Faerie Queene*' *ELH* XVI (1949) 194–228

Notes

PREFACE

1 Hood *Letters of Robert Browning* 134
2 McLuhan 'Introduction' to *Alfred Lord Tennyson: Selected Poetry* xv–xvi
3 McLuhan 'Tennyson and the Romantic Epic' and 'Tennyson and Picturesque Poetry' in *Critical Essays on the Poetry of Tennyson* 87, 71
4 Abrams *The Mirror and the Lamp* 3–29

CHAPTER 1

1 Newman *London Review* I (February 1829) 169, 171
2 Ibid 159
3 Hallam 'On some of the Characteristics of Modern Poetry, and on the Lyrical Poems of Alfred Tennyson' 617
4 Ibid 621
5 Mill 'The Two kinds of Poetry' 715–16
6 Smith 'The Philosophy of Poetry' 832
7 This phrase, which so succinctly characterizes the school, appears in the anonymous review called 'Sensation Novels' in *London Quarterly Review* 252
8 Dobell *Thoughts on Art, Philosophy, and Religion* 73. Hereafter page references to this edition will be inserted in the text.

9 Preyer 'Sydney Dobell and the Victorian Epic'
10 Ibid 177
11 E. J[olly] *The Life and Letters of Sydney Dobell* II 31
12 Ibid I 232
13 Fox *Monthly Repository* 253–4
14 This note appears on the back of the page bearing the motto from Cornelius Agrippa.
15 Ibid 71
16 Collins *Robert Browning's Moral-Aesthetic Theory 1833–1855* 9
17 Ibid 5
18 Heraud 'Historical Romance' 521–2
19 Lister *Edinburgh Review* 1–24
20 *Correspondence of Henry Taylor* 106
21 Ibid 50–5
22 Ibid 73
23 Lister *Edinburgh Review* 4. Hereafter page references to this review will be inserted in the text.
24 Priestley 'The Ironic Pattern of Browning's *Paracelsus*'
25 Ibid 80
26 Anonymous review, *Quarterly Review* x 332
27 As Harold Wiener points out, 'Byron and the East: Literary Sources of the "Turkish Tales" ' 129
28 Jeffrey *Edinburgh Review* 201–3
29 Anonymous review *Quarterly Review* XI 457
30 Stempel 'Browning's *Sordello*: The Art of the Makers-see'
31 Kintner *The Letters of Robert Browning* I 342
32 Grote *A History of Greece* I 344. Further references will be inserted in the text.
33 As Michael Mason has pointed out: 'The Importance of *Sordello*' in Armstrong *The Major Victorian Poets* 141–2

CHAPTER 2

1 Macready *The Diaries* I 277
2 Merivale *Edinburgh Review* 133
3 Fitzball *Thirty-Five Years of a Dramatic Author's Life* II 166
4 DeVane and Knickerbocker *New Letters of Robert Browning* 32
5 Lytton *The Dramatic Works* 110
6 Kintner *The Letters of Robert Browning* I 150
7 Ibid I 411
8 Ibid I 381
9 Honan *Browning's Characters* 51
10 Macready *The Diaries* I 383
11 Ibid I 362
12 As Park Honan has pointed out: *Browning's Characters* 66–7
13 Orr *Life and Letters of Robert Browning* 97
14 In a letter to John Forster, quoted by Forster in his *Works and Life of Walter Savage Landor* I 388
15 Landor *Complete Works* XIII 391
16 Ibid 161
17 Cook 'The Meaning and Structure of *Pippa Passes*' 426. Further references will be inserted in the text.

18 Griffin and Minchin *The Life of Robert Browning* 126
19 Macready *The Diaries* II 23
20 DeVane and Knickerbocker *New Letters of Robert Browning* 25
21 Ibid 25
22 Hood *Letters of Robert Browning* 5
23 Dickens greatly admired Browning's treatment of Mildred, who may, in fact, be the prototype of Little Em'ly. See Forster *Life of Charles Dickens* II 24–5
24 Charlton 'Browning as Dramatist' 50
25 Lounsbury *The Early Literary Career of Robert Browning* 141
26 Ibid 132–8
27 Tinker 408, Beinecke Rare Book and Manuscript Library. In this manuscript the play has been copied by Sarianna Browning, and revised by Browning himself. In addition, the manuscript includes the cuts and revisions proposed by Macready. Most of these are listed and described by Joseph W. Reed, jr, 'Browning and Macready: The Final Quarrel.' The quotations from the manuscript are published here with the permission of the Yale University Library.
28 Hood *Letters of Robert Browning* 9
29 Kenyon *Robert Browning and Alfred Domett* 106
30 Kintner *The Letters of Robert Browning* I 251
31 Ibid I 26
32 Ibid I 411
33 Ibid I 77
34 In this discussion of fantasy I am indebted to Graham 'The "Caricature Value" of Parody and Fantasy in *Orlando*'
35 Kintner *The Letters of Robert Browning* I 411
36 Ibid I 26
37 Ibid II 732
38 Ibid I 455
39 Ibid I 26
40 Ibid I 551
41 Kenyon *Robert Browning and Alfred Domett* 127–8
42 Kintner *The Letters of Robert Browning* I 455

CHAPTER 3

1 Anonymous 'Narrative and Romantic Poems of the Italians' 498
2 Scott *Essays on Chivalry, Romance, and the Drama* 65
3 Heraud 'Historical Romance' 521–2
4 Scott *Essays on Chivalry, Romance, and the Drama* 65
5 Lundgren 'The Function of Romance in *Martin Chuzzlewit, Dombey and Son* and *Hard Times*' 2. Throughout my discussion of romance I am indebted to this thesis and to Lundgren's supervisor, Richard M. Stingle.
6 Marston *Gerald: A Dramatic Poem* 42
7 Frye *Anatomy of Criticism* 187
8 Marston *Gerald: A Dramatic Poem* 131–2
9 Hood *Letters of Robert Browning* 7
10 Kintner *The Letters of Robert Browning* I 47
11 DeVane *A Browning Handbook* 176
12 Shaw *The Dialectical Temper* 73–4
13 DeVane *A Browning Handbook* 182–3

14 Kintner *The Letters of Robert Browning* I 135
15 Ibid
16 As Eugene Kintgen points out in 'Childe Roland and the Perversity of Mind' 256
17 Hood *Letters of Robert Browning* 235
18 Browning 'Introductory Essay' 7
19 McLuhan 'Introduction to *Alfred Lord Tennyson: Selected Poetry* xxi. See also 'Tennyson and Picturesque Poetry' and 'Tennyson and the Romantic Epic.'
20 Quoted by Brockington, in 'Robert Browning's answers to questions concerning some of his poems' 176
21 See Peter *Complaint and Satire in Early English Literature* passim
22 Kintner *The Letters of Robert Browning* I 356
23 Ibid
24 Ibid
25 Ibid I 356–7
26 Quoted by Brockington, in 'Robert Browning's answers to questions concerning some of his poems' 176
27 DeVane *A Browning Handbook* 212
28 In dealing with the *Dramatic Lyrics* I am indebted to Northrop Frye, *Anatomy of Criticism*, especially to the section called 'Specific Thematic Forms (Lyric and Epos)' 293–303
29 Both letters are quoted in DeVane *A Browning Handbook* 207
30 Honan *Browning's Characters* 122
31 Langbaum *The Poetry of Experience* 137
32 Ibid 77
33 Kintner *The Letters of Robert Browning* II 732
34 Orr 'Mrs. Orr's Classification of Browning's Poems' 235
35 Sessions 'The Dramatic Monologue' 503n
36 Browning 'Introductory Essay' 6
37 Fairchild 'Browning the Simple-Hearted Casuist'
38 Langbaum *The Poetry of Experience* 85
39 Milsand 'La poésie expressive et dramatique en Angleterre: M. Robert Browning'
40 Curle *Robert Browning and Julia Wedgwood* 172–3, 176
41 Quoted by Collingwood *The Life and Work of John Ruskin* I 232
42 As Robert Langbaum points out in his review of Honan's *Browning's Characters*, 271
43 This ironic reading of the poem was first suggested by F.E.L. Priestley, and is more fully developed in his article, 'Browning's Irony.'
44 King *The Bow and the Lyre* 33
45 Ibid 12
46 As Roma King points out, in ibid 27
47 Shaw *The Dialectical Temper* 163
48 Ruskin *Modern Painters* IV 379
49 As Priestley has pointed out, in 'Blougram's Apologetics'

CHAPTER 4

1 James 'The Novel in *The Ring and the Book*' 306, 312
2 Curle *Robert Browning and Julia Wedgwood* 159
3 As A.S.P. Woodhouse has pointed out, in 'Nature and Grace in *The Faerie Queene*' 198

4 McElderry 'The Narrative Structure of Browning's *The Ring and the Book*' 211
5 Curle *Robert Browning and Julia Wedgwood* 161
6 See Woodhouse 'The Argument of Milton's *Comus*' and 'Nature and Grace in *The Faerie Queene.*'
7 As C.W. Smith has pointed out: *Browning's Star-Imagery* 202
8 Curle *Robert Browning and Julia Wedgwood* 176
9 Ibid 167
10 Ibid 177
11 Ibid 176–7
12 Atkins *English Literary Criticism* 24 and passim
13 Gest *The Old Yellow Book* 47
14 Altick and Loucks *Browning's Roman Murder Story* 88–90
15 Quoted by Griffin and Minchin *The Life of Robert Browning* 297
16 James 'The Novel in *The Ring and the Book*' 314

CONCLUSION

1 Kintner *The Letters of Robert Browning* I 17

Index

This book
was designed by
PETER DORN
and was printed by
University of
Toronto
Press